PREFACE

This volume describes some of the main forces and tendencies which served to bring the people of Finland, in the course of the nineteenth century, to nationalist-conscious citizenship, enabled them to withstand the attempts at Russification which were made especially during the two decades preceding 1914, and contributed to the attainment of political independence after the collapse of Imperial Russia in 1917.

Concerning the content of this volume, two general remarks should be made. In the first place, the amount of labor entailed by the study was so large that some topics had to be left out of the picture. For example, no attempt is made to delineate the consequences of the nationalist movement in the field of art. Another omission that no doubt strikes the reader is the economic basis of the movement. The former topic was omitted for the reason that the available data seemed insufficient for detailed treatment and too refractory for more superficial summary. As for the latter, it became evident, as the work progressed, that at least the first fifty or sixty years of the history of nationalism in Finland lacked the economic basis which we conventionally associate with developments of the kind that constitute the subject matter of this book. It would probably be precipitate to insist that economic factors have been equally absent during the past half a century, but it appears that their importance was not sufficiently great to influence

the course of events as related in these pages. While it seems that the predominantly literary and academic affiliations of the nationalist leaders account for this fact, a final statement of the economic aspects of the nationalist endeavors in Finland can be offered only after considerable further research.

Secondly, in Finland as elsewhere the development of nationalism as a purposeful doctrine was accompanied by a good deal of philosophizing concerning the larger aspects and meaning of nationalist principles and "isms." Such speculative phases of the subject have not been omitted, but they have been relegated to a secondary place. Attention has been fixed primarily upon those outstanding consequences of the nationalist movement which transformed the ideals and objectives of a handful of zealous patriots into vital nationalist creeds accepted by a substantial part of the Finnish citizenry, and effected in a multitude of ways many phases of the intellectual, social, and political history of the country.

Despite the complexity of the story as here presented — a complexity that persists in spite of the broad outline which the author has intentionally followed — it is hoped that the reader will perchance discover that in the history of nationalism in Finland there inheres a good deal of material illustrative of the manner in which modern nationalism has shaped the course particularly of the lesser nations of the Western European culture area.

In order to avoid confusing repetitiousness in the use of place names, the author has followed Professor Eugene Van Cleef's example in his *Finland — the Republic Farthest North* by giving the Swedish form in parenthesis when mentioning for the first time a place name for which Swedish as well as Finnish is used. Subsequent references are in Finnish only.

The kindness and courteous coöperation of the librarians and their assistants of the Library of the University of Helsinki and of the State Archives in Stockholm are gratefully acknowledged. Among the persons to whom the author is glad to assign much of the credit for the completion of the study, he wishes especially to mention Professors Y. Hirn and G. Suolahti of the University of Helsinki, the Late Librarian of the University of Helsinki, Dr. G. Schauman, and Mr. E. F. Rautela, A.M.

Several members of the Department of History at Columbia University have likewise left their imprint upon the pages of this book. The author is indebted to Professor Carlton J. H. Hayes, under whose guidance the preliminary studies of the subject were undertaken several years ago, for a critical reading of the manuscript; to Professor Geroid T. Robinson, who painstakingly reviewed the manuscript and the proof and thereby eliminated errors and added greatly to the clarity of the narrative; and to Messrs. Thomas P. Peardon, D. Rankin McBride and George C. Groce, Jr., for helpful suggestions. He wishes also to express his obligation to Columbia University Press for permission to use material which has previously appeared in his *The Prohibition Experiment in Finland*, and to his wife for aid in the preparation of the manuscript and the reading of the proof.

JOHN H. WUORINEN

COLUMBIA UNIVERSITY
     August, 1931.

CONTENTS

I. INTRODUCTION 1
    Finland as a Part of the Swedish Kingdom . 3
    Finnish Particularism 9
    Patriotic Studies 18
    Summary 26

II. SEED-TIME, 1810-1820 29
    Under a New Roof 29
    Public Opinion and the New Order . . . 32
    Critics of the New Order 39
    The Language Situation 42
    Adolf Iwar Arwidsson 47
    Summary 54

III. TWO DECADES OF GROWTH, 1820-1840 . . 56
    The Lay of the Land 56
    Historical Studies 59
    Finnish and Education 62
    Folklore Studies 66
    The Saturday Club 76
    The Press 79

IV. NEW SOURCES OF STRENGTH, 1840-1860 . . 83
    The Outlook 83
    Johan Vilhelm Snellman 87
    Early Gains 95
    Additions to Nationalist Ideology . . . 98
    Opposition and Victory 100

V. Dissension within the Ranks, 1850-1870   .   107
    Scandinavianism and Independence Schemes .   107
    Swede-Finn Nationalism   .   .   .   115
    New Influences   123
    Aggressive Fennomen   127

VI. The Old Order Changes   .   .   .   141
    Language Legislation   141
    Education and the Nationalist Movement   .   154
    Labor and Nationalism   169
    Russification — the Test of Strength   .   .   187

VII. The Last Twenty-five Years   .   .   204
    The Language Problem and Politics   .   .   204
    Russification, the World War and Independence   214
    Reconstruction   222
    Swede-Finn Demands and New Language
      Legislation   224
    The Outlook   228
    The Nature of the Problem   .   .   .   234

Notes   239

Bibliography   281

Index   295

Chapter I

INTRODUCTION

It has long been recognized that the rise of nationalism, especially among subject nationalities in Europe, has been the result mainly of two factors: first, the awakening of linguistic groups to a consciousness of cultural unity; and, secondly, the development among such linguistic groups of an ambition to achieve political independence. In most cases, also, the latter objective appears to have been the product of the former, though the two have been so closely intertwined that it is dangerous to dogmatize as to their relative importance or the order of their appearance.

In the case of Finland, for example, nationalism, properly so called,[1] began to emerge after the separation from Sweden in 1809. It arose primarily from the apprehension, especially among some of the younger Finns, lest the union with Russia should be followed by an absorption into the Russian empire. It did not seem to these patriots that the status of Finland, as an autonomous state in a personal union with Russia, constituted an adequate guaranty against such an eventuality. They believed that absorption could be prevented only if the people were set off sharply from the Russians by the possession of a distinct national culture and by a consciousness of distinct nationality which this cultural separateness would give. Thus while the motive was the maintenance and strengthening of political autonomy in the face of an anticipated policy of Russification, the means came to be the stimulus of national culture. But in the work of erecting this barrier against Russia, it too, tended to become an end in itself; and it is more than likely that many a nineteenth-century Finnish patriot was more conscious of its importance than of the existence of the original objective.

A century and a quarter ago, the inhabitants of Finland did not constitute a united linguistic group. The population was bilingual — it had been bilingual since time immemorial. The people were not moved by the sort of consciousness of cultural unity which we recognize in our day as one of the earmarks of patriotic citizenship. As regards aspirations for political independence, it is doubtful if any such aspirations were nurtured before the middle decades of the last century. Even at that time political independence was, as far as is known, the secret dream of the few rather than the avowed ambition of the many. It seemed therefore that the country was singularly ill-prepared for the emergency which the patriots saw ahead. Undaunted, they set to work. Briefly expressed, the cardinal points in their program were the development of Finnish into a literary language, the creation of a Finnish national literature, and the elevation of Finnish to the status of an official language alongside Swedish. In a word, the appearance of nationalist aspirations in Finland meant, in common with nationalist movements in many other lands, the emergence of a demand for a far-reaching linguistic reform.

Prior to the nineteenth century Finnish had been the language neither of educators, government officials, nor literary men. Now it was to be made to serve them all. The philologist joined hands with the littérateur, and both were assisted by the historian and the newspaper man. In their hands dialects spoken by the country folk were welded into a national language of surprising elasticity and abundant resource of expression. The cornerstones of an impressive nationalist movement were thus laid. The main edifice constructed later could never have been erected except for these linguistic and literary labors. The story of nationalism in Finland is thus largely the story of the tortuous course that had to be traversed before the use of the Finnish languge spread into the home of the academician and the man of business, into the lecture rooms of school and university, into the halls of parliament as well as the council chambers of ministers of state.

A study of nationalism in Finland must center, then, upon the nineteenth century. Its objectives become intelligible and most phases of its growth can be described only in the light of events that occurred after 1809. But it is also true that some of the ground work for these nineteenth century developments reposes in the century preceding. Figuratively speaking, the period before 1809 produced a part of the brick and mortar which went into the structure erected after that date. It is therefore no mere antiquarian interest which prompts a brief consideration of some features of Finland's history during the Swedish period.

Finland as a Part of the Swedish Kingdom

When Sweden was arbitrarily halved in 1809 and the eastern section, Finland, became a part of the Russian empire, a union of more than six hundred years came to a close. During those centuries Finland had become an integral part of the Swedish kingdom.

The Swedish conquest of Finland began about the middle of the twelfth century and was completed by the close of the thirteenth. At that time Sweden was not yet a unified state. The kingdom consisted of several confederated provinces ("land"). Each of these had its own assembly ("landsting"), judge and laws. These provincial assemblies were the only law-making bodies in existence. No province recognized the binding force of any but its own customs and enactments. Through their "lagman" they participated in the selection of the common king. The king chosen had to obtain a confirmation of his election from the several assemblies, whose laws he solemnly agreed to observe. No permanent central organ capable of exercising legislative, judicial or administrative functions had as yet developed.[2] A centralized state, in other words, had not yet come into being, and the "Swedish" conquest of the twelfth century was more a provincial Uppland undertaking[3] than an enterprise carried out by a unified government. National unification was fully achieved only with the growth of royal power and the development of a central administration and a national legislative body.

In Sweden, the royal prerogative encroached but slowly and intermittently upon the functions of the provincial "landsting." While the right of king and council to legislate in matters upon which the provincial laws were silent was claimed as early as 1285, the precarious character of the kingship, especially during the troublesome Kalmar Union period (1397-1523), reduced attempts actually to exercise this power to relatively unimportant dimensions. In fact, the royal prerogative was successfully asserted only after the establishment of a hereditary national monarchy under

Gustavus Vasa, in the sixteenth century. On the other hand, the importance and power of the King's Council grew more rapidly. Having been originally an extra-legal, irregular, purely advisory body, it assumed a permanence and authority which enabled it to supercede the provincial assemblies in the field of legislation and quite frequently the powers of the king as well. Out of it grew in the course of time the national parliament, the Riksdag.

Prior to the sixteenth century the Council dealt for the most part only with such questions as adherence to or rejection of the Kalmar Union, the choice of the king, and the like. It concerned itself but rarely with the making of laws or the raising of taxes. These matters were considered as falling within the domain of the provincial assemblies which continued to function throughout the Middle Ages. Indeed, their authority, especially during the latter half of the fifteenth century, was at times decisive even in political questions involving the entire kingdom. It was only in the sixteenth century that the "landsting" began to lose ground, and even then the decisions of the Riksdag were occasionally submitted to them for confirmation. This was done as late as 1605. However, when in 1617 the Riksdag obtained legal status it was clear that the day of the provincial bodies had passed. After the year 1634 the decisions of the Riksdag were conclusive and final. A truly national legislative body had come into being.[4]

It was of fundamental importance that Finland became a part of Sweden centuries before the process of unification had destroyed the province as the basic unit of political organization. Finland's position in the kingdom and, more important still, the basic aspects of the institutional development of the country during the period covered by this study, can be understood only in the light of the fact that the union took place before concepts of law, administrative practices and political authority had come to have a clearly defined meaning outside and independent of the province.]

Our knowledge of the internal conditions in Finland during the twelfth and thirteenth centuries is scant, and we know but little of the changes caused by the Swedish conquest. There is good reason to believe that local customs and institutions were at first not radically affected by the closer contact with the Swedes. In the course of time, changes of no small consequence began to appear. The Catholic Church was established on a firm foundation. By the close of the thirteenth century, "Swedish law" was applied throughout the country — the first law code for the provinces of Sweden proper had been completed some fifty years earlier — and by that time Finland had come to occupy, one might say, the position of one of the provinces of the kingdom; the bonds uniting Finland to Sweden were probably no less close than the ties which held together the Swedish "lands" in the elective monarchy briefly sketched. Later, when centralization began to gain ground at the expense of local institutions, the resulting amalgamation proceeded in general equally on both sides of the Gulf of Bothnia. The provinces slowly coalesced and grew into a larger, more compact unit. The process was completed by Gustavus Vasa, who established a hereditary monarchy and whose successful personal rule contributed truly national organs of law and administration. Yet nothing illustrates better the slow process whereby these changes were taking place than the fact that, as we have noted, many decades

elapsed after the reign of Gustavus before the Estates of the
Realm, in Riksdag assembled, obtained recognition in law.
When this happened in 1617, the Riksdag began to exercise
legally the powers that it had partly appropriated at the
expense of the provincial assemblies generations earlier.[5]

The political and legal rights of Finland's inhabitants
illustrate more specifically the position of the country in the
kingdom. They possessed all the prerogatives enjoyed by
the inhabitants of Sweden proper. Finland participated in
the election of the king beginning in 1362. In that year Finland's right in the matter was definitely embodied in an
enactment which read in part: "As twelve men from each
bishopric . . . with their judge, shall choose the king on behalf of all the people, and as Finland is a bishopric . . . it
is reasonable that [the Finns] be given in the future the
honor enjoyed by the other bishoprics . . . so that whenever
a king shall be chosen, the judge shall come, with priests
and twelve men of the common people, to choose the king
on behalf of all the people . . . "[6] This privilege was never
questioned while the elective kingship lasted. To be sure, the
right of election became more than once merely a right to
confirm an election already held. This applies particularly
to the fifteenth century. During the constant wars caused
by the Kalmar Union, legal forms in the elections were seldom observed. The magnates were all-powerful and decided
all questions to suit themselves. As a consequence the more
distant parts of the kingdom had at best only an opportunity
to recognize what the leading members of the nobility had
already agreed upon.[7]

Important as participation in the election of the king may
have been, it was in all likelihood of less moment than other

rights of more local significance. In the administration of
justice, the jury system provided participation by the common man in judicial decisions which often concerned him
more, and touched his life more intimately, than the choice
of this or that contender for the throne ever could.[8] Also,
the Finns were legally "native Swedes" as regards appointments to governmental positions. Nor was representation in
the Riksdag ever denied them. The *Riksdagsordning* of
1617 and subsequent laws which established and defined the
composition, functions and powers of the national parliament, provided representation for the four Estates in
Sweden and Finland alike. The same qualifications for the
right to vote, eligibility to seats in the Riksdag, and method
of selecting members, prevailed in both sections of the kingdom.[9]

These circumstances seem to have been responsible for
the absence of that antagonism between the Swedes and the
Finns which frequently appears when two linguistic groups
are brought into contact with each other. But it is safe to
say that other factors were no less important. The Finns and
the Swedes had not been widely and securely separated before the conquest in the twelfth century. Swedish-speaking
inhabitants were found in Finland centuries before that
time. Contrary to the popular notion, the Vikings did not
always go forth as robbers and plunderers; that they carried
on trade with the people in Finland is amply demonstrated.
No profound differences existed in the culture of the two
groups or in the stage of social development reached by
them. Nor did the conquest mean a discovery of regions
particularly suited for material exploitation. The backward-
ness of economic development in Sweden, the absence of a

strong centralized government, and the paucity of valuable natural resources in sparsely populated Finland appear to account for the absence of economic exploitation as a concomitant of the conquest. Hence prejudices and antipathies found poor soil in which to grow and economic interest had no appreciable chance to strengthen them.[10]

FINNISH PARTICULARISM

What has been said by way of suggesting the bold outlines of the position of Finland in the Swedish kingdom and of the political rights which placed the inhabitants of both parts of the kingdom upon a footing of equality, should not obscure the presence of forces and trends that made internal unification far from perfect. Especially during the last hundred years of the Swedish period in Finnish history, we discover evidences of increasing particularism. Geographic conditions, language, local economic interests, provincial patriotism and the ambition of individuals occasionally combined to throw into relief the fact that Finland was after all separate from Sweden proper. The reasons for the particularist trends include causes difficult if not impossible to analyze and others sufficiently concrete to invite specific appraisal.

Consider the influence of geography. Until the steamer replaced the sailing vessel and before the locomotive rendered the stagecoach obsolete, the distance separating Finland from Sweden was considerable. At certain seasons of the year, communications were often completely severed for months. As a consequence, administrative unity and control were at times of the loosest description. At no time was Finland so closely united with the rest of the kingdom as completely to eliminate the dissolving influence of distance. The consequent absence of easy and regular communication served to give a longer lease of life to local institutions and interests and not only invited, but on occasion made imperative, policies and practices dictated by local considerations. That such local policies and practices were not always, or necessarily, in keeping with the desires of the central administration in Stockholm goes without saying.

Finnish particularism was fed also by the actual as contrasted with the theoretical functions and importance of the national parliament. It was observed above that while the Riksdag had become an organ in the Swedish governmental mechanism long before the seventeenth century, its constitutionality was fixed only in 1617. Its powers as then stated were indefinite and were exercised for many years parallel with those of the provincial assemblies. Even after the latter had permanently given way to the national parliament composed of the four Estates of nobles, clergy, burghers and land-owning peasants, the inadequacies of the Riksdag as a body representing the citizenry of the country reduced its significance to very moderate proportions. Not all its members actually participated in its labors. Beginning in 1627, it became customary to appoint a Secret Committee for the transaction of all important business. Its membership represented only the three higher Estates, and only on rare occasions could the peasants make their voice heard in its deliberations. This committee decided questions on behalf of the whole Riksdag. Its influence was out of all proportion to its numbers. It tended at times to replace the parliament altogether, in that not infrequently only members of the Secret Committee constituted the whole parliament.[11]

[These inadequacies of popular participation in government were naturally operative in the kingdom as a whole, but they had a relatively greater bearing upon Finland than upon the rest of the realm] Even in a full Riksdag, Finland was never adequately represented. In the rump parliaments this representation tended at times to disappear altogether. This was particularly the case in time of war. When peace prevailed and inclement weather did not prevent attendance at a regular Riksdag, Finnish representatives had no telling opportunity to make their influence decisive in matters of purely local, Finnish concern — much less in questions of greater import — because they were distributed among the four Estates. In each they constituted only a minority and Finnish members had thus but little say in determining questions and policies which frequently concerned them most intimately, such as war and taxation. To be sure, the absence of a strong, centralized government especially before the seventeenth century had placed much of the actual administrative authority in the hands of local lay and clerical dignitaries who often did much to overcome the effects of ineffectual participation in the Riksdag. But this condition of affairs was likely to lead to arbitrary exercise of power and the imposition of unlawful exactions which the distant central government at Stockholm was unable to prevent. Dissatisfaction was the unavoidable result.

Furthermore, Finland was becoming a less important part of the kingdom than had been the case formerly. Sweden's participation in the Thirty Years' War placed this hitherto unimportant state in the forefront of European nations, and brought her new provinces. More important than these additions of territory, or the acquisitions made along the south-

ern littoral of the Baltic during the first half of Gustavus
Adolphus' reign, were the gains in 1658 whereby Sweden
obtained her natural boundaries to the south. These latter
annexations were contiguous to Swedish territory. Through
them, not only was the area of Sweden proper enlarged, but
her population was increased as well. In this growing Baltic
empire Finland became of less moment and began to assume
the position of a frontier province. This trend continued
later, especially during the wars of Charles XII which
brought the kingdom to the brink of ruin. The economic
life of the country was paralyzed by ever mounting taxes.
Agriculture suffered from the ravages of man as well as
nature. Shipping and commerce well-nigh disappeared. All
of Finland was conquered and occupied by the Russians for
nearly ten years and it has been estimated that about one-
third of the population was wiped out during the two decades which preceded the conclusion of peace at Nystad in
1721. That peace resulted in the cession of southeastern
Finland to Russia and ushered in a period more conspicuously marked by Finnish particularist trends than any before it. It appears that much of this particularism arose from
the changing position of Finland within the kingdom, and
was fed by the feeling that Finnish interests were unduly
subordinated to those of Sweden proper.

During the years following the close of the Northern
War, internal reconstruction dominated Swedish politics
and statesmanship. In this work, the main emphasis was
placed upon raising the kingdom from the abyss of material
exhaustion into which it had fallen. Particular attention was
paid to conditions in Finland. Various Riksdag committees
were appointed on several occasions for the purpose of

investigating the havoc wrought by the war and to propose ways and means to rehabilitate the country. A great deal of information on nearly every phase of life in Finland was collected. Scores of petitions, memorials and complaints were received by the authorities in Stockholm. One of the complaints of the Finns which stands out somewhat prominently among many others had to do with an old difficulty which was becoming increasingly conspicuous during the middle decades of the eighteenth century.

The practice of appointing Swedes to administrative, judicial and other positions in Finland was of old standing. After 1721 it became more frequent and created resentment among the peasantry and jealousy among the gentry. Such appointments were particularly objectionable when the incumbent knew little or no Finnish. For example, at the Riksdag of 1738-1739 the Finns complained of the inefficiency of the customs officials. They alleged that the customs personnel neglected their duties and compelled the people to submit to all manner of inconveniences. "The situation," they said, "is made worse by reason of the fact that the Customs Service in Finland is manned by Swedes who do not even understand Finnish. It therefore often happens that goods are incorrectly recorded although they have been properly declared, and are confiscated . . . without any fraud having actually been committed. . . . " [12] Another complaint at the same Riksdag found fault with the appointment of Swedes to various judicial positions. It is impossible to present a case to a judge or official who knows only Swedish, the argument ran, and hence recourse must be had to interpreters "who feel under no obligation to help the poor Finnish peasant or to see that justice is done. All kinds of errors and confusion result, to say nothing of the fact that our own deserving, honorable and able countrymen are excluded from higher positions." [13] The demand was presented that Finnish officials be appointed to the various branches of the central government in Stockholm to facilitate the transaction of Finnish business. Failing this, the establishment of what really amounted to a Finnish central government was suggested. These petitions were ultimately buried in the files of a committee appointed to act upon them.

The attitude of the government toward complaints of this kind was in all probability that of a Swedish judge who foresaw dire calamities ahead if the proposed reforms were adopted. "Through them," he said, "the door would be opened to internal misunderstanding and jealousy which could but bring harm to the country. If the inhabitants of other provinces also were to demand that only officials born in a given province be appointed to serve in it, it is to be feared that we should soon see as many republics as there are provinces, and that would mean setting fire to the whole State." [14] Nevertheless, a Royal Resolution of the year 1739 recognized the essential justice in the demand of the Finns that Finnish speaking officials be appointed. It stated that only persons who knew Finnish should be appointed to judgeships and other offices, "as far as circumstances, the qualifications, and the length of term of the applicants' previous service permit." However, the loop-holes in this qualifying clause of the Resolution were adequate to nullify its intent, as is shown by the persistence of the same grievance during ensuing years. [15]

Another concrete illustration of the attitude of the Finns toward this question is given by a project formulated by the

so-called Finnish Riksdag Deputation nearly a decade later.
About two-thirds of its thirty members were Finns or
Swedes long resident in Finland, and it is perhaps safe to
consider their views representative of opinions current in
Finland. The report of the Deputation, dated January 29,
1747, included most of the important features of the scores
of petitions and memorials presented at the Riksdag during
the preceding quarter century.[16] There is good reason to be-
live that it was drafted with the complaints presented in
1738-1739 as a model.

Having surveyed the destruction and havoc wrought by
the wars during the preceding four decades, the report continued: "That the administration of justice — and, therefore, the life and property of Finland's inhabitants — has
been entrusted to men more dependent upon translators in
the discharge of their duties than on their own abilities and
integrity, has ever been one of the most bitter complaints in
Finland. The result of this condition has been despair among
the common people, and the gentry have been robbed of all
incentive to educate their children, because they have observed that lately native, lesser officials have been but infrequently promoted to higher positions in those branches of
the government service in which Finnish is indispensable."
To remove this and other enumerated abuses, the Deputation proposed several measures for adoption by the Riksdag.
It was urged that a "permanent rule be adopted to the effect
that petitions from Finland shall take precedence over all
other matters that come before the Royal Council, the Supreme Court and the various governmental departments;
that all offices whose incumbents come into direct contact
with the common people [in Finland] be filled with native

Finns and such as do not need an interpreter in dealing with
the peasants or burghers; that at least two-thirds of the
seats of the Turku (Åbo) Court and of the professorships at
the University in Turku be in the hands of Finnish men; that
all lower officials be wholly recruited from among the natives and that all Swedes appointed to public office in Finland should know Finnish"; and that at least one Finn be
appointed to every department of the central government.
Other less important suggestions were also made. These
proposals were sufficiently comprehensive to have removed
most of the causes for complaint, but the recommendations
of the Report were not accepted, and the question of government jobs remained for years a source of irritation.[17]

In the seventeen-fifties, the University in Turku became the center of a controversy in which this same element was conspicuously present. "At the Convocation of
somewhat more than two years ago," runs a report from
the year 1756, "the Academy was the object of insulting,
scurrilous attacks, partly by letters and partly by means of
posters in public places. Hatred against God-fearing, well-
meaning men of Swedish birth and sympathies begins to
gain ground in such a way that it will soon be difficult to
attend to the duties of one's office," especially since students
at the University had become contaminated by it.[18] This
instance of professional jealousy appears to have been sufficiently novel and extreme to warrant special mention in a
report to the Chancellor of the institution, but the underly-
ing opposition among Finnish academicians against the appointment of Swedish professors to Turku was of an older
date. Nearly a century earlier, Pehr Brahe, the founder of
the University, mentioned it. "The Finnish nation and those

who have been connected with the Academy for a longer period," he wrote in 1666, "feel resentful toward outsiders who have been appointed from time to time. I would therefore suggest that no member of the University or of the province — if he is able and available — be in any way discriminated against. No cause for complaint should be given. . . . " [19] Needless to say, this counsel did not prevent the appearance of the evil Brahe would have avoided. Nor did the Church escape it. In the year 1755, an election was held in Turku to fill the vacant seat of the bishop. Vitriolic pamphlets and noisy student demonstrations characterized the campaign.[20] The candidacy of one contender for the office was urged on the grounds that he was a Finn — an attempt sharply rebuked by the King in person. The viewpoint of the leading men in Sweden was stated by Count Tessin, the Chancellor of the University at the time. He deplored the "discord and dissension between the Swedish and the Finnish nations" which the election had brought to light and repudiated the charge that discrimination or favoritism influenced university or other appointments. "All the inhabitants are subjects of the same state and constitute one people," he stated, and hence internal jealousy must not be tolerated.[21]

Whether these controversies in the seventeen-fifties served to open the eyes of the authorities to the fact that their relatively uncompromising and indifferent attitude was deepening the gulf which had begun to separate Finland from Sweden, it is impossible to say. While an attempt was made to observe the Royal Resolution of 1739, it is obvious that family connections and a host of other factors tended to render it inoperative. However, the prohibition in 1760 against absentee office holding, ecclesiastical pluralities and sinecures in Finland, by removing a real source of inefficiency and corruption, ushered in a tangible reform. The agitation began to disappear, and its absence during the closing decades of the century suggests that the vexing question of appointments had assumed more manageable proportions.[22]

PATRIOTIC STUDIES

The difficulties mentioned in the preceding paragraphs may be said to have reflected grievances and the existence of personal or class ambitions. Without attempting at this point to determine whether they should be considered as having reflected nationalist aspirations, we may proceed to take note of certain other influences which were appearing during the period. Historical and philological research was beginning to make contributions to the materials which a later generation used in the formulation of a nationalist creed. It was partly in the atmosphere of dissatisfaction and protest which prevailed during the middle decades of the eighteenth century that the notions of a Finnish fatherland and a separate Finnish nationality were being slowly formulated and the foundations of a national history laid.

At the very time when Charles XII was embarking upon the disastrous wars that nearly wrecked his country, an obscure scholar in Turku was finishing a study which appeared in the year 1700. The scholar was Daniel Juslenius, and the work bore the title *Aboa Vetus et Nova*. It was intended to deal with the then capital of Finland but its content went considerably beyond the limits of a local history. Unreliable earlier writers, tradition, folk tales, mythology, chance similarities in names or words, were indiscriminately drawn upon in the construction of a wondrous tale of wholly imaginary national greatness in the distant past. The Finns were described as descendants of one of the Jewish tribes who had founded a mighty state under the leadership of one of Noah's descendants. Their powerful kings were enumerated in an imposing list. That both the kings and the state never actually existed, seems to have bothered Juslenius not at all.[23] Yet, because *Åbo, Old and New* contained a good deal of material descriptive of contemporary conditions, it was redeemed from the more complete surrender to the vagaries of fancy which characterized his second work, published three years later. In the pages of the *Vindiciae Fennorum* the author was able to free himself from all constraint. His whole fatherland was now his domain. The treatise was a militant defense of Finland, its inhabitants and their language against all criticism, depreciation and slander. It described the country as singularly fertile and rich in valuable minerals, its climate as uncommonly salubrious and conducive to extraordinary physical and mental attainment. The Finns were blessed with no small list of virtues: they were brave, honest, of temperate habits, God-fearing, hospitable and endowed with marked all-round ability; among their many contributions to civilization was the art of writing.[24]

The writings of Juslenius, who later attained to professorial dignity and a bishopric, are of small importance as historical works. Their significance lies in the fact that in them is found the first effective expression of the contention that Finland and its people could claim excellencies inferior to none. Love of the fatherland was strongly emphasized by

them. To be numbered among the Finns, an illustrious people, was a source of pride for Juslenius personally, and his
uncritical readers, especially in later times, were only too
likely to share this view. Many of the unhistorical and ex-
travagant ideas expressed by him became for decades classic
models for many writers. They were quoted as authority by
enthusiastic students, and even sober academicians of a
later and more critical age have found them on occasion
both useful and pertinent.

This interest in the fatherland received a strong impulse
during the decades following the collapse of Sweden in
1721. The manifold efforts made to regain at least some of
the economic prosperity which the Northern War had destroyed were based in the main upon the belief that conditions could be improved only by increasing the productivity
of farming and the development of industry and commerce.
The natural resources of the kingdom were investigated as
never before, with a view to discovering means for utilizing
them more effectively. Even the character and earlier history of individual trades were scrutinized in the hope that
ways leading to greater prosperity might be discovered.
Relatively unknown sections of the country were surveyed,
plans were made for new roads, schemes for rendering
more useful the immense water ways of the kingdom were
drafted, and a much needed revision of the land laws was
begun.

In this work, the University in Turku participated in an
active way and brought forth a type of academic productivity which may be said to have contributed more to the
strengthening of the feeling and aspirations voiced by Juslenius than to a notable hastening of economic reconstruc-

tion. Historical surveys of towns, villages, bishoprics, provinces and trades became frequent products of scholarly work. These surveys differed from the naïve products of earlier times in that they dealt nearly always with only contemporary conditions and questions which left but little chance for excursions into a fabulous past. They were descriptions of economic enterprise, administrative organization, or religious conditions, in which inaccuracy of fact was at least partly redeemed by the sobriety of approach. During the years 1730-1800 about one hundred such studies saw the light of day. This interest in the fatherland received the approbation of the academic authorities and of the leaders within the Church. The Vice-Chancellor of the University suggested in 1750 that the professors should urge students who intended to present a dissertation to select some subject concerning "our beloved fatherland," and four years later the Cathedral Chapter in Turku emphasized the importance of knowing the history of the country and advised the publication of books on that subject.[25]

Through these studies, the history of Finland was placed upon a sounder basis. Through them, a greater knowledge and appreciation of Finland was spread, especially among the upper classes. It was discovered that the home town, or district, was a part of a larger unit, a common fatherland, and that the Finns constituted a people separate from the Swedes. "Patria" began to connote Finland rather than the kingdom as a whole. By their emphasis upon practical matters, by dealing with questions closely connected with the life of the peasant and the artisan, no less than with the life of the burgher or the gentry, they raised hitherto neglected fields of investigation to the dignity of scholarly

analysis and exposition. Most important of all, they provided not a little of the material with which a later, more
nationalist generation proceeded to construct a national history of considerable dimensions.[26]

This interest in the existing conditions and past history
of Finland was paralleled by another. Academicians and also
members of the clergy began to find the Finnish language a
subject worthy of study, and Finnish folklore and folk
songs sufficiently interesting to justify their collection and
analysis. Minor efforts had been made along these lines as
early as the middle of the sixteenth century, but it was the
eighteenth that furnished the proper background for the
gigantic work which ultimately culminated in the appearance
of the *Kalevala*, the Finnish national epic, in the eighteen-
thirties. The increasing solicitude for Finnish led in turn
to the writing of grammars and dictionaries. Juslenius
among others manifested an active interest in such labors,
and the dictionary he produced in 1739 remained the outstanding work in the field for upwards of eighty years.[27]

No account of the developments here surveyed would be
complete without a mention of Henrik Gabriel Porthan.
Born in 1739, Porthan grew to manhood during the period
when Finnish studies, in the wider sense of these words,
were becoming something more than isolated illustrations
of more or less meaningless academic antiquarianism. He
matriculated at the University in Turku at the age of fifteen.
A nephew of Juslenius, he was brought under the influence of the patriotic studies and interest which still per-
sisted in the circle of the Juslenius family in Turku. He
began his career as educator in 1762 as *Dozent* in Eloquence
and became professor in 1777. Till his death in 1804, his

connection with the University remained unbroken. The importance of Porthan during this period is perhaps best suggested by the fact that the phrase "Porthan Era" has long since become synonymous with the most flourishing period in the history of the University before 1809.

Porthan made a two-fold contribution to studies concerning his country and its people. A few years after the publication of Macpherson's *Ossian* (1760), but in all probability before it became known in Sweden-Finland, and before Herder had commenced to invite the attention of contemporary Europeans to the beauties and significance of folk poetry, Porthan began to investigate the character and forms of the abundant Finnish material which he found near at had. His first important publication was an extensive collection and analysis of Finnish folk poetry, *Dissertatio de Poesi Fennica*, which appeared serially in five parts between the years 1766 and 1778. This was the first attempt made in Finland to deal with material of this kind in a detached, scientific spirit, without the fantastic extravagance of an enthusiast of the type of Juslenius. While Porthan never finished the investigations thus started he was instrumental in promoting similar or related studies among his students, especially after a sojourn at the University of Göttingen in 1789 had brought him into contact with the Romantic movement sponsored by Herder and his folowers.[28]

From studies of this type, Porthan was gradually led to the field of Finnish history. His most notable researches in this subject appeared in a series of fifty-six publications (1784-1800) in which he amassed a wealth of materials hitherto unknown. Porthan attempted no systematic presentation of Finland's history as a whole. On the contrary, he was avowedly a collector and compiler of facts, interested in ferreting new information out of old, long-forgotten documents discovered in dusty archives in Turku and elsewhere. During his forty-two years' service at the University, he either wrote or assisted his students in preparing more than two hundred publications, the greater number of which dealt with problems in Finnish history, philology or related subjects. One may say that he left untouched no major phase of Finland's history and institutions. Both the magnitude of the studies he made, or sponsored, and the scientific spirit evident in everything he undertook abundantly justify the title "Father of Finnish history" which posterity has bestowed upon him.[29]

Porthan's interest in his country carried him considerably beyond the confines of academic activity. He was instrumental in founding, in 1770, the Aurora Society, whose membership included many leading persons of the day. One of the aims of the Aurora Society was the promotion and development of the Finnish language and the dissemination of knowledge about the fatherland. A newspaper was founded in 1771 to aid in the work. The first point in its program was to the effect that it would print contributions dealing with Finland, its characteristics, history and the language of its people. By spreading information about Finland, the newspaper aimed to arouse the patriotism of its readers. In its pages were published many an article from the pen of Porthan on a multitude of subjects. Neither the Aurora Society nor its paper was long-lived, but both illustrated the influence of Porthan in stimulating studies of his fatherland.[30]

In evaluating Porthan's significance to Finland, one of the well known Finnish scholars wrote nearly twenty years ago that in all probability the development of no people in recent times has been more profoundly influenced by the labors of one man than Finland has been influenced by Porthan's work.[31] Certain it is that his work furnished much of the basis upon which Finnish nationalism was builded in the course of the nineteenth century. Already the generation following him appears to have sensed its value and later, when the nationalist movement had left its swaddling clothes, the recognition of Porthan's significance became increasingly definite. "The fatherland is beginning increasingly to understand," runs a statement from the year 1864, "that the new Finnish era which is now commencing was begun by Porthan. . . His spirit will live as long as there are Finns in Finland." He became "the mighty oak in whose shade the Finnish people gather at the close of day to measure their accomplishments and to gather new strength for the morrow." [32] Porthan "taught us," says another writer of a more recent date, "that we were something more than a fragment of the Swedish state, and showed us that we are a separate people and nation." [33] While living he founded Finnish historiography and the study of Finnish folklore, divorced researches in Finnish philology from the absurdly unscientific approach of his predecessors, and was singularly successful in arousing among his contemporaries an interest in studies dealing with the language and history of his country; after his death he became the maker of a nation to a degree which only men no longer living can attain.

Before proceeding to estimate the general nationalist significance of the trends surveyed in this chapter, passing mention must be made of an instance of eighteenth-century Finnish separatist activities which aimed at the establishment of Finland's independence.

The dissolution of Sweden's Baltic empire during the first half of the eighteenth century resulted not only in the loss of the provinces south of the Gulf of Finland, but also in the cession of a part of southeastern Finland to the growing Russian colossus. The inability of the kingdom to prevent the periodic destruction of the eastern part of the realm by the Russians, whose expansion seemed to spell a complete partition of Sweden-Finland in no distant future, later created the conviction among some of the leading military men in Finland that the country could be saved from destruction only by the establishment of its independence under Russian protection. The course of the Russo-Swedish war of 1788-1790 seemed to justify this conviction and brought about a military conspiracy among a considerable number of the army officers stationed in Finland. The conspiracy failed, largely because most of the men involved were actually more interested in the reëstablishment of peace with Russia and in curbing the powers of the king, whom they considered too autocratic, than in the question of Finland's independence. Another reason for its failure was the loyal attitude of the country as a whole. The conspirators were denounced as traitors and many of them were compelled to escape to Russia, whose service they entered.[34]

Summary

This brief account of Finland's history during the Swedish period may be closed with the question, Is it justifiable, in the light of the eighteenth-century trends discussed, to speak of Finnish nationalism prior to the nineteenth century? The answer must be in the negative.

Finnish nationalist sentiment cannot be said to have been the basis for the numerous Riksdag complaints and petitions of which mention has been made. Most of them dealt with economic questions of one kind or another, such as taxation, trading privileges and the like.[35] It is also important to observe that these petitions and protests were never stiffened by nationalist sentiment into the inflexibility of the ultimatum. Juslenius in his earlier years rose to defend the honor and achievements of his country and its people, and in doing so contributed to the heightening of an interest in things Finnish, but he was no nationalist agitator. He considered himself "a good Swede" and ended a long and useful life as a respected bishop in Sweden.[36] Porthan's historical researches, as we have noted, were of fundamental importance, but it is worthy of note that to him the "history of the Fatherland" appears to have meant, in the last analysis, the history of the Swedish state.[37] So far as is known, he never devoted a single lecture to Finnish history, and one searches in vain for references to the subject in his other lectures.[38] Much of his scholarly effort was devoted to studies of the Finnish language, yet his class room references to his mother tongue were exceedingly rare.[39] An academician interested in Finnish studies in the wider sense of the word, he was totally devoid of nationalist ambitions. The abortive attempt to detach Finland from Sweden in 1788 he considered reprehensible, and was convinced that "this foolish, criminal attempt is detested by all, excepting possibly a few windbags among our nobility who probably hope that they can transform their fellow citizens into serfs on the Livonian or Courland model. . . . " [40] Finally, the conspiracy of 1788, far from being a nationalist uprising, was an enterprise in which the grudges and ambitions of a handful of military men from Finland and Sweden furnished the motive force.

One is compelled to conclude, therefore, that what many Finnish writers have interpreted as nationalism in eighteenth-century Finland,[41] consisted of a growing feeling that the people of the country "belonged" to a geographical area — local patriotism — and was not based upon a conscious realization that they consituted a distinct cultural group or nationality. It was only after the developments of 1808-1809 had taken place that this local patriotism began to metamorphose into nationalism in the modern sense of the word. It is to these events that we now turn.

CHAPTER II

SEED-TIME, 1810-1820

UNDER A NEW ROOF

When Finland's century-long connection with Sweden was severed in 1808-1809, the separation came as an incidental result of the Napoleonic wars. At the time the population of the country numbered about 863,000 souls. This figure was increased to 1,053,000 in 1811 when those sections of southeastern Finland, which had been ceded to Russia in 1721 and 1743, were reunited to Finland. Of the total population some 40,800 lived in cities, of which only one had more than 10,000 inhabitants.[1] Agriculture was the mainstay of the people. Modern methods of agriculture, diversification of crops, and drainage, had not yet become safeguards against the crop failures which a hostile climate and a grudging soil frequently caused. While Finland was agriculturally self-sufficient, having no need to depend upon outside sources for grain, the general standard of living was modest at best. A failure of crops usualy meant poverty or death to thousands. Means of communication were poor. Even in the relatively thickly populated parts of the country, the network of roads revealed many a gap. The age of canals and railways was still in the future, and as for the steamship, more than a decade was to elapse before it began to break down the isolation of this part of northern Europe.[2]

The enormous timber resources, which constitute a basic
factor in the economic life of present-day Finland with its
growing industrialization, were as yet unused on a large
scale. A struggling iron industry surviving from earlier
days and a textile industry hardly worthy of the name constituted the meager beginnings of a later machine age.[3]
Law and the administration of justice, governmental organization and educational and religious life were institu-
tionalized according to patterns which had been slowly
evolved in Sweden-Finland in the course of preceding
centuries.

Finland's existence as a part of the Russian Empire was
begun not as a subject province but as an autonomous, constitutional state. The government under which Finland assumed this new status was established while the Russo-
Swedish war of 1808-1809 was still in progress. Several
months before the conclusion of peace in the fall of 1809,
Alexander I convened at Porvoo (Borgå) a Diet representing the whole country. The Diet began its deliberations in
March of that year. It was not called upon to legislate in
the ordinary meaning of the word. Taking the administration of the country as it had been while Sweden and Finland
were one, it molded that administration into conformity
with the new order brought about by the victory of Russia's
arms. Swedish institutions were retained with only such
changes as the new situation made imperative. An appointive
Government Council modelled on the Swedish Council of
State was created to form the central administration. It
combined advisory, executive and judicial functions and consisted of two divisions, the Department of Economy and
the Department of Justice. The former was in charge of

the various branches of the administration while the latter
constituted the Supreme Court of Finland. The chairman of
the Government Council — the name of the Council was
changed in 1816 to the Imperial Senate of Finland — was
the Governor-General appointed by the Tsar. Local administration and law courts underwent no change worthy of
mention.

It was also necessary to create an agency through which
the Finnish government could communicate and deal with
the authorities in St. Petersburg. In the Russian capital Finnish affairs were at first entrusted to a Russian official. This
temporary arrangement was abandoned in 1811 when the
Finnish State Secretariat was established. The Secretariat
consisted of a committee of Finns and a Minister-Secretary
of State — also a Finn — whose function it was to communicate directly with the Tsar on all matters affecting him
as Grand Duke of Finland. According to the constitution in
operation in the Swedish kingdom at the time when Russia
annexed Finland, there were certain things that had to be
done by and with the consent of the representatives of the
four Estates, and others requiring only the executive decree
of the Monarch. It was for advice respecting this latter class
of matters that Alexander, who according to the Constitution had succeeded to the position of the Swedish king as
supreme executive of the country, established the Secretariat.[4]

The character of the autonomy granted to Finland and
solemnly confirmed by Alexander may be summarized as
follows. The right of all Finnish citizens to enjoy the protection of the laws of the country was specifically recognized.
The Lutheran Church retained its former previleged posi-

tion as State Church. Only Finnish citizens of this religious persuasion could be appointed to public office.[5] Acting through the Diet, the people could decide as regards the imposition of new taxes — all taxes were to be expended in Finland — and the changing of old and the enactment of new laws. However, the Diet could be convened only at the instance of the Grand Duke, and the enactments of the legislature were subject to his approval. The establishment of the Government Council meant that the government of Finland would rest in the hands of native Finns. Perhaps of greater immediate importance as regards the practical fruits of this autonomy was the creation of the Finnish State Secretariat at St. Petersburg. If Finnish affairs at the Russian capital had been left in the hands of Russian ministers, it is probable that Finnish constitutional prerogatives would have soon disappeared and the country would have drifted into the position of a Russian province. Especially during the early years of the union with Russia, the Finnish Senate was, one might say, more the center of a provincial government with relatively extensive powers, than the central administration of a constitutional state. The center of gravity of the government was for many years in St. Petersburg, and there the Finnish State Secretariat proved the best bulwark against deviations from and disregard of the fundamental laws of the Grand Duchy.

PUBLIC OPINION AND THE NEW ORDER

On the whole, public opinion seems to have considered the new order quite acceptable. This is true at least of the expressions of opinion found in letters and other similar records of the period; of the views of the inarticulate bulk of the nation little or nothing is known. To many it seemed that the grant of constitutional government was the result of the noble generosity of a great ruler whose intention it was to unite a small, unimportant nation to his empire with bonds of lasting gratitude. Alexander had sent his armies to Finland not for plunder and murder but to defend and confirm its inhabitants in the enjoyment of time-honored institutions. He had convened the Diet not only to give advice, but to participate in the making of important decisions. His efforts would bring the country to the road leading to peaceful growth and orderly development. But what about the future? What assurance existed that the political autonomy established by Alexander, and the inviolability of Finnish laws and institutions guaranteed by him, would be observed by his successors? In spite of constitutions and the like, Finland's political existence depended in the last analysis upon the person of the Tsar and his interpretation of the binding character of the limitations the Constitution placed upon him, as well as upon his willingness to hold in check the attacks which might be made on Finland's privileged position in the empire. The nature of the settlement effected in 1809 tended to contribute to these fears. Through the establishment of the Senate and the Finnish State Secretariat, Finland came to stand in a direct relation to and dependence upon the Grand Duke. The Russian conquest came to be thought of by many as an event leading to submission to the person of the Tsar, rather than as an event leading to incorporation in the empire. "I have no connection with Russia," wrote G. M. Armfelt, one of the most important personages in the Finland of that day, "for I am a Finn and can be nothing else, but I am bound to the benefactor of my country, Tsar Alexander, who," he added with disarming candor, "has treated me and mine with extraordinary kindness." [6] Armfelt was not alone in holding these views, for the plenitude of imperial favor was extended to many sufficiently prominent to warrant special attention. To find fault with the new régime was out of the question, as far as such men were concerned, but uncertainty about the future could hardly be avoided.

The submission to Russia was made easier by a legitimate fear of the disasters which a renewed war between Sweden and Russia would bring with it. The elevation of Finland to the status of an autonomous state invited comparison with its earlier position as a part of the Swedish kingdom and raised the query, in the minds of many of the leading men, whether reunion with Sweden would be advantageous to the country — and incidentally, to themselves. Newly acquired economic and political advantages, and an avid acceptance of favors of one kind or another had in some cases disclosed unblushing servility in personal conduct, and a haste in the acceptance of the Russian order, which could ill afford close scrutiny and investigation. A return to Sweden would mean strict accountability, with dire consequences to many who were riding the crest of the wave. In their eyes the "hated Russian sceptre" became a guaranty of future progress and well-being. [7]

The defeat of Sweden had suddenly given to Finland some of the things for which her spokesmen at many a Riksdag had petitioned with but indifferent success. A local autonomous constitutional government, manned by Finns, had been created. Taxes had been temporarily reduced and no longer would the revenue collected in Finland disappear into the royal treasury in Stockholm, to be disbursed according to needs and considerations frequently foreign to Finland. Incorporation into Russia had brought peace, and would in all probability mean the end of the countless wars of the past. There was something more than rhetoric in the words of one of the leading military men of the time when he said, in surveying the effects of the Russian conquest, "We are a free people, as heretofore. We are governed according to our old established laws. We have chosen our own men to administer justice. . . If we are permitted to enjoy the advantages we now have, Finland will be, considering her position, the happiest country in all of Europe." Contrasting the lot of his country before 1809 with the present, he summarized the effects of Finland's former union with Sweden by saying:

Finland was a scene of war for centuries. Our fields were fertilized, at intervals of twenty years, by the blood of Finnish citizens. Thousands of persons were lost in every war, to the eternal loss of the country. This is the reason why one-third of our country is still uncultivated. When a couple of decades of peace had repaired some of the damage and the population began to grow and material well-being increased on every hand, war was again upon us. Every peace brought added taxes and burdens — heavier at times than those borne by the Swedes. This was our fate for centuries. This is the advantage we derived from being a Swedish province. It is my belief that as long as we enjoy the protection of the ruler of Russia and as long as the Russian monarchy exists Finland will never again become a theater of war. It is in these respects that I consider Finland more fortunate now than under Sweden.[8]

The army officer whose salary and other privileges had been confirmed by Alexander; the petty official who had been

permitted to retain his post with an increase in salary or
who enjoyed an increased pension; the senator whose income
was commensurate with his social prestige and political
influence; the university professor buoyed by increased
grants to his university; the bishop whose interests were
sufficiently worldly to enable him to aspire to the title of
this or the ribbon of that — these and many others found
it easy to consider the new dispensation superior to the old.
The actual as well as the imaginary benefits to Finland of
her union with Russia were interpreted largely in terms of
personal advantage. This fact more than any other accounts
for the zeal with which some of the leading Finns tried to
meet the wishes of all-powerful Alexander and the demands
of Russian policy in general. The defeat of Napoleon, which
confirmed Russia's control of Finland, seemed to prove the
wisdom of this attitude and gave it the prestige of patriotic
duty and farseeing statesmanship.[9] And as for the petty
bourgeoisie, their view appears to have been well expressed
by a writer some years later who pointed out the wider
opportunities offered to Finns by Russia. Into Russia's
armies entered, he stated, " a considerable part of our young
gentlemen, and many a father and mother, many a sweet-
heart, will find the most precious interests life holds dependent upon the success of her arms." With an eye to the future
he added: "I believe that nobody will contradict me if I
call Finland our place of birth and Russia the country which
will increasingly become our fatherland — that is, the country upon which our existence and happiness will ultimately
depend." [10] Both the present and the future seemed to place
a premium upon the new order.[11]

This attitude of subservience was illustrated by a question

which arose during these years, that of introducing Russian into the schools of Finland. Already in 1811, when the Turku University received increased grants, it was made clear that the promotion of the study of Russian was expected of the University authorities. They were not slow to respond. Two Russians were appointed to give instruction in the subject, in the following year, and two Finns were granted subsidies for language studies in Russia. The whole question became a subject of imperial concern in the same year when a decree was issued in June, stating that instructors in Russian should be appointed to the secondary schools at the earliest possible date, and that five years after the appointment of such instructors, all persons aspiring to positions in the civil or military service, or in the Church, must pass examinations showing a satisfactory command of the language.[12] By 1815, many of the secondary schools had added Russian-language instructors to their staffs.[13] The process was hastened by another decree in November, 1817, which fixed May 1, 1818, as the date after which all candidates for public office were required to comply with the provisions of the decree.[14] To be sure, certain modifications in the application of these decrees were introduced later. Students preparing for the ministry were exempt from them in 1824, and school teachers were likewise exempt after 1831.[15] But beginning in 1817, all students entering the University were required to pass an entrance examination in Russian.[16]

The impetus to the introduction of Russian came from the Russian authorities, but the men active in promoting the cause were Finns. G. M. Armfelt, mentioned above, left no stone unturned in his efforts to hasten the process. He seems to have been responsible for the decree of 1812. He was convinced that Finland's welfare would depend primarily upon the retention of the government of the country in the hands of native sons. A thorough familiarity with Russian on the part of the Finns would reduce, or perhaps eliminate, the danger to Finland's newly-established autonomy which the appointment of Russians to office would involve.[17] His knowledge of Russia and the Russians convinced him, furthermore, that the empire offered numerous opportunities for rapid advancement to young Finns willing to surmount the linguistic barrier. Nor was Armfelt the only man who held these views. Bishop Tengström, the primate of the Lutheran Evangelical Church, displayed a similar solicitude and considered the sending of Finnish students to Russia "the first strand in the tie which will unite, even in the realm of letters, the Russians and the Finns into one people." [18] In 1808, before Finland's political status had been fixed, a prominent Finnish army officer proposed to Alexander that contingents of Russian troops should be incorporated into the Finnish army for the purpose of facilitating the linguistic amalgamation which he considered desirable.[19] Six years later an educator soberly maintained that "Finland's progress in the future . . . seems to make it necessary that her inhabitants be brought into closer contact with the Russians. In any case, the education of the youth of the land must be planned with this in view, partly because it will mean larger incomes and more rapid advancement, and partly because it will give them a chance to uphold and strengthen, even outside of Finland, the honor of the country and a confidence in her fitness for higher intellectual accomplishment. It is for these reasons that Russian should

be increasingly introduced into Finland's schools." [2] In
1822 — to mention one more example — the lecturer in
Russian at the University wrote, in discussing the decrees
mentioned, that through them "the Russian tongue was
placed in the position which properly belongs to the language
of the conqueror within a nation united to him." [21]

CRITICS OF THE NEW ORDER

However, there were others who hoped that Russia's
annexation would be only temporary, and dreamed of a reunion with Sweden. In 1812 the two emperors whose agree-
ment at Tilsit five years earlier had caused the political dis-
turbance in the North were again engaged in a war. The
outcome of Napoleon's Russian campaign, these men believed, might cancel the settlement of 1808-1809.[22] They held
furthermore that the ultimate fate of Finland would be
largely determined by the attitude of Sweden. The shifting
currents of opinion in the Swedish governmental circles
were therefore closely followed by those hostile to the Russian régime and desirous of reëstablishing the old connection with Sweden.

The loss of Finland was not at first considered permanent
by the leading men in Sweden. King Charles XIII exclaimed in 1811, upon being informed by the prominent
statesman G. M. Armfelt of the latter's intention to return
to his native land, "We shall meet again, God helping us,
for Finland will return to us yet."[23] In the same year, Bernadotte, who had been chosen heir-apparent to the Swedish
throne in August, 1810, confided to the representative of
France in Stockholm that "When the Estates chose me they
did so only in order to please the Emperor [Napoleon] and

with the hope that the first result of his favor and protection would be the return of this province [Finland]. When I arrived, this foolish scheme occupied everybody's mind." [24] This attitude was strengthened by the growing tension between Napoleon and Alexander. When the final break between them came, however, these hopes were blasted. Sweden's foreign policy received a new definition at the hands of the man who had been looked upon as the future liberator of Finland. Bernadotte considered Finland as an unimportant province and a perennial subject of contention between Sweden and Russia. [25] In February, 1812, he convinced the Swedish State Council that any attempt to recover Finland would be hazardous and unwise and that in no event would Sweden be able to retain Finland permanently, even if Alexander's preoccupation with Napoleon should spell temporary success for Swedish arms. In April Sweden and Russia concluded secret agreements whereby each engaged to respect the territories of the other. The cession of Finland was thus again confirmed. The new liaison was solemnized in August of the same year when Alexander and Bernadotte met in Turku and the former guaranteed the latter's succession to the Swedish throne. An understanding was also effected relative to the cession of Norway to Sweden, and Russia was once more confirmed in the possession of Finland. [26]

These events deprived those Finns who hoped that the Russian régime was only temporary, of their only real support. Even those unable to view the situation in the wider perspective of the realities of international politics had no difficulty in interpreting the meeting of Alexander and Bernadotte as an event sealing the doom of the country. As far as Sweden was concerned, the new order in Finland had come to stay. If the verdict rendered by the war of 1808-1809 were to be changed, new sources of strength would have to be discovered.

The younger patriots who considered the union with Russia a misfortune were a mere handful of enthusiasts devoid of power and influence. Filled with apprehension when they contemplated the meaning of Finland's position in the empire — to them it seemed to spell unavoidable political and linguistic Russification — they cast about for safeguards against the calamity that beckoned in the future. They found this safeguard in what might be somewhat loosely termed internal, national unification. If the people of the country could be made to sense the danger, and if they could be welded into a nation conscious of a separate, distinct nationality, a new source of strength would in fact have been found. The feeling of national distinctiveness would be the rock upon which the future of the country could be founded, even if the Constitution were as chaff in the storm and political autonomy subject to the caprices of imperial policy.

The desired national unity, it was believed, could be builded only upon linguistic unity. We noted in the first chapter that Finland was divided linguistically into two parts. Confronted by this internal linguistic division, the early patriots proclaimed that it must be eradicated. Because Finnish was the language of the overwhelming majority, they concluded that Finnish should become the national language of the people. They fixed their attention particularly upon the fact that the middle and upper classes were predominantly Swedish in speech and maintained that these classes must be Finnicized. Because of the significance which the language situation began to assume in the program of the sponsors of the nationalist movement, and in view of the central position it came to occupy in the history of the movement during the greater part of the last century, it is necessary to turn back at this point for a glance at its antecedents during the Swedish period.

THE LANGUAGE SITUATION

In the main, the Swedish-speaking middle and upper classes were of Finnish origin. That Swedish had gained ground at the expense of Finnish among them was natural and unavoidable in view of Finland's position in the Swedish kingdom. In the process of Swedization, the schools had played an important part. It appears that as long as Latin remained the language of education, and until the centralization of the Swedish government had proceeded to the point where it began to eliminate localisms of every kind, Finnish remained the language spoken by a substantial part of the upper classes in Finland. In the course of the eighteenth century Latin began to lose ground in school and university, and Swedish became predominant in the field of education. The result was that a knowledge of Swedish became an unavoidable prerequisite for education in all parts of the realm. Whether a Finn aspired to become a servant of the State or the Church or desired to enter the professions, circumstances forced him to master Swedish. Of course, this necessity had been present even before the eighteenth century, but it became more impelling during the last hundred years of Finland's union with Sweden. "All who are educated for official positions and receive instruction in the schools," observed a professor in Turku in the seventeen-eighties, "are taught to understand and speak Swedish. Nobody considers this a cause for complaint. . . The advantage which the youth expect to gain from a knowledge of Swedish makes them anxious to submit to this trouble." [27] Even the elementary schools were apt to require a knowledge of Swedish as a condition for admission, and parents were therefore often compelled to obtain for their children at least a modicum of familiarity with the language before sending them to school.[28]

In school the difficulties of mastering studies in an unfamiliar tongue were frequently great, and education in general was likely to suffer, in that instruction in Swedish absorbed a goodly part of the pupils' time and effort. School principals and teachers occasionally complained of the situation. One of the main difficulties in the way of studies, wrote a school principal in 1802, was that "we are compelled to admit children who, while they are able to read Swedish, in most cases do not understand, much less speak Swedish." [29] In 1803, the exclusion of such children was proposed as a measure which would improve instruction in one of the provincial schools,[30] while a School Resolution from 1760 suggested another supplementary method: "Whereas Finnish has come into general use among the students, and considering the harm which lies therein, it has been decided that every instructor should see to it that this deep-rooted, harmful habit be eradicated. . . . " [31] It was with understandable concern that the Cathedral Chapter at Turku wrote in 1754: "If one considers the position of Finnish youth who frequently do not know a single word of Swedish before they are compelled to read a Swedish Catechism and a Latin grammar, one may well wonder that the greater part of the

pupils have actually succeeded." [32] Later it went on record
as being opposed to any policy which would discriminate
against the Finnish-speaking students by definitely compelling them to master Swedish before admission into the
schools. [33]

In view of these circumstances it is easy to understand
why Swedish, once acquired, tended to become permanent.
It was a valuable economic asset. In the course of the eighteenth century, it became increasingly the language of the
home of the educated and of good society in general. According to the testimony of an observer in 1779, "the gentry
and those who have obtained any education at all, understand and even speak Swedish." [34] A dozen years later the
same writer stated, in words which clearly suggest the
change that was taking place: "As recently as the beginning
of the present century the clergy, most of the gentry and the
greater part of the city traders and burghers spoke predominantly Finnish. . . But how great has been the change
since then." [35]

The process of Swedization was hastened, during the decades when Swedish was thus taking the place of Finnish
among the upper classes, by the gradual break-down of the
earlier sharp distinctions between noble and commoner.
Educational opportunity, formerly the exclusive privilege
of the few, became increasingly the possession of the bourgeoisie and even of the less well-to-do farmer and artisan. [36]
But as the act of embracing this opportunity meant per-
force the mastery and adoption of the Swedish language,
the middle and upper classes in general became more exclusively Swedish while Finnish tended to become a patois
spoken by the untutored town laborer and peasant.

That the gentry should have been particularly influenced by the ascendancy of Swedish was natural. Although largely of Finnish extraction and in many cases still Finnish in speech as late as the seventeen-seventies, the gentry more than any other class was affected by the growing monopoly of Swedish in the schools and in public life in general. This eighteenth-century remnant of an earlier influential landed aristocracy had become an office-holding aristocracy whose livelihood and prestige depended upon civil or military appointment, and consequently upon the prerequisites for such appointments. As a class, furthermore, it had been seriously depleted by the stormy years of the Northern War. During the decade of Russian occupation which preceded the conclusion of peace in 1721, all who could had escaped to Sweden and many remained there permanently. With the return of peace not a few native Swedes were appointed to positions in Finland. Such appointments contributed a good deal to the appearance of those wranglings about office holding which were mentioned in the preceding chapter, as well as to the further Swedization of the upper class. The ultimate result was that the gentry became more sharply separated from the bulk of the Finnish people than would have been the case if social stratification had rested only on birth and wealth.[37]

While the clergy was also influenced by the Swedization process, it never became as Swedish in speech as the gentry. The ministers of the gospel were frequently of Finnish parentage and with relatively few exceptions their mother tongue was that of their parishioners. When this was not originally the case, the position and functions of the clergyman, by bringing him into close and constant contact with the common man, made a mastery of Finnish inevitable. The clergy had used Finnish in religious services even during the Catholic period and had raised the vernacular to the stature of a written language in the first half of the sixteenth century. By the close of the eighteenth century the clergy represented, putting it broadly, the only group among the educated classes that was still Finnish in speech.[38]

As regards the bourgeoisie, they had largely become Swedish in speech by the nineteenth century. The trend toward social democratization which became fairly marked in the second half of the eighteenth century was reflected particularly in the increasing influence of this class whose wealth and culture had considerably increased during the preceding two hundred years. The climb of the enterprising man of business up the ladder of economic well-being, educational opportunity and political influence meant the adoption of the Swedish language. A generation or two usually sufficed to transform the successful Finnish-speaking artisan, shop-keeper or farmer into a Swedish-speaking burgher, government official, or member of the professions. The taking of a Swedish name was ordinarily the beginning of the metamorphosis; Swedization was as a rule the consequence of even moderate success in business, and the changing of Finnish names into Swedish was by no means uncommon even among the lowliest classes.

By far the greater part of the Finnish-speaking as well as the Swedish-speaking groups were farmers and fishermen. They appear to have lived and died but little touched or troubled by the ascendancy of the Swedish language. Before the rapid growth of population in the nineteenth century and before mechanical inventions revolutionized the means of communication and quickened every phase of national life, the lowly Finn and the humble Swede-Finn came into frequent contact with each other only in the cities and in those parts of western and southern Finland where they had lived side by side for centuries. Language seems to have caused no appreciable friction between them. Even in bilingual communities where questions of practical import had to be solved — such as the use of a common church, or problems connected with the care of the religious needs of a bilingual community too small to employ two ministers — the difficulties that arose were eliminated with ease. At times the spirit of mutual helpfulness assumed forms which showed uncommon considerateness and coöperation. The controversies which arose on occasion were more often consequences of the short-sighted selfishness of the local gentry, or the laziness and incompetence of the clergy or local officials, than the result of any antagonism among the common folk arising out of linguistic differences.[39]

It would be stressing the point a good deal to maintain that the language situation as outlined above was fully perceived and understood during the years covered by our discussion. As a matter of fact, it appears to have been but partly understood. However, a growing concern over some of its aspects was definitely making its appearance and before the union with Russia was a dozen years old, it had brought into being the beginnings of the Finnish nationalist movement. Its most important spokesman was Adolf Iwar Arwidsson.

Adolf Iwar Arwidsson

A poet, historian and newspaper man, Arwidsson was one of those who considered the separation from Sweden a calamity. Thoroughly versed in Swedish history and anti-

quities and keenly conscious of the superiority of the culture
and institutions of his country over those of Russia,[40] he
contemplated with horror the prospect of Finland as a part
of Russia. His anti-Russian feelings had led him as a boy
in his teens to participate in the pulling down of the imperial
shield from the city gates of Porvoo, shortly before Alexander's arrival to open the Diet in 1809. He saw no adequate
guaranties in the political autonomy solemnly granted to
Finland at Porvoo. He studied in Sweden in 1817-1818 and
while there became convinced of the need for a Finnish
nationalist awakening. "Through my sojourn in Sweden,"
he states in his autobiography, penned a few years later,
"my concepts of state and people became clear and vital,
especially after my return to Finland, when I had a chance
to compare the government of a constitutional state with
the submission of a defeated people, driven under the
yoke." [41] He noted the ignorance, indifference and venality
of the ruling classes. Their selfish chase for pensions, titles
and the like left them no time or inclination to consider and
work for the welfare of the country as a whole.[42] "Anger
fills my soul," he wrote to a friend in 1821, "when I consider how little the words 'people' and 'fatherland' are understood by our flint-hearted contemporaries"; and he concluded his indictment by exclaiming: "Oh, to have a real
fatherland, to be a citizen of a State, and not a squatter in
a mangy province governed by stupid asses and sly foxes." [43]
He proceeded to arouse his countrymen to the dangers he
perceived; he was determined to disturb the tranquillity of
both ass and fox.

The opening gun of his attack was fired in 1820. "In
order to bring my countrymen to their senses," he wrote a

couple of years later in giving an account of the incident,
"and to disturb the long sleep of the authorities, I decided
that something must be risked. . . Already in the early days
[of 1820] I dispatched a short essay, 'Letters from Finland.
By a Traveling Swede,' [to a friend in Sweden] with the
request that he approach the printer Imnelius with the proposition that he publish them, on his own responsiblity. The
two letters contained a frank discussion, especially of our
Senate, and I intended to add to them a third on the University and a fourth on the internal conditions of the country. . . To avoid suspicion . . . the letters were dated as of
July, 1819, because a group of Swedes visited Turku at
that time." Arwidsson got into difficulties with the printer,
and did not write the contemplated additional letters. But
the first two "Imnelius printed in his paper. . ."[44] He was
hauled to court for it and given three months in jail. The
articles created a terrific furor here at home [in Finland].
They were circulated in hundreds of copies. The general
discontent in the country, which had hitherto lacked definite
expression, used them as a whip which could at least be
brandished at the disliked Senate. The pompous dignitaries
of the Senate raised a horrible howl; the public gave un-
stinted praise . . . And as for me, I certainly was satisfied." [45]

The tenor of the "Letters" can be surmised even from
this somewhat exaggerated account by their author. A few
brief quotations will suffice to illustrate their content. Re-
ferring to the organization of the Finnish state in 1809 and
the years following, Arwidsson charged the leading men of
that day with gross incompetence.

They considered it quite enough to secure their own economic
interests. . . Servile boot licking was deemed the best way leading

to personal preferment. . . Their humble, solemn prayer was:
'Give us *today* our daily bread' and that secured, the rest could
take care of itself. . . The main feature of the new status of Finland was the disarming of the country, whose defense was left to
Russian troops. The teeth of the country were thus extracted by
her own men and placed on a silken cushion at the foot of the
conqueror's throne. Rather to be fed like a toothless old man in
the Home for Invalids maintained by the great empire, they felt,
than to rely upon one's own ability to make a living.[46]

This wholesale condemnation was accompanied by an
equally complimentary evaluation of the members of the
Finnish Senate. Arwidsson admitted that they were acceptable as officials appointed to to carry out orders, but as real
administrators and statesmen he found them hopeless. "The
greatest misfortune is that the future gives us no promise of
improvement. It is wasted effort to try to find among the
younger members men with real competence and thorough
training. A few utilize their spare time wisely; most of them
waste it on women and cards." [47]

These reflections were hazardous even in an foreign
paper, and would have been quite impossible in Finland.
There the attack had to be made in a less militant manner.
Arwidsson realized this full well. While he chose the press
as his weapon and became the ablest editor of his time, he
attempted to keep within the limits imposed by the prevailing
censorship. In the year 1821 he founded a paper of his own,
the *Åbo Morgonblad* (*Åbo Morning News*). It was in its
pages that he began to prod his countrymen to a new realization of the needs of the time.

Already in the second issue of his paper, Arwidsson presented the interpretation of the new position of Finland
upon which most of his nationalist argument was later to

rest. Finland was no longer a province, he pointed out, but a constitutional state. Self-government created conditions and demands which could not be met by the sterile efficiency of a bureaucratic officialdom. Statesmen of larger stature were needed; and above all an unselfish love of country and the people should replace the narrow provincial patriotism of earlier days, which only too frequently failed to free itself from grasping self-interest. The people must be reborn; a more enlightened view of public questions must be inculcated. This could be achieved only by the coming generation; hence the education and training of the youth should be the major concern of all true patriots. The educational system must be thoroughly overhauled, and infused with a "national aim" which it had hitherto lacked. In explaining the meaning of this "national aim," Arwidsson pointed out that one of the consequences of Finland's long union with Sweden had been a partial Swedization of the Finns. The disruption of that union had brought about a realization of how much had been lost by this de-nationalizing process. "All the Finns ought now to constitute a united whole, every citizen ought to feel deep in his heart that he is a Finn and nothing else,"— and yet, was not the country hopelessly divided by the fact that a language barrier separated the upper classes from the lower? The national aim of which Arwidsson spoke could be attained only if the teaching of Finnish should become general and education, instead of being limited to the Swedish-speaking classes — and thus continuing the Swedization process — should become the possession of the nation as a whole. Finland's future would never be secure until its people became united, until a consciousness of separate nationality permeated them, welding

them into a whole and endowing them with the strength
which only the consciousness of a separate nationality can
give.[48]

[In presenting these and similar views to his readers,
Arwidsson evolved a theory of nationality which requires
brief mention because many ideas contained in it became
permanent parts of the Finnish nationalist creed of later
years. According to him, language is the main criterion of
nationality. All who speak a common tongue constitute a
natural indivisible whole. They are united by ties stronger
by far than the bonds through which a set of institutions or
a state bind people together. Language reflects the "dis-
position, character and habits of a people"; it is "the result
of age-long changes to which climate, political institutions, trade, agriculture, industry, science and art, as well
as political fortunes, have alike contributed." [49] The highest
aim and aspiration of a people should be the retention and
development of its individuality, which consists of everything that definitely marks one nation from another. Among
these distinguishing marks language is the most conspicuous. The welfare of mankind requires that nationalities
exist, for only through them can mankind in general be
raised to ever higher levels of cultural achievement and material well-being. Every nation which fails to retain its
individuality is therefore guilty of "cowardly, treasonous
surrender of the place assigned to it; it has revolted against
the Eternal Order" and has forfeited its right to exist.[50]]

Considering thus that language was the *sine qua non* of
national existence, Arwidsson demanded repeatedly that provision be made for the greater use of Finnish in school,
government and society. The overwhelming majority of the
population of Finland was Finnish-speaking. This majority

could never become the real beneficiary of educational advance unless its language replaced Swedish as the language of the schools. The majority could never feel a vital interest in the maintenance of Finland's government and judicial institutions so long as Swedish enjoyed its privileged position as the sole official language of the country. Finally, the Finns could never become a truly united nation while the upper classes were separated from the lower by a linguistic gulf. The gulf could be bridged and the people united only by reversing the process which had made the upper classes increasingly Swedish. In a word, they would have to adopt Finnish as their mother tongue.[51]

Unless national education solidly founded upon Finnish became general and progressive, it would be impossible to contemplate Finland's future without grave misgivings. It is safe to say that Arwidsson had Russia and Russification in mind when he declared that only a people which enjoys such national education "will be endowed with that strength and perseverance which rulers must take into account, and which the fatherland can depend upon to give courage in battle and a spirit of devoted sacrifice in the hour of danger." He recited with vigor the calamities which attend upon nationalities unable to retain their language and the purity of their culture. Dishonesty and a lack of loyalty were the characteristics of their family life, and political subordination to other peoples was their lot. There was no misunderstanding his solemn words: "Change us into half-Finns or half-Russians . . . and we shall soon sink to the level of full-fledged Moldavians, Wallachians or Serbs." Nor was it an accident that these Slavic peoples were made to serve as examples of extreme national degradation.[52]

It did not take long before the authorities, disturbed by

Arwidsson's activities, decided to silence him. He had been
under suspicion ever since the publication of the devastating
"Letters" in the fall of 1820, and in October, 1821, his paper
was discontinued. He refused to be muzzled, however. In
February of the following year he published an article in
another Turku paper. It appeared under the heading "Observations" and contained a pessimistic survey of the conditions
in Finland. The article included an incidental reference to
the military, whom he dismissed by saying: "A straight
back, a tight-fitting coat, social graces, a good supply of
curses — and the picture is complete." [53] This bit of analysis
cost the writer dear. The authorities sensed revolution as
well as insult in it. An investigation was held and resulted
in permanent expulsion from the University. Unable to find
satisfactory employment elsewhere because of the interfer-
ence of the enraged authorities, the young *Dozent* emigrated
in 1823 to Sweden, where he later became librarian of the
Royal Library in Stockholm.[54]

SUMMARY

There were many among Arwidsson's contemporaries
who shared his views. His advocacy of the elevation of the
Finnish language to the position of a national language in
the real meaning of the word was sympathetically received.
His demand that the use of Finnish should be stimulated in
order that the upper classes should become Finnish in
speech, and a Finnish national literature could be developed,
was admitted to be timely. Nor was he the first among
Finnish writers to define the basic importance of language
for nationality.[55] But Arwidsson alone seems to have considered Finnish as an indispensable support for the con-

tinuation of Finland's political autonomy. He was the first to point out that unless the people were united by the elimination of the linguistic gulf which separated the classes from the masses, political autonomy would break down at the first gust of ill wind from Russia. He was the first to identify the future security and progress of the country with a complete linguistic reform. The demand for a frank recognition of the fact that Finnish was the language of some seven-eighths of the Finns and that a unified Finnish nation would of necessity mean a nation Finnish in speech; that national unification could be achievd only by making Finnish the official language of the country and the language of the upper classes as well; that Finland's political autonomy meant little as long as it meant only the existence of a Finnish government, but might mean everything if intelligent, nationalist public opinion could be created and spread until the people became united in a self-conscious nationality able to bend the government to its will — these and kindred ideas Arwidsson bequeathed to his countrymen when circumstances compelled him to leave his country. The seed he sowed was destined to yield abundantly, although some twenty years elapsed before other men took up the task where he had left it.

CHAPTER III

TWO DECADES OF GROWTH, 1820-1840

THE LAY OF THE LAND

IF ARWIDSSON's collision with the authorities was applauded by like-minded patriots and if his departure for Sweden was regretted by them, neither the applause nor the regret was strong enough to disturb the tranquillity which characterized the conditions in Finland during the eighteen-twenties. Already before Arwidsson wrote himself out of the country, his articles had caused many a worthy to frown at the ideas he was propounding, and during the nine months the *Åbo Morning News* succeeded in staying within the limits imposed by the censor its list of subscribers grew ever shorter.[1] In the main, the following words may be applied to the decade following Arwidsson's disappearance from the scene: "Somnolescence and apprehension characterized our political life, and the same was also true of everything else."[2] Public affairs continued to be dominated by a small official class. Careful side-stepping of issues likely to disturb the existing order, nepotism, and a strong aversion to publicity, were conspicuous among those responsible for the administration of the country. Discussions concerning politics were seldom lifted above a live concern in vacancies, appointments, backstairs approaches to places of influence in the Russian capital, and the like. At the Turku

University, which was the center of the higher intellectual life of Finland, quietism and reaction reigned supreme. The European reactionary trend, which the mere mention of the Carlsbad Decrees brings to mind, extended to Finland also. Pedantic conservatism rather than progressive scholarship and interests met the student on every hand, and as for the professors, dismissal or even imprisonment for failure to accept unquestioningly the prevailing order was not unknown.[3] Arwidsson's statement to the effect that his agitation "broke over the authorities like the sound of the hunter's horn"[4] was true, but it was true primarily in the sense that it aroused some of Arwidsson's own countrymen to start the proceedings that resulted in his dismissal from the University. It did not bring them to an acceptance of the creed offered by the *Åbo Morning News*; less still did Arwidsson succeed in enlisting them in the nationalist effort he advocated.

Freedom of the press was non-existent. Arwidsson's arguments in favor of a free press had brought no tangible results and the printed word continued to be subjected to rigorous control. Efforts had been made already in 1810 to prevent dangerous literature from reaching the reading public. In that year the importation of almanacs printed in Sweden was forbidden, partly because these products of the printing press "would undoubtely cause trouble among the common people." In 1823 all books prohibited in Russian were declared equally prohibited in Finland.[5] A more comprehensive enactment was passed in 1829. Works dealing with artistic, literary or scientific subjects were strictly forbidden if they were objectionable from the point of view of the Christian religion, or if they disclosed a

lack of respect for the members of the Russian Imperial
family, for good morals or for the reputation of individual
citizens. A special Censorship Administration with a number of branches was also established to supervise the work
of the censors.[7] In 1831 the provincial governors in Finland
were charged with the responsibility of forwarding to the
Third Section of the Russian Imperial Chancery copies of
all newspapers and periodicals published in the country —
a measure which indicated that a double control over the
press was deemed necessary.[8]

After the *Åbo Morning News* ceased to disturb the authorities, problems of nationality and the like were for several years but seldom publicly discussed. The attitude of the
intellectual and social élite toward such questions during the
twenties and early thirties appears to have been well expressed by a contemporary who summarized the situation in
the following words: "A return to the former union with
Sweden was not thought of, and nobody wanted to think
of a complete amalgamation with Russia. . . We considered
Finland . . . our fatherland, and felt that Finland was an
entity by itself which could no longer become Swedish and
ought never to become Russian. In other words, we felt that
we were Finns, members of a Finnish nation. . . . " However, "if one can say that national consciousness existed at
the time, it certainly lacked a firm foundation; it was not
based upon a hopeful confidence in the future. . . It was
thought wisest to think little and talk less about the future. . . . "[9] Furthermore, "we had neither books nor
pictures dealing specifically with Finland and its historic
past. . . Everything we learned about our own country was
based on hearsay and discussion."[10] "Nobody deemed it

advisable to renew the efforts at arousing our national consciousness which had been made by the academic littérateurs" of the type of Arwidsson.[11] Enthusiastic patriotism did not disturb the solemn loyalty of the classes toward the Russian régime.[12]

But while the Arwidssonian nationalist agitation appeared to have vanished, leaving only the files of the *Åbo Morning News* as tangible evidence of its intent, the nationalist movement had by no means come to an end. Not only was the so-called Porthan tradition of the preceding generation kept alive; it was actually strengthened. The eighteenth-century interest in Finnish studies to which Porthan had made such notable contributions, obtained many new converts in the course of the eighteen-twenties and thirties. Putting it broadly, the nationalist cause was served for some twenty years after Arwidsson's premature labors by (1) work in the field of historical studies; (2) a growing interest in the introduction of Finnish into the schools; and (3) the discovery, compilation and publication of new stores of folklore.

HISTORICAL STUDIES

After the death of Porthan in 1804, Finnish historical scholarship produced only meager results for well over a quarter of a century. Whatever the reason may have been, it was not a failure on the part of the patriots to appreciate the value of history as an aid in the nationalist awakening. On the contrary, they seem to have realized fully the influence of national history in the attainment of their aims. "A people can be reborn only through its history. It is in the honor and renown of his forefathers that the young citizen finds sustenance for his patriotism and support for all his aspirations and deeds," stated the author of an article published in 1822 which emphasized the value of history as a stimulant of nationalist sentiment.[13] Three years earlier the School Commission had made an unsuccessful attempt to encourage scholars to undertake the writing of a history of Finland by offering a moderate money-prize for a suitable text book. The aim of the Commission was to bring forth a "text book . . . in the history of the Fatherland, written with a greater emphasis on the national development of the Finnish people than we find in Swedish histories. . . . " However, the conservative objectives of the Commission were clearly revealed by the provision that the contemplated book should be written in Swedish and should not provide entertaining reading for the layman.[14]

Nevertheless, the historical works that appeared during these years were few in number, and insignificant as sources of nationalist inspiration. They were for the most part cumbersome institutional accounts, overgrown chronologies, or arid biographical studies.[15] But while historical works of importance were as yet wanting, enthusiasm for the collection of historical sources was gaining ground. For example, the Turku Cathedral Chapter urged the clergy in 1820 to collect and preserve documents of value.[16] The collection of source materials was considerably stimulated by a great calamity in 1827. The greater part of Turku, the historic capital of the country, was destroyed by fire in that year, and most of the library of the University was lost. The loss was keenly felt and led to efforts to repair the damage by appeals for contributions by the nation, the attention of which was thus called to the significance of preserving the

records of bygone generations. The results of the appeal
exceeded all expectation, and ultimately the printed materials lost were almost completely duplicated by the dona-
tions of generous citizens.[17]

The teaching of national history was far removed from
that treatment of subject matter which in our day has
made instruction in history a powerful instrument in the
propagation of nationalist sentiment. In the primary and
secondary schools, national history was not taught at all;
instruction in history was limited to the ancient and medie-
val periods. The text books used were forbidding compendia.
As far as we can tell, no patriotic fervor on the part of the
teachers elevated instruction in history above the level of
dry factuality, or tempted them to follow such by-paths of
history as might have easily led to the exploitation of those
phases of the national past which were, in the eyes of the
patriots, most charged with nationalist meaning.[18] In the
absence of national history from the schools it is not surprising to find that for years after 1809, Sweden was considered by many as the Fatherland, and that the concept
"history of the Fatherland" often meant the history of the
old mother country.[19] As regards the University, Finland's
history appeared among the lectures offered in 1816 and
became a regular part of the curriculum some years later.
But it appears that here also no nationalist approach enliv-
ened the usual professorial exposition. The lectures were
largely based on the sober researches of Porthan and on
other similar sources; pre-history and distant periods in
general were cultivated to the exclusion of more recent
developments.[20] A dispassionate, semi-Romantic interest in
human life and institutions in earlier ages is disclosed by

the meager evidence we have of the nature of university studies in this field; it would be going beyond the evidence to say that the historical discourse was consciously employed to inspire the soul and quicken the heart.[21]

FINNISH AND EDUCATION

Of somewhat greater and more immediate importance than the writing or teaching of history, were the attempts made to extend the use of the Finnish language in educational institutions. It will be recalled that within less than a decade of the annexation of Finland by Russia, voices were raised urging that the educated classes should "nationalize" themselves by adopting Finnish as the language of their homes, and that, furthermore, they should bend every effort to effect a change in certain features of the educational system. The point particularly stressed was that unless the Finnish language were speedily adopted as the language of education, the educated classes could not become a truly integral part of the nation, and national unity could never be fully realized. Two brief quotations will suffice to illustrate the emphasis placed upon the necessity for eliminating the monopoly in school and university which the Swedish language enjoyed. "Without Finnish we are not Finns," proclaimed a writer in 1823, yet by every right the language of the majority of the nation "ought to be taught and used more extensively. . . Without its development, we shall never enjoy the advantage of becoming a united people."[22] Two years earlier, another writer declared that ". . . if we Finns ever hope to nationalize ourselves, the study of our mother tongue and its literature must be taken up in a serious manner at our University; it must not be considered less important than any other academic study." [23]

We have surveyed in another connection [24] the part which the educational system in Finland had played, before the nineteenth century, in the Swedization of the Finns, and the story need not be repeated here. But a brief statement concerning the language situation which existed for several decades after the separation from Sweden will not be amiss, for it will enable us to understand more clearly the reasons why the demand for a linguistic reform became a persistent part of the nationalist program.

According to an official survey of the educational institutions, made in 1826, Swedish was at the time the language of instruction in all the important schools in Finland. The exceptions were few save in the Viipuri or southeastern part of the country where German held the field to the exclusion of Swedish. Finnish was used only in the lowest schools in Finnish-speaking parishes. These parish schools were unpretentious establishments whose educational program did not extend beyond the art of reading and writing and elementary religious instruction. Neither in the secondary schools nor in the University was Finnish included among the subjects studied.[25]

The consequences of this state of affairs were detrimental to the Finnish-speaking students, as well as to educational advance in general. The complaint that the presence of students who knew little or no Swedish slowed the work of the schools was frequently heard.[26] In their efforts to cope with a difficult situation, the teachers at times tried to exclude Finnish-speaking students altogether, as is shown by a report in 1829 to the effect that extra fees were demanded of such students before admission was granted.[27] Under these circumstances, it was not necessary to urge the introduction of Finnish into the schools because of its significance to the nationalist creed; a concern in educational work and progress *per se* was sufficient to lead to the conclusion that something ought to be done. This is amply shown by a sober communication of the Turku Cathedral Chapter, in 1826, addressed to the School Commission. It stated in part that "although Finnish is the original and true mother tongue of our country, and therefore of necessity would seem to deserve careful attention and further development — as is the case among other civilized peoples — little or no attention was paid to it when our educational institutions were founded. Yet a knowledge of Finnish is not only desirable but well-nigh indispensable" in every walk of life. The Cathedral Chapter suggested that provision be made for the teaching of Finnish "at least in the primary schools" in which "an occasional hour or two" weekly should be devoted to the subject.[28] The suggestion led to no action, and is significant primarily as an illustration of the fact that even conservative leaders within the Church appreciated the awkwardness of an educational system which was rendered sterile because it inevitably and permanently excluded from its advantages the Finnish-speaking majority of the country.

The predominance of Swedish outside the class room and lecture hall was unquestioned, as far as the middle and upper classes were concerned. In the homes of the gentry Swedish held undisputed sway, although a fair familiarity with Finnish was common.[29] The absence of formal instruction in Finnish in the schools meant, however, that Finnish did not easily lend itself to the demands of polite society or of the world of letters. Probably the best illustration of the situation is the fact that nearly all the important nationalist argument down to past the middle of the century was written in Swedish by men who knew Finnish only poorly but who nevertheless considered it their mother tongue. Their view of the language situation appears to have been well stated by Th. Rein, one of the important figures in the nationalist movement, in the following words: "That higher education was the monopoly of a class sharply separated from the bulk of the nation by its language, and that the language of this class was almost solely used in the schools, the administration, legislation and literature of the country, was indeed a serious obstacle to educational advance, as well as a crying injustice toward the majority of the nation." [30] The obstacle could be removed and the injustice righted only by a thoroughgoing, democratic educational reform.

During the two decades following 1820, relatively little was accomplished by way of providing room for Finnish in the curriculum of the schools and of the University. A substantial step forward was taken in 1828 when the first lectureship in Finnish was established at the University. Thirteen years later Finnish was introduced into the secondary schools. In both cases the language became a subject of study only. To be sure, it was made obligatory in the secondary schools, but at the University it remained optional.[31] That the authorities were beginning to realize the need of a greater emphasis upon Finnish is also shown by the fact that after 1824 clergymen appointed to serve in Finnish parishes were required to present evidence of a satisfactory command of the language of their charges.[32] However, these reforms cannot be considered as reflections of a frank recognition of the place of Finnish in the field of higher education. This was rather conclusively shown at the dedication in 1832 of the new university buildings in Helsinki (Helsingfors) whither the University had been moved in 1828, the year following the disastrous Turku fire. The dedication ceremonies included appropriate addresses in Swedish and Russian but none in Finnish.[33] The whole question of obtaining for Finnish its "natural rights" in education appears to have assumed larger proportions in press discussions than in the minds of those responsible for the formulation of the educational policies of the country.[34]

FOLKLORE STUDIES

We have noted earlier that already in the course of the eighteenth century several Finnish academicians — notably Porthan — began to collect and study Finnish folklore. Speaking in general terms, the interest in folklore and related matters continued without marked interruption during the century following the publication of Porthan's *Dissertatio de Poesi Fennica* in 1766-1778; indeed, folklore studies have remained a respected and popular field down to our day. Yet it is necessary, in speaking of the development of nationalism in Finland, to take note of an important distinction between these studies before and after Finland's separation from Sweden in 1808-1809. Before 1808-1809, folklore, folk legends and folk songs were the concern primarily of academicians of no striking nationalist bent, although they often disclosed something more than a purely scientific exultation over their findings. On the other hand, after Finland had become a part of the Russian empire, the interest in folklore and related things took on a new meaning. In a very special sense it contributed to the nationalist

developments surveyed in the second chapter. One is justified in saying that Finnish nationalism as a purposeful
doctrine was formulated largely under the inspiration of
folklore studies which fall, from the point of view of time,
within the years 1810-1840. ⌐

⌐Probably the main reason for the greater significance of
folklore studies for Finnish nationalism during this period
was the appearance of Romanticism in Finland. Largely an
intellectual and aesthetic reaction against the cosmopol-
itanism and classicism of the eighteenth century, Romanticism gave a powerful stimulus to an interest in the common man and common things in general. Prominent among
its standard bearers were men like Herder and the Schlegels
in Germany, Scott in England and Chateaubriand in France.
The romantic movement ultimately influenced many fields of
scholarship, notably philology and history. It brought into
being or gave wider currency to many of our notions about
national distinctions, national consciousness and national
excellencies — ideas which are frequently compounds of
imaginative untruths and half-truths.[35] In a very direct and
striking way, Romanticism furnished a most important impulse to the Finnish nationalist movement by stimulating
that interest in folklore which led to the publication of the
Kalevala, the Finnish national epic, in 1835. ⌐

For many years after Porthan's death in 1804, much of
his work remained buried in a long series of learned dis-
courses. It was only after the disturbances of the war of
1808-1809 had passed into history that his work began to
obtain new and active followers. The severance of the connection with Sweden appears to have done much to turn the
minds of many Finns to various questions and problems

which easily took on a nationalist tinge when tackled by men of Arwidsson's stamp. [Folklore in particular became charged with new significance: it came to be considered as the very embodiment of those national differences and characteristics upon whose cultivation Finland's future would depend. It is a significant fact that the spark that revealed to the eyes of the patriots the true importance of the treasures buried in folklore was furnished by foreigners. Probably the most important among them was Herder.]

Herder [36] entered the picture in the following manner. In the fall of 1812 a young student, A. J. Sjögren by name, began reading Herder's *Andrastea* which he had chanced to find in the school library of his home town. Sjögren had already become acquainted with a work on Finnish mythology which had appeared under Porthan's influence some fifteen years earlier. The pages of *Andrastea* opened a new world to the young student. His attention was fixed upon Herder's ideas: a people in order to fulfill its "destiny" must develop its culture; culture is the result of the workings not of individuals but of folk-character; language is the basic and most important expression of this folk-character. Discussions of Macpherson's *Ossian*, Shakespeare, etc., made up a goodly part of *Andrastea*. Sjögren read everything, copied lengthy extracts and made notes. The effect produced by this reading is suggested by the words he confided to his diary: Herder's "writings held a magic charm for me. . . I have never given greater attention to any work than to Herder's *Andrastea*," and "I shall never forget the impression it made on me." [37]

The enthusiasm aroused by Herder was communicated to a small group of students.[38] A collection of Swedish folk songs which appeared in 1814, and Macpherson's *Ossian* which fell into their hands in the same year, served to keep them hewing to the line marked out by Herder. Several of the young enthusiasts went to Sweden in 1817 to continue their studies at Uppsala University. There their Finnish patriotism was kindled by the observations they made of the nationalist tendencies among the Swedes. The nature of their reactions to the new environment is suggested by a letter written by a member of the group. It stated in part that "we would like to show the Swedes that we can exist without their language or customs — yes, even without their Thor and Odin. . . If we ever want to obtain the respect of foreigners, we must be ourselves, and not try to be everything, for that means trying to be nothing. . . Let us not solemnly throw away everything that is ours; let us not offer as much as a cat's mew to Balder and Brage. . . ." No, "it is by reawakening the spirit of Porthan and thereby creating interest in our history and national language" that something of real worth will be accomplished. This should be done in order that "our posterity will not be a meaningless compound of a Russian and a Swede, which means a zero — but a nation independent at least in the realm of the intellect and the spirit. . . . " [39] The appeal to Porthan meant fundamentally but one thing: folklore. "No independent nation can exist without a fatherland," declared one of these young patriots, in words that might well be Herder's, "and no fatherland can exist without folk poetry. Poetry is nothing more than the crystal in which a nationality can mirror itself; it is the spring which brings to the surface the truly original in the folk-soul. . . ." [40]

The most immediate result of the patriotic zeal of the

group at Uppsala was the work of Hans Rudolph von Schröter. Von Schröter was a German lawyer who studied Swedish literature at Uppsala in 1818. He came into contact with the Finnish clique and developed an active interest in Finnish folklore and folk songs. With the aid of the Finns, he translated a number of specimens and published them in 1819.[41] Despite its meager content, the book became an important landmark in the history of Finnish folklore studies. In Sweden it served to spread a knowledge of Finnish folk poetry. In Finland it brought new converts to the patriots' cause and gave added point to their arguments. It is interesting to note that Arwidsson's first article of unmistakably nationalist content was a lengthy review of von Schröter's collection.[42] The collection became both a challenge and a promise — a challenge in that it urged Finns to take up a study which a foreigner had found not unworthy of attention, and a promise because it suggested that more important compilations of similar material might perhaps be produced if only men could be brought to address themselves to the task of unearthing new folklore treasures.

Some months before the appearance of von Schröter's *Finnische Runen*, another foreign influence entered the stage. The famous Danish philologist R. K. Rask visited Finland in 1818. He became familiar with some of the eighteenth-century academic treatises which had been produced under Porthan's guidance and learned of the existence of unpublished folk songs. He urged the further collection and study of the unique materials, and converted to his views one of the Finnish professors, Reinhold von Becker. Von Becker made one of the first extended tours of his country for the purpose of collecting folklore, and his findings and conclusions had a fundamental effect upon the work of Elias Lönnrot whose labors in turn culminated in the publication of the *Kalevala*.[43]

⟨With von Becker we enter upon a new phase in the history of Finnish folklore collection and study during the nineteenth century. The earlier period, characterized more by a Romantic, enthusiastic appreciation of the import of folklore than by a systematic, sustained collection of these treasures of an older age, now comes to an end, and the period of active collection and publication may be said to begin. In the course of the twenties, the work of preserving for later generations what remained of the songs and poetry of the forefathers was continued without interruption.⟩ Its first important results were embodied in a series of four publications by Z. Topelius — the father of the poet — which appeared between 1822 and 1831. In the place of the fragmentary earlier compilations, Topelius was able to offer lengthy epic poems collected among the common folk, especially from the eastern part of the country. He proved conclusively that folk poetry had not yet disappeared from Finland and that much might still be salvaged, and thus he stimulated others to follow in his footsteps.

Elias Lönnrot (1802-1884) entered the University in 1822 and at once identified himself with those who had begun to labor for the Finnish language. He came under the influence of von Becker, under whose guidance he was introduced to folklore studies. In 1827 he completed his first study in this field, an analysis of Väinämöinen, the central figure in Finnish epic poetry.[44] This investigation necessitated a thorough familiarity with Porthan's researches and the methods of von Becker. The contributions of Topelius were also utilized.[45] From the latter, Lönnrot received that love for Finnish folklore and mythology which ultimately enabled him to become the greatest of all Finnish collectors of folklore. In view of the significant consequences which flowed from Lönnrot's labors, his work and achievements must be summarized at this point.

Following the example of several earlier runo collectors, Lönnrot undertook to unearth songs and poetry mong the common folk in eastern Finland where the ancient art of rune singing had not yet disappeared. The first journey for this purpose was made in 1828. Others followed and were ultimately extended to Russian Carelia where Lönnrot found the richest stores of folklore and folk songs. The first results of these discoveries were published in four minor collections between 1828 and 1831. Having completed his medical studies in 1832, the young doctor moved to a distant inland town and continued his work of rune collector with renewed vigor. He tramped hundreds of miles, visited and made friends of the peasants skilled in rune singing, paid them for their services in money whenever necessary and on occasion had recourse to liquor to arouse spirits and loosen tongues. The results were astounding, and in a few years Lönnrot had collected thousands of items of songs. Their content was varied but the stories told in them were sufficiently unified and related to suggest that they might be combined in a unified whole.[46] The collector undertook the task of weaving a complete story out of the countless strands he had found and ultimately produced a connected poem of twenty-five runes, containing roughly 12,000 lines. Lönnrot named it the *Kalevala* and published it in two volumes in 1835.[47]

Because of the part played by Lönnrot in the compilation
of the *Kalevala*, the question has been raised whether the
Finnish epic is a national epic in the ordinary sense of the
word or whether it should be considered the creation of
the man responsible for its publication. It is obvious that the
Kalevala as it appeared in 1835 [48] had never been sung by
the rustic poets who furnished Lönnrot with its content, nor
is there any reason to believe that all of it was ever known
to them. It was gathered from various sources in the course
of several years, and the poems recorded by Lönnrot represented numerous variations of theme as well as marked
dialectic divergencies. In reducing this miscellaneous material into a unified whole, Lönnrot adopted a rather free
procedure. While he attempted to retain the order in which
the poems had been sung to him, his own arrangement tried
to follow the content and meaning of the poems themselves
and when they yielded no convincing clue, he made changes,
effected new combinations of a given theme, and on occasion
furnished lines or passages of his own. In making his additions, he followed the direction of the content of the poems
and cast his own contributions into a form indigenous to the
material obtained from the rune singers. In the course of
this work, Lönnrot's became in fact one of the rune singers,
for his procedure was not different from that used by the
singers in their less pretentious presentations of the songs
they had learned. Lönnrot thus became the last and the
greatest of the Finnish rune singers. It may be said therefore that if we consider the *Kalevala* as a complete poetic
product, most of it is Lönnrot's work, but if we consider the
episodes in it, nearly all of it came from the common folk
of eastern Finland and Russian Carelia. [49]

To the generation of the thirties, the appearance of the *Kalevala* was an event of first rate importance. It was hailed as a relic from a distant, heroic age — an impressive, Homeric poem which the people had brought forth in times immemorial. It had been handed down from generation to generation, and in the course of centuries it had dissolved into thousands of fragments which Lönnrot had recovered and joined into a mighty monument to the genius of the Finnish people. Its content was thought to be genuinely national — no foreign influences had ever marred it. As a historical source and a storehouse of mythology it was naïvely believed to be both dependable and unique. It disclosed a golden age of novel customs which charmed an age captivated by a Romanticist appreciation of ancient rusticity and the spell of a culture hitherto unknown. Probably more than anything else, the *Kalevala* gave life and inspiration to the nationalist movement of the thirties and early forties, and during the last hundred years it has left a deep imprint on many phases of Finland's cultural development.[50]

Critical scholarship during the past two generations has conclusively shown that most of the content of the *Kalevala* originated in western Finland; that instead of having come down from a hoary age it dates from the Middle Ages or later periods and that parts of it were composed — if this word may be applied to the Finnish epic — as late as the eighteenth century; that its episodes deal with Gotland and expeditions to Sweden; that many of the heroes and names in the epic show an unmistakable Germanic origin; and that, as has been discovered in the case of the Icelandic *Edda,* the runes in the *Kalevala* contain a good deal of material

directly traceable to Christianity and are not indigenous to
the pagan period of antiquity.[51] But while these conclusions
have robbed the epic of its earlier authority as a reliable
source for prehistoric Finnish life and culture, they have
failed to reduce its significance for the growth of the Finnish nationalist movement. It brought to light, it was held,
a fecund poetic genius of well-nigh national proportions
which compelled admiration. Also — and this was in many
ways more important at the time when the epic appeared —
it revealed the startling resources of the Finnish language
and came to play a decisive part in the development of
modern Finnish both as a spoken tongue and as a literary
vehicle.

When Lönnrot entered the University in 1822, the institution was in the throes of a lively controversy usually called
the "dialect struggle." The literary Finnish then in use had
evolved since the Reformation in the sixteenth century.
Based mainly on the West Finnish dialect, it was heavily
freighted with Swedicisms and was withal both clumsy and
inadequate. One phase of the nationalist movement was the
so-called "Finnization" of the literary Finnish which meant
that it should be purged of foreign words and idioms so as
to render it more national and more easily understood by
the common man. The supporters of this demand looked to
the richer eastern Finnish dialect as the future literary language while those who opposed it clung to the usage made
familiar by more than two centuries of literary tradition.
In this controversy, Lönnrot took a middle position, and the
language of the *Kalevala* represents an effort to find a compromise acceptable to the contending parties. Because most
of the poems were from eastern Finland and Russian Care-

lia, Lönnrot accepted the eastern dialect as his medium but made many important changes in it in favor of the western dialect. It is probable that this procedure was dictated by his desire to make the *Kalevala* sufficiently readable in all parts of the country to assure it the place and popularity of a real people's book. He failed in this objective,[52] but his choice of vehicle in the *Kalevala* as well as his later work as newspaper editor, translator, grammarian and lexicographer was decisive in determining the foundation upon which the Finnish language has rested since his day.[53]

The Saturday Club

We must turn back at this point to take note of an organization that played an important part in making Lönnrot's work successful and exercised a considerable influence upon the whole nationalist movement during the greater part of the last century.

Some years before the removal of the University to Helsinki in 1828, there was formed among the students an informal discussion club whose membership included several of the most prominent of the academic youth of the day. When the University was transferred to the capital, the organization became an important agency in the furtherance of the general nationalist program. It was called the Saturday Club and counted among its members nearly all the men then living who were destined to prominence, especially in the field of letters and of education, during the second and third quarters of the nineteenth century. Among them were Elias Lönnrot, Johan Vilhelm Snellman, Johan Ludvig Runeberg and Zachris Topelius, around whose names the history of one of the most important periods of the Finnish nationalist movement must largely be written. The central aim of the Saturday Club was the promotion of Finnish national consciousness and the improvement of the material and intellectual life of the nation. While literary and scientific matters and events like the Polish Revolt of 1831 were eagerly discussed at its weekly meetings, it was the patriotic ideal that furnished the real inspiration. Two results which flowed from the activities of the Saturday Club stand out. The first was the founding of the Lyceum in 1831 — a landmark in the modernization of the secondary schools in Finland. More important was the formation in the same year of the Finnish Literature Society.[54]

The main reason for the organization of this society was the desire of some of the members of the Saturday Club to enable Lönnrot to continue the publication of folk songs. Its general objectives were stated in the following words:

Because it is the Society's aim to work for the cultivation of all subjects that are related to a knowledge of the Fatherland or to the development of the Finnish language, the Society intends to collect all printed and written records concerning Finland's antiquity, mythology, geography, statistics, and the Finnish language and poetry; Finnish songs, old sayings and antique objects, as well as all publications, irrespective of subject matter, written in Finnish; and whenever possible, to publish works useful for the development of the Finnish language, history and literature; to give encouragement, by means of prizes, to the writing and translation of books on these subjects by competent authors . . . and to the study of specific problems related to Finland's history, literature and language.

The first and greatest single accomplishment of the Society was the *Kalevala,* the publication of which was made possible by the funds raised by the Society. In the course of the ensuing years, it became the center of patriotic studies of every description. Beginning in 1841, it sponsored the publication of *Suomi*, an annual learned review which has appeared since that year. As the headquarters for the publication of folk poetry and related material, innumerable text books, dictionaries and scientific works of every description, the Finnish Literature Society soon began to exert an influence upon the course of the nationalist movement and the intellectual development of the country which no other organization was able to equal. When the Saturday Club faded from the scene in the closing thirties, its main progeny had already grown to dimensions which the parent body never succeeded in attaining.[55]

The Saturday Club is associated with still another important impulse given to the nationalist movement during these years. In its patriotic atmosphere Johan Ludvig Runeberg (1804-1877) nurtured his interest in the lot of the Finnish peasant. In 1832 he published the first of a number of poems destined to have a profound influence upon high and low. The *Elgskyttarne* (*The Elk Hunters*) was a long hexametric poem describing the life of the peasants in central Finland. In the lowly tiller of the soil Runeberg discovered "patriarchal simplicity, a profound manly endurance, an inborn clear comprehension of life's most intimate aspects." These characteristics he threw into high relief in *The Elk Hunters*, which was acclaimed as the first great national poem of modern Finland. It placed for the first time living examples of the Finnish-speaking peasant before the upper classes, in word pictures that opened new vistas to the patriots. Among the friends of the nationalist cause Runeberg speedily came to be considered as the man who really knew the Finnish common folk and was able to impart his knowledge to others in a singularly captivating form. In his poems, said one of his contemporaries, "we recognized ourselves and felt that we were one people, that we had a fatherland and were Finns." "We are Finns, the voice of the poet told us, in Swedish, and we understood him." [56] The nationalists before Runeberg had spoken and written of the necessity of raising the bulk of the nation to higher levels of material well-being and cultural progress; it was Runeberg who fixed their attention upon the people they were trying to save. *The Elk Hunters* and other early poetic products of Runeberg were of greater immediate significance to the nationalist movement than the *Kalevala* for one may say that through them the Swedish-speaking upper class intellectuals found the people. [57]

THE PRESS

For approximately twenty years after the *Åbo Morning News* was killed by the fiat of the authorities, the press in Finland failed to carry on Arwidssons' work in the spirit in which he had begun it. Yet journalistic enterprise continued to play a part in the nationalist awakening. It gave currency to the aspirations and ambitions which led to the foundation of the Finnish Literature Society and the publication of the *Kalevala*. The nationalist significance of the journalism of this period, although it appears tepid and curiously deficient by comparison with the press of the last two generations, was sufficiently great to require brief summary.

While the first newspaper in Finnish had appeared as early as 1776, the Finnish-language press really began its history in 1820 when the *Turun Viikkosanomia* (*The Turku Weekly News*) was established for the purpose of furnishing the country folk with miscellaneous practical advice and cultivating their higher faculties. Natural history, geography, historical sketches and related subjects were given considerable space in its columns. It never became a propaganda paper, any more than its Swedish-language contemporaries, but its contribution was notable. It was well written and acted as a steadying influence in the "dialect controversy" and thus promoted the development of modern literary Finnish. *Oulun Viikkosanomia* (*The Oulu Weekly News*) offered sprightly articles on all manner of practical matters and kept its readers informed on the progress of folklore collection and other patriotic studies during the eleven years of its existence (1829-1840). The *Sanansaattaja Viipurista* (*The Viipuri Messenger*) was edited along similar lines between 1833 and 1841. Probably the most important among these papers was the *Mehiläinen* (*The Bee*) which Elias Lönnrot edited during the years 1836-1837 and 1839-1840. It approximated more than the others a real people's paper, and its purpose was to spread knowledge and love of the fatherland. It was in its pages in particular that Lönnrot laid the foundation for modern Finnish by lending his authority to the compromise between the western and eastern dialects.[58]

As regards the number of newspapers, the press was unpretentious in the extreme. In 1820 there were not more than three with total yearly issues amounting to 416. Ten years later, eight papers with 780 issues yearly were published, and as late as 1840 the corresponding figures were thirteen and 1,109. The circulation of the individual papers was correspondingly low. In 1833, the total circulation of the press was approximately 3,000, and eleven years later it was still somewhat under 6,000. Nor were the papers long-lived, as a rule. For example, the decade of the twenties witnessed thirteen journalistic enterprises of which only three were able to carry on for any length of time. The Swedish-language papers definitely outdistanced those printed in Finnish. In 1820 one appeared in Finnish and two in Swedish; in 1830 the figures were two and six; in 1837, three and seven; and in 1840, three and ten.[59] The Swedish-language papers were particularly important in the spread of the nationalist ideas, for they addressed themselves to the educated classes and their content was nearly always designed to arouse the patriotism of the reader.[60] However, some of the Finnish-language papers had a considerable circulation. When the *Turku Weekly News* in the closing twenties printed editions of 2,000 copies, the figure was considered phenomenal and remained a record for many years.[61]

The files of the newspapers reflect in varying degree the nationalist interest of the time. The importance of historical studies and descriptions was not infrequently emphasized, although the significance of history in the growth of a robust patriotism was often presented in a way that disclosed a Romantic appreciation of the past rather than a real understanding of history as a vitalizing force in the formation of nationalist ideology.[62] In general, the newspapers made no persistent attempt to popularize national history. History was left by them to take form at the hands of academic compilers who, as we have noted, were as yet but very moderately successful in forging history into an instrument for nationalist emancipation. Also, while the problems and interests of Finland were often discussed in a manner indicative of a clear-cut distinction between Finland and the Russian empire, the concept of fatherland had not yet been charged with sufficient patriotic meaning to prevent the occasional inclusion of dispatches from Russia under the heading "Domestic News." [63]

A significant feature of journalism during these years was an active concern in the advancement of the Finnish language. Even before the molders of public opinion had been startled by the resources of vocabulary and richness of idiom revealed by the *Kalevala*, the newspapers often discoursed on the beauties of Finnish and stressed the importance of its mastery for the upper classes. The appearance of the Finnish Literature Society in 1831 was greeted with expressions of satisfaction, and the efforts of those who labored for the preservation of folklore, or were engaged in writing grammars, were encouraged and considered as promises of better days ahead. The introduction of Finnish into the schools was likewise frequently urged.[64] On occasion the concern with "patriotic subjects"— a phrase much used at the time — was given added emphasis by appropriate foreign news. For example, articles on the then contemporary situation in Ireland and the work of Daniel O'Connel are found among the offerings of the newspapers.[65] However, it was only in the course of the eighteenforties that the press began to serve as an effective instrument of the nationalist propaganda.

CHAPTER IV

NEW SOURCES OF STRENGTH, 1840-1860

THE OUTLOOK

THE period from 1809 to the closing thirties marked, as we have seen, the dawn of Finnish nationalism. Nearly every variety of those intellectual interests and tendencies which our day and age recognizes as giving life and substance to nationalism began to contribute to the formulation of the creed expressed in the words, "We are not Swedes, we cannot become Russians, therefore let us be Finns." [1] Efforts were made to change historical studies from the calling of the academician or the pastime of gentlemen of leisure into a discipline for patriots. Many of the more obvious shortcomings of the existing educational system were discovered, and discussions concerning the "natural rights" of the Finnish language — with consequent demands that it be given a place in school and university — meet us with increasing frequency. The press began slowly to direct public opinion into channels leading to an understanding of the ideal which men like Arwidsson considered an impelling necessity: a united nation. And the work of collecting folklore, myths and songs was carried to a point where it was beginning to serve as a source of inspiration not only for learned investigators but for middle and upper class intellectuals as a group — was, in fact, unfolding a new promise to all who cared to read. Over most of this nationalist advance — for advance there was — Romanticism was writ large.

But in surveying these developments, we have been viewing only the face of the medal. The reverse carried a different relief. Its shadows began to show, by the early eighteen-forties, that while considerable progress had been made, the work was by no means completed.

In the first place, the nationalist endeavor still remained a purely middle and upper class movement. Its leaders were enthusiastic collectors of folklore and men of letters who drew inspiration from the results of their labors and extolled the virtues of the people who had treasured these evidences of poetic accomplishments and originality. They failed almost completely, however, to achieve the aim which was fundamental in the Arwidssonian program, namely, the spanning of the linguistic gulf which separated the Swedish-speaking classes from the Finnish-speaking masses. It was obvious that the eradication of the line which divided the nation could be achieved in no other way than by the Finnization of the classes. Yet this process of "nationalization" had made only inconspicuous headway by the forties. "Finnish is my mother tongue and Finland is my fatherland" was proclaimed often enough — in Swedish — but relatively few were able or willing to translate this slogan into an actual accomplishment.[2] To do so required not only the enthusiasm of volatile youth but the persevering effort of the mature man, and not many were able to contribute the latter to the furtherance of the cause.[3] The leading nationalists were more apt to debate the meaning of Finnish nationality than to try to become Finnish in speech.[4] The

nature of a goodly part of the nationalist agitation was
suggested by a newspaper in 1844 when it declared that
the time had come "to make less noise by writing and really
to do something for the Finnish language and the education
of the people." [5]

Secondly, the educational system still bore the stamp of
class rigidity and had yielded but imperceptibly to the nationalists' demands for reform. In spite of their frequent
discussions of the shortcomings of the schools, the patriots
had succeeded but very moderately in their effort to breast
the current which carried the existing order along its familiar course. The masses profited by the existing schools only
to the extent of acquiring the barest rudiments of learning
seasoned with the exhortations of the clergy who were more
interested in preparing the common man for his portion in
the world to come than in fitting him for nationalist-conscious citizenship in this. And as regards historical studies,
it may be said that on the whole they tended as yet to bring
forth a cult dedicated to the worship of bygone ages, rather
than men with a clear perception of the needs of the day.
For the time being at least, historical research appears to
have created a tendency to "bury oneself in the graves of
the past," rather than a determination to shape the present
and delineate the future in terms of a specific nationalist
objective. [6]

Thirdly, while the newspapers furnished the most important medium for the dissemination of the nationalist
gospel, they failed to free themselves from the limitations
which their middle and upper class antecedents and control
imposed upon them. The press was not partisan, for political
parties appeared in Finland only after the convocation of

the Diet in 1863. The papers contained mostly literary articles, reviews and the like, partly because of the prevailing censorship, and partly because reviews and magazines had not yet appeared to furnish a refuge for literary writing. The newspapers were not democratic in tone; less still were they independent in viewpoint or judgment. Their tenor was as a rule subdued and dignified; persuasive news was seldom matched by vitality or controversial intemperance. Pompous contemptuousness rather than spicy invective or compelling logic was the weapon used in the petty editorial combats that at times vitalized the compound of anecdotes and bits of gossip which were usually the liveliest items of editorial offerings. The Finnish-language papers were read by the common people, but they contained relatively little of direct nationalist argument, were few in number, and succumbed easily to economic reverses. The Swedish-language papers found their subscribers mostly among the middle and upper-class intellectuals and were unable to carry their ideas to the masses because they were presented in a language that was not understood by the bulk of the nation.[7]

Finally, the nationalist movement was almost wholly centered in the capital and extended but little beyond the limits of the university group which had given it birth and sustenance. The Swedish-speaking capital with its Swedish-language university was immeasurably removed from the life in the provinces. On the shores of the countless lakes, in the river valleys and on the plains of the interior lived the farmer and the artisan, the merchant and the petty official, almost wholly untouched by the nationalist awakening in the capital. To be sure, Runeberg had brought the Finnish peasant within the intellectuals' ken of consciousness, and

Lönnrot had endowed him with glory by showing that it was among the common folk that the stuff for the *Kalevala* had awaited the collector, but the peasant remained nevertheless outside the nationalist movement. The nation which the nationalists wanted to save by effecting the union of the classes and the masses was only too often thought of in terms of a Romantic concept to be idealized, rather than as a group of men, women, and children whose language was worth learning and whose life and problems required study if the nation were to be raised to a higher level of material and intellectual well-being. The new dispensation hardly penetrated beyond the circle of light shed by the academician's lamp.

Speaking in general terms, then, it may be said that by the opening of the forties the country had hardly attained to nationalist adolescence. In the course of this decade, however, the nationalist movement developed with unprecedented rapidity. The man who contributed most toward its growth was Johan Vilhelm Snellman, often called the Father of Finnish nationalism.

JOHAN VILHELM SNELLMAN

Snellman's background was typical of the antecedents of most of the nationalist leaders of the day. Born in 1806 in Stockholm during his parents' temporary sojourn in the Swedish capital, he came from one of the many Swedicized Finnish bourgeois families which contributed most of the leadership to the nationalist movement during the last century. He matriculated at Turku University in 1822, where he became associated with the Saturday Club and the interests of men of Runeberg's and Lönnrot's stamp. After the

Turku fire in 1827, Snellman continued his studies in Helsinki, took his degree in 1831 and was appointed *Dozent* in philosophy in 1835. His connection with the University was terminated four years later as the result of a controversy between the young *Dozent* and the University authorities precipitated by Snellman's desire to deliver a course of lectures on The True Nature of Academic Freedom. Disheartened by the opposition of the conservative elements which held the reins at the University, Snellman undertook a journey abroad in 1839. During the following three years he resided in Sweden, Denmark and Germany where he continued his philosophical studies and acquired an outlook on the problems of his country which was destined to have far-reaching consequences.[8]

Before leaving Finland, Snellman began his career as a newspaper man by publishing the *Spanska Flugan* (*The Spanish Fly*). The first issue appeared in the fall of 1839 and the remainder after Snellman had left the country. The *Spanish Fly* was designed to arouse the authorities and awaken the public by concentrating criticism on the weak spots of the existing order. Nor did the sting of the *Spanish Fly* miss the mark. In spite of the fact that its wings were badly clipped by the censor, the buzz of the *Fly* was sufficient to annoy and arouse its older colleagues; in general, Snellman's first newspaper adventure was sufficiently successful to mark the beginning of the end of the Romanticist, more or less ineffectual journalism which had held the field since the days of Arwidsson's *Åbo Morning News*. However, the *Spanish Fly* was not a carrier of the nationalist gospel. Its function was to sting and irritate, rather than to preach and instruct.[9]

During his stay in Sweden Snellman took an active part
in the endeavors of the younger Swedish intellectuals of the
day and began his serious newspaper work. His reactions
to the Swedish milieu and to his experiences in Denmark and
Germany appear not to have been unlike Arwidsson's during the latter's sojourn in Sweden some twenty-five years
earlier. That Snellman received in Sweden a powerful stimulus for his later work as the outstanding leader of the
nationalist cause in Finland is rather conclusively shown by
a letter penned in 1840. Writing to a close friend, he delineated the problems of his country and the outlines of the
program which he adopted as his own for more than a
generation.

> Our poor fatherland's age-long lack of independence [he said]
> is the reason for the total absence of patriotism among us. . . The
> educated class has *not the slightest* interest in the physical or
> spiritual well-being of the masses. Who among the men running
> the country are touched by the misery of the rural regions? What
> university graduate cares to lift a finger for the education of the
> Finnish common folk? . . . The mass of the people are turned in-
> ward because of long-continued oppression. They might possibly
> dare to find fault with the sheriff or the clergyman, but a governor
> is looked upon as a little god and a senator is considered a *non
> plus ultra*. They have hardly ever had an interest in the commune,
> parish, province or country, or a thought that conditions might be
> better. . . The bulk of the nation can never be raised as long as
> Swedish remains the language of administration and instruction.

The attitude of the upper classes, Snellman continued,
branded them as incapable of understanding what the situation of the country demanded. At best the classes believed
that "they could form an aristocracy capable of withstanding
the baneful influences of the east.[10] The result is a subser-

vient, oppressive aristocracy of bureaucrats. The educated
do not comprehend the situation and if they did, it would
be against their interests to work for its improvement."
According to Snellman, the country could be saved from
the dangers that threatened only if it were clearly recognized that "Finland can achieve nothing by force; the country can be saved only by the might that resides in education."
And as regards his own course of action, Snellman declared:
"I shall have done my share if I cry to the winds of heaven
what I have here whispered, and illustrate the argument
by references to the history of our country since 1809. . . ." [11]

Upon returning to Finland in 1842, Snellman made an
unsuccessful attempt to obtain a position at the University.
He was already considered an objectionable radical, and
even the leading newspapers refused to employ him. Find-
ing all doors closed at the capital, he accepted in 1843 the
principalship of a secondary school in Kuopio, one of the
small provincial cities. It was there that Snellman began to
labor in earnest for the nationalist cause, in the spirit disclosed by the letter quoted. A new phase in the history of
the Finnish movement was beginning; a more militant
nationalist agitation was making its appearance.

Two weekly newspapers, established by Snellman in 1844,
served as mouthpieces for his propaganda. The *Maanmiehen
Ystävä* (*The Farmer's Friend*) was printed in Finnish and
was designed for the masses. It was edited primarily with
a view to providing the common folk with useful reading
matter and contained but little direct nationalist argument.
More important was the *Saima* which addressed itself to
the Swedish-speaking upper classes. From the point of
view of both content and policy, the *Saima* speedily became

the leading paper in the country. It was nearly always filled with thought-provoking challenge, and its style was ever vigorous and at times blunt and intemperate. In the history of Finnish journalism as well as in the history of Finnish nationalism, the *Saima* marked the end of one period and the beginning of another. As regards the former, it provided real editorial leadership where well-meaning Romanticist littérateurs had previously held the field; as regards the latter, it presented a definite program and urged speedy action where its predecessors had been in the main content with wordy counsel.

The philosophical bases of Snellman's nationalist principles may be summarized as follows. In the life of the individual, he held, morality furnishes the only dependable guide. Morality consists in living and acting in accordance with the dictates of one's conscience as to what is right and what is wrong. However, the dictates of one's conscience are purely subjective and therefore are not infallible guides of conduct. One must therefore depend upon some objective norm for one's actions which is outside and independent of one's will. Such an objective norm is found in human society. Effort in behalf of the society of which the individual is a part furnishes him with the guiding star he needs — is in fact, fully in accordance with the strict demands of highest morality.

Man's morality attains to its fullest stature within the State or, in other words, in the field of politics. In political action man is laboring for the good of his nation. If he draws his inspiration not only from a deep love for his fatherland — a subjective element — but also accepts the spirit of his nation — the objective check upon the subjec-

tive inspiration — as a directive for his efforts in behalf of
the common good, he fulfills his obligations both as citizen
and as human being. But what the spirit of the nation is,
and what its demands, cannot easily be determined. Parliaments, constitutions and the actions of statesmen frequently
fail to disclose it or to indicate the demands of the hour.
The indispensable objective norm must be sought elsewhere.
It is found and resides only in the spirit of nationalism
which animates a people. The dictates of this spirit of nationalism must guide the average citizen as well as the legis-
lator and the statesman. It follows that this spirit of
nationalism, which is based upon a clear perception and
systematic development of the individuality of the nation to
which the individual belongs, serves in the last analysis as
the only directive for the life and labor of the true patriot.[12]

Having thus defined the general substance of intelligent
and useful citizenship, Snellman proceeded to indicate what
these principles required of all Finns mindful of the welfare
and progress of their country. According to Snellman, it
was self-evident that the Finnish nation consisted of the
Finnish-speaking majority. The Swedish-speaking upper
classes he pronounced to be a denationalized appendage of
the population. Their duty was to amalgamate themselves
with the Finnish part of the people from whose ranks most
of the Swedicized Finns had originally risen. "The Swedish
language and nationality belong to a foreign nation" and
not to the Finns, he declared. Hence Swedish literature in
Finland could never become a part of the national Finnish
tradition. Furthermore, it was denied all lasting significance
by reason of the fact that it was not clothed in the language
of the nation. But while the Finnization of the classes was

demanded by circumstances, the bridging of the linguistic gulf which separated the classes from the masses would be but one step toward the goal which must be attained. The educational system must be reorganized, for it could never become an effective or national agency for the elevation of the Finnish people as long as it was freighted with the short-comings of an undemocratic age. It should be renewed from top to bottom so as to meet the needs of a democratic era determined to instruct the many as well as educate the few. No less important was the emphasis which Snellman placed upon the necessity of elevating Finnish to the position of the official language of the country. He held that the administration of law was bound to be inadequate at best, and both hateful and foreign at worst, as long as Finnish was not recognized by law as the language of the law courts and of the administration in general.[13]

The course marked by Snellman was clear: the exclusiveness and inadequacy of the University and of the schools in general must be exposed and provision made for the introduction of Finnish into the educational system; lest the true interests of the fatherland be jeopardized by the continuation of internal linguistic disunion, the upper classes must become Finnish in speech; more lasting literary achievements in Finnish should replace the literary accomplishments in Swedish which were meaningless and inadequate from the viewpoint of the nationalist cause; and Finnish must be made the second official language, if the Finnish-speaking part of the population were to be brought to a realization of the fact that it had an interest at stake in the future and welfare of the country. It was to urge this comprehensive program of Finnization that the *Saima* was published. The highest duty of the individual and the pressing demands of far-seeing statesmanship demanded, according to its editor, that the program be carried out. "A house divided against itself cannot stand." [14]

Despite the prevailing censorship which prohibited all direct political discussion, Snellman was able to prove to his fellow journalists that many questions of vital public interest could be safely and profitably explored. The development of industry, the need for a more enlightened tariff policy, the importance of railways, and of public schools — every conceivable subject provided grist for the *Saima's* mill and was discussed in its pages. However, it was not permitted to carry on for long. Snellman's activity began soon to disconcert the authorities. His criticism of the somnolescence of the so-called intelligent public and the shafts directed at the shortcomings of academic and other dignitaries and their policies brought him enemies, many of whom considered him a dangerous visionary. At the close of 1846, the paper was silenced. But Snellman refused to be silenced. By the spring of 1847 he was editing the *Litteraturblad för Allmän Medborgerlig Bildning* (*The Literary News for the Citizens' Education*), a monthly review founded by one of his friends but in fact edited and controlled by Snellman. The content of the monthly was more exclusively literary than had been the case with the *Saima*, but its pages carried the message of its predecessor.[15] Snellman thus continued to prove to his readers that the usual plea of the Finnish journalists, "we write what we can and not what we would," was only too often a blind for incompetence or indifference or both.

EARLY GAINS

By the time the *Saima* disappeared from the scene, its propaganda for the nationalist cause was beginning to produce results and by the middle of the century the Snellman program had become a vital creed accepted by many. An impressive demonstration of the strength which the Finnish movement had attained was furnished by the annual student celebration in 1848. A student festival on Flora Day (May 13) had been long a part of the University tradition. It had been prohibited since 1836, but the prohibition was revoked in 1848. The occasion developed into a nationalist demonstration the like of which the country had never witnessed. Fredrick Cygnaeus, a poet and the ablest speaker of his day, electrified the thousands present with a compelling oration on Finland's Name in which he described the beauties of the fatherland and urged his hearers to live and die for Finland. The climax of the celebration was reached with the singing of "Our Country." The poem had been written by Runeberg two years earlier and set to music in the spring of 1848. It was sung over and over again, amid indescribable enthusiasm. The dramatic introduction of the song served to establish it, within a few years, as the national anthem of the country. The following stanzas illustrate the sentiments it expressed — sentiments that have served as a source of inspiration for three generations of Finns.[16]

> Our country dear, our Fatherland!
> Ring out, oh precious sound!
> No rising hill, no mountain grand,
> No sloping dale, no sea-washed strand,
> More dearly loved, can e'er be found,
> Than this, our fathers' ground.

Our land is poor, and poor shall be,
To him who gold doth crave.
Strangers pass here proudly by, but we
Shall always love this land. We see
In moor and fell and isle and wave,
A golden land, so brave.

We love our rippling brooks, so bright,
Our rapid streams, so strong,
The whisper of dark woods at night,
Our starry skies, our summer's light,
All, all that we in heart and song,
Have felt and cherished long.

Here fought our fathers, without fear,
With sword and plough and thought.
And here, in darkened times, and clear,
With fortune far away or near,
Their Finnish hearts have beat and wrought
And borne what fortune brought.

Who tells, of all the fights, the tale,
In which this folk withstood,
When war did rage from dale to dale,
When frost set in with hunger's wail?
Who measured all their wasted blood,
And all their patience good?

.   .   .   .   .   .

And if we once were made to rise
To gold clouds, from below,
And if we lived in starry skies,
Where no one weeps, where no one sighs,
To this poor, lovely country, though,
Our longing hearts would go.

The concluding stanza gave an optimistic promise of a
happy future which an all-pervading love of the fatherland
would make possible:

Thy blossom, hidden now from sight,
Shall burst its bud ere long.
From our love shall rise, so bright,
Thy splendor, hope, and joy and light,
And higher then shall ring, more strong,
Our patriotic song.

The exultation of the Flora Day celebration[17] was kept alive and strengthened by *Fänrik Ståls Sägner* (*The Tales of Ensign Stål*) which appeared in December of the same year. Having kindled the imagination of his countrymen twelve years earlier by his *Elk Hunters*, Runeberg now brought forth a collection of seventeen poems which speedily became a veritable treasure house of patriotic inspiration. The poems dealt with the events of the disastrous war of 1808-1809 which had made Finland a part of the Russian empire. They were portraits of men and incidents, drawn with consummate poetic skill and animated by a deep love of the fatherland. That the poet endowed thick-headed privates and simple peasants with the same brand of sublime heroism that he found in the actions of generals and other representatives of the presumably more intellectual classes, mattered little to the generation that was introduced to the *Tales of Ensign Stål* during the Christmas holidays of 1848. "We rejoiced, we sighed, we were enraptured [by them]," wrote a contemporary, "and our hearts beat faster than before. We felt more than ever that we belonged to a nation worthy of being preserved. This feeling no arbitrary decree could ever hope to suppress." [18] From that day to this, the *Tales of Ensign Stål* have remained among the sacred books of Finnish patriotic writing.[19]

ADDITIONS TO NATIONALIST IDEOLOGY

Finnish nationalist ideology was considerably developed in the course of the forties. The sustenance it received from the *Kalevala* has been mentioned in another connection. The *Tales of Ensign Stål* were also of inestimable value in endowing the heroes of 1808-1809 with endearing and inspiring qualities, worthy to serve as ideals for young and old. According to a journalist, the *Tales* taught those who did not already know it that the Finns were a brave and manly people; "a realization of this fact permeated the national consciousness." [20] But however important these sources were in the development of the Finnish nationalist psychology, they were in many ways no more important than the contribution made by M. A. Castrén (1803-1852).

Castrén entered the University in 1830. During the following half-dozen years he fell under the influence of the work which centered in the Saturday Club and the Finnish Literature Society and became an enthusiastic supporter of the Finnish program. The appearance of the *Kalevala* in 1835 decided his choice of vocation. He determined to devote himself to Finnish philology with the hope of being able to throw light upon the distant past of his people and their relation to the rest of mankind. His first conspicuous achievement was the publication of a Swedish translation of the national epic, an accomplishment of great significance in that it made the national epic fully available to the upper classes, many of whom were unable to read the Finnish original. During the decade that followed, he made several extensive journeys into European and Asiatic Russia and collected an impressive amount of philological data. The results of these investigations have influenced Finnish nationalists down to our day.

Writing to Snellman about his philological undertakings in the fall of 1844, Castrén made the following statement:

My work and ambition in this world are worth but little. But while one lives he must try to labor earnestly for the cause whose spokesman one is. There is only *one* thing by which I have been deeply moved, and I can live only for it — everything else is of secondary importance. I have decided to prove to the people of Finland that we are not a . . . nation isolated from the world and world history but that we are related to at least one-seventh of the people of the globe. If the cause of this nation is thereby served, all will be well . . . Grammars are not my objective, but without them I cannot attain my goal.[21]

His conclusions relative to the past and the racial affiliations of the Finns were drawn under the influence of this pretentious nationalist ambition. Five years after the lines quoted were penned, the conclusions were presented. Classifying the Finns with the Turco-Tataric, Mongol and Manchu-Tungus language groups, Castrén maintained that they all originated in the Altaic region; and thus he formulated the Ural-Altaic concept. The scientist-patriot achieved his ambition to establish a relationship between his people and a sizable part of the earth's population.

That this theory was a compound of the work of a nationalist visionary and the conclusions of an able philologist and grammarian, and that Castrén's interpretation of the racial connection between the Finns and the peoples mentioned is devoid of value, has been fully demonstrated since his time. For example, as regards the purely philological classification of Finno-Ugrian languages, and the racial connection which Castrén believed he had not only discovered but proved, an eminent authority tells us that "no valid reasons for this classification have yet been produced. The term 'Turanian' is equally devoid of value. . . ." Furthermore, "Finnish and Hungarian, though related, are about as widely separated from each other as English and Persian." [22] Another, in discussing the alleged connection between the Finns, the Magyars and the Lapps, concludes that "nothing could be more absurd than to assert a community of physical origin for the three. . ." and adds that "In race, as in religion, the Finns are truly indigenous to Western Europe." [23] However, more than two generations of Finnish historians and popular writers, as well as Finnish nationalists in general, have continued to accept as fact the naïve conclusions of Castrén — an interesting illustration of the nationalist will to greatness.[24]

OPPOSITION AND VICTORY

Already before the *Saima's* voice was stilled by the censor's fiat, Snellman's energetic journalism had caused uneasiness and opposition among the more conservatively inclined. Their unwillingness to follow the path marked by Snellman led him to maintain, in 1845, that Finland's hope lay in the hands of the younger generation which was willing and able not only to love the fatherland but to make Finnish its language. The younger generation was in fact beginning to participate in the nationalist movement in a manner that gave it a force it had previously lacked.

In 1843, a number of the more enthusiastic students at the University published a coöperative work designed to give Finland the real beginnings of a truly nationalist modern literature. Another followed in 1845.[25] In the latter year, one of the student corporations published the first volume of *Readings for the Benefit of the People of Finland* which appeared in three parts between 1845 and 1847. The *Readings* contained information on Finland's constitution — the most important parts of which were translated into Finnish — government, history and internal administration, and in general reflected an unmistakable nationalist feeling.[26] Also, Finnish began to gain an entry into the corporate life of the student "nations" whose official language had hitherto been Swedish.[27] In 1846, the Academic Reading Club, sponsored by students and the younger members of the University faculty, was established. It provided a forum and literature for those interested in the literary and nationalist developments abroad.[28] In the same year appeared the first issue of *Fosterländskt Album* (*The Patriotic Album*) which was wholly dedicated to exclusively national, Finnish interests.[29] A few years later, the students became active in the founding of rural libraries designed to stimulate the reading habit among the common folk, and offering them appropriate reading matter.[30] In keeping with these general tendencies, propaganda for the Finnish language was beginning to find converts among the teachers.[31] In a word, the younger generation was unmistakably enlisting in support of the nationalist cause.[32]

These and other similar gains were made in the teeth of a periodic opposition which threatened on more than one occasion during the forties to strangle the nationalist movement. The suppression of the *Saima* in 1846 has been noted. Its fate was shared by several other papers. The Finnish language papers in particular fared ill at the hands of the censor, probably because of their possible disquieting effect upon the masses. The culmination of the authorities' opposition to the new awakening was reached in 1850 when the publication of all books in Finnish, excepting those aiming at "religious edification or economic usefulness" was categorically forbidden.[33]

Curiously inconsistent with this reaction were certain measures to which the friends of the Finnish movement could point, by the decade of the fifties, as evidences of tangible success. In 1846 it was decreed that "considering the importance of having ministers who are fully familiar with Finnish" appointed to serve the needs of the people, provision should be made for the establishment of fellowships for those students at the University who "devote themselves to Finnish studies," and that in the filling of vacancies within the Church, a good command of Finnish should be considered a more important qualification for appointment than the term of previous service.[34] A year later another enactment provided that in the future no person should be permitted to teach in the lower grades of the elementary schools who "fails to show a satisfactory knowledge" of the Finnish language.[35] A third, dated February 8, 1851, made it incumbent upon the provincial Courts of Appeal to take into consideration the linguistic equipment of judges serving in "those parts of the country where Finnish is spoken," but the phrasing of the ordinance suggested that the requirement might be waived in the presence of other pertinent merits.[36] In December of the same year, a fourth law stated that servants of the state could expect promotion in the Finnish parts of the country only if they could present evidence of a knowledge of Finnish.[37] A more conspicuous victory for the cause was registered in 1850 — the very year of the sweeping censorship edict mentioned above — when the first professorship in Finnish was established at the University. M. A. Castrén became its first incumbent, by imperial decree. Both the new chair and the appointment of the patriot-scholar were interpreted as a signal triumph of the nationalist program.[38]

Nor was this all. The objectionable censorship measure of 1850 was practically rescinded in 1854 and the publication of Finnish works could thus be freely resumed. During the Crimean War and the following years the press was given a freer rein. The result was that the nationalistic Finnish-language papers in particular grew rapidly and obtained circulations that were considered astounding. For example, the *Suometar*, founded in the capital in 1851, had a list of subscribers during the middle fifties that approximated 5,000 — a figure several times larger than the *Saima,* or any other newspaper of the period, had been able to reach.[39] Another indication of the more liberal trend of these years was given in 1856 when Snellman was appointed to a professorship at the University. While the appointment was made in recognition of his accomplishments as a scholar and was by no means the result of the part he had played in the Finnish movement — his leadership of the Finnish cause had lost him the opportunity to succeed to a chair in 1848 — it appeared to mean that the day for fuller realization of the hopes of Arwidsson, Runeberg, Snellman and other nationalists was slowly coming. Furthermore, the importance of national history was given official recognition in 1856 when the first chair in Finnish history was founded. It was entrusted to Zachris Topelius, a strongly

nationalist poet, editor and scholar who had rendered inestimable services to the patriots' cause for nearly twenty
years.[40]

Most of these concessions to the nationalist cause were
obtained in the closing years of the rule of Nicholas I. When
he was succeeded by Alexander II (1855-1881), the nationalists looked forward to still further gains under the auspices of the benevolent Alexander. Despite his notable reforms in Russia, it may perhaps be said that he governed
Russia in the manner of an absolute ruler: the Reforming
Tsar's reign was still that of an Autocrat of All the Rus-
sias. In Finland his rule was different, however. He reigned
there, not as a monarch with unlimited powers, but as the
Grand Duke of a constitutional state. His liberalism made
possible the convocation of the Finnish Diet in 1863, which
led to the revival of the political life and more active self-
government in the Grand Duchy. The title "Reforming
Tsar" is perhaps no less justified by Alexander's policies
toward Finland than by the reforms and changes he was
able to carry out in the Empire.

Under the auspices of the benevolent progressivism of
Alexander's Finnish policy — which has prompted a recent Finnish historian to remark that "he ruled [Finland]
like a Western European over a part of Western Europe," [41]
— the nationalist movement was able to reach one of its
most important objectives: legislation elevating Finnish to
the status of an official language. The first definite step toward the introduction of Finnish into the administration of
the country was taken in 1856 when provision was made for
the appointment of translators to the provincial governments
for the purpose of issuing necessary public documents in

Finnish. Two years later it was decreed that beginning in 1859, Finnish would be the official language of the proceedings at Church and County Assemblies in the Finnish parts of the country. This measure brought to an end the antiquated and cumbersome custom, formerly required by law, of using Swedish as the official medium at such assemblies.[42] However, these measures did not touch the core of the matter. The monopoly which Swedish had long enjoyed in the law courts and the central and local government remained practically intact until the promulgation of the famous Language Ordinance of August 1, 1863, which has been called "the cornerstone of the future progress of the Finnish people."

The main provisions of this important measure were:

(1) Although Swedish still remains the official language of the country, the Finnish language is hereby declared to be on a footing of complete equality with Swedish in all matters which directly concern the Finnish-speaking part of the population. As a consequence hereof, documents and records in Finnish shall henceforth be freely accepted at all law courts and administrative offices in Finland. (2) Not later than the close of the year 1883, the aforementioned rights of the Finnish language shall have become fully operative even as regards the issuance of documents and records by law courts and administrative offices; judges and other servants of the state who already possess an adequate command of the language may issue protocols and other official documents whenever they are requested to do so.

The Finnish Senate was charged with the responsibility of proposing "ways and means for the gradual introduction of Finnish into the legal and administrative offices of the country, and for other measures demanded in consequence of this . . . ordinance." [43]

Superficially considered, the Language Ordinance of 1863 seemed to mark a great victory for the Finnish nationalist movement, for after twenty years Finnish would be official beside Swedish. The realization of this important objective would not mean the fulfillment of the whole nationalist program, however. Its content went considerably beyond the elevation of Finnish to the position of an official language. Furthermore, the nationalists were prompted to additional effort by the fact that for several years before 1863, active resistance to the nationalist movement had been making its appearance. By 1863 the opposition was strong enough to have become a factor of some consequence. In the next chapter, we turn to survey the rise of the opposition to the Finnish cause.

CHAPTER V

DISSENSION WITHIN THE RANKS, 1850-1870

SCANDINAVIANISM AND INDEPENDENCE SCHEMES

WHEN Snellman began his nationalist agitation in the eighteen-forties, his worst enemies were the prevailing censorship, the suspicion of the authorities toward everything savoring of innovation or change, and the conservative inclinations of the class to whom his message was primarily addressed. The Censorship Administration saw to it that the *Saima* did not venture too far into the forbidden fields of journalistic enterprise, and when the energetic editor proved too difficult to handle, his paper was suppressed. The unfriendly attitude of those who sat in high places was perhaps most clearly shown by the refusal of the university authorities to appoint him to the chair in philosophy that became vacant in 1848, for which he was amply fitted. The conservatively inclined upper classes frowned only too often upon the attempt to raise the masses to articulate, more intelligent citizenship, especially as the process involved, according to Snellman, the Finnization of the classes. Some considered such ideas revolutionary and dangerous, others pronounced the talk about Finnish nationality and its importance foolish and useless, while still others were willing to proceed only with utmost care and deliberation in the direction indicated by Snellman. Neither outright hostility

nor latent opposition, however, prevented the advance which
had brought the nationalist cause, by the close of the fifties,
far beyond the point reached thirty years earlier under the
stimulus of Arwidsson. The younger generation was largely
responsible for the advance, although it appears that the nature of the nationalist movement — it will be recalled that
it was still limited to literary and related enterprises — during the period partly accounts for the gains made.[1]

The first indications of a more wide-spread and active
opposition to the Finnish cause were intimately connected
with Scandinavianism. Scandinavianism was a movement
among university students and academicians and dated from
the eighteen-forties. Its main aim was to sponsor closer
cultural and intellectual relations between Norway, Sweden,
Finland and Denmark. In addition to working for a closer
rapprochement along these lines between the four countries,
some of its supporters were interested in certain political
questions of international import. Not a few of the Danish
Scandinavians contemplated enlisting the aid of their northern neighbors in the solution of the Schleswig-Holstein
problem, and the Swedish Scandinavians included men
deeply interested in the possibilities of recovering Finland
from Russia. The nationalist movements in Finland and
Norway, however, had created a somewhat less favorable
soil for the seed from which, the more ambitious Scandinavians hoped, a rejuvenated and strong North would in time
grow.

The Scandinavian movement was considerably strengthened by the political constellation in Europe during the
Crimean War. The widening anti-Russian coalition seemed
to spell the possibility of a paralyzing Russian defeat, lead-

ing to at least a partial dismemberment of the Tsar's domin-
ions and the liberation of Finland from Russian control.
One of the most important spokesmen of the more active
Scandinavianism which came into being under the stimulus
of these hopes was E. von Qvanten, a Finnish émigré resident in Sweden. An enthusiastic supporter of Finnish nationalism as defined by Snellman, he saw in the war the
opportunity for attaining the ultimate goal of Snellman and
his followers. The formula von Qvanten proposed was
simple: Sweden's participation in the war against Russia,
the liberation of Finland and the formation of a new Scandinavian state, a greater Sweden-Finland. A constitutional
king and common budget, army, navy, foreign affairs, and a
periodic Union parliament would constitute the broad basis
of the contemplated state, while separate administration,
national parliaments and independent control of the expen-
diture of taxes would guarantee the realization of distinctly
national objectives. Within this framework Scandinavia
would be united — for Norway had been united to Sweden
since the Napoleonic period — and the North would attain
to new and greater eminence.[2]

In spite of the efforts of the censor, von Qvanten's bro-
chures and Swedish newspapers containing discussions of
Sweden's foreign policy were extensively circulated in Finland and caused considerable discussion. Many Finns of the
younger academic group in particular became inspired by
von Qvanten's idea of an autonomous Finland united to
Sweden. Despite the five decades that had elapsed since the
age-long union between them had been severed, Finnish
sympathies for the old mother country were strong and
deep. More than six centuries of common traditions had

left an indelible imprint upon the two countries; their institutional life was identical in many respects, and it was not
difficult to consider them as parts of a united whole. It required no great effort to convince the enthusiasts that the
program delineated by von Qvanten represented not only an
alluring possibility but a reasonable certainty and that under
no circumstances should the chances for its success be decreased by a display of indifference toward it in Finland.
Converts to the new scheme for the political emancipation of
Finland debated the constitutional arrangements of the contemplated Sweden-Finland, scanned the columns of the
Swedish newspapers for news favorable to the success of
the project and drank toasts to English admirals and French
generals. Finnish Scandinavians, in a word, were heart and
soul for the von Qvanten program.[3]

Most of the Finnish nationalists, however, refused to be
carried away by the optimism of von Qvanten's supporters.
To the former, the collapse of Russia seemed but a most
remote possibility — especially as long as the hoped-for
larger anti-Russian coalition had not actually come into being — and the liberation of Finland a vain hope. Even if an
unexpected turn of the wheel of fortune were to make a reunion with Sweden possible, the union might not prove an
unmixed blessing. It would almost certainly place new
obstacles in the path of the Finnish nationalist movement in
that it would give an undue prominence to the Swedish-
language group in the country. Yet the further development
of the nationalist movement would be no less important if
Finland became a part of Sweden than it was while Finland
was chained to Russia. Sweden could retain Finland only as
long as the international situation in Europe was favorable

and no longer. The time would come sooner or later when Finland would again be at the mercy of Russia. When this time arrived — and it was certain to arrive — Finland would unquestionably be denied the constitutional and other privileges which had enabled the country to exist as an autonomous state since 1809. In fine, the seasoned workers in the Finnish nationalist vineyard were convinced that although Finland's position in the Russian empire was fraught with dangers, it was preferable for the time being to the uncertainties inherent in the von Qvanten scheme, the fulfillment of which was more than unlikely.

The rejection of the von Qvanten program — and with it, the chances for overthrowing Russia's domination that might have resided in it, in case the Finns had risen as one man to do battle for independence, and if Sweden had sponsored the cause — did not mean that the nationalists were not desirous of reaching out for political independence. On the contrary, some of them had come to consider political independence the ultimate objective of the nationalist movement and were of the opinion that it was specifically directed toward that goal. Speaking of Snellman's agitation, A. M. Castrén, the philologist, wrote as early as the fall of 1844:

Go ahead and call forth opposition [to Russia]. But if it is to reach far enough and bring us the result we desire, it must be political — it must be an opposition of the sword. If such an opposition were created at the present time, the result would inevitably be Finland's ruin. . . I consider all our undertakings nothing less than preparations for revolt. Not that we can expect to engineer such an enterprise single-handed, but we can abide our opportunities. Russia will sooner or later collide with the Turks . . . and Poland is only waiting for a chance to leap to arms. When the trouble begins, we too shall raise the cry . . . 'Down with the

Muscovite.' But I feel that for the time being we must make no noise. . . We shall proceed defensively as long as we are too weak to attack the enemy. War is our goal, but for the present we can only gather strength. We shall bring forth children; we shall write books; we shall cherish our patriotism and love of country; we shall all labor to the best of our ability, and God shall be with us. The Russian will never obtain power over us, least of all spiritual and intellectual power — this I know, for I have seen the terrible barbarism of Mogul's land.[4]

The idea of freedom from Russia was also clearly implied in the more guarded words of Y. Koskinen written in 1857, within a year of the Peace of Paris which closed the international conflict that the Scandinavians had hoped would lead to a redrafting of the political map of northern Europe. "We may hope," he said, "that Russia's desire for power will bring her into another contest with Europe and that we shall be destined to serve as the vanguard of Western civilization [against Russia]. We must prepare ourselves for this task of honor — and all the work for the furtherance of education in this country is preparation for it. Would that we could boast some day that in no other country has education permeated the common people more completely than in ours! Were that the case, we should be fully as strong in every respect as other, more populous nations." [5] That these words were written by a man who was emerging at the time as one of the leaders of the younger and more radical Fennomen who were destined to give greater definiteness and new direction to the nationalist movement during the second half of the last century, suggests that aversion to political independence was by no means the reason for the rejection of von Qvanten's scheme. Ordinary caution and political sagacity seemed to make its acceptance impossible.

The foreign policy of the Swedish government during the war, and the Treaty of Paris that brought it to a close in 1856, showed clearly that the older Fennomen's attitude toward the designs of the Finnish émigré was well warranted. But many of the optimistic Scandinavians in Finland refused to abandon the path upon which the alluring speculations of a Finland united to Sweden had placed them. While their political aspirations were crushed by forces and events over which they had no control, they felt that all was not lost and that another way remained which would lead ultimately to the sought-for goal. They reasoned that if Finland could not be brought into political association with the former mother country, a closer cultural and linguistic union was still possible — was, in fact, rendered imperative by the very circumstances that had prevented the realization of more ambitions aspirations.

The basic ideas formulated by the Finns who subscribed to the idea that the outcome of the Crimean War made such a linguistic and cultural rapprochement necessary may be briefly summarized as follows. The so-called Swedish tradition in Finland, a priceless heritage from bygone ages, should be maintained and strengthened. More specifically, the existing educational, judicial and administrative institutions — reflecting as they did the Swedish tradition — should be guarded against all change that might make them less Swedish. Therefore the Finnish nationalist program, with its insistence upon a progressive introduction of the Finnish language into all phases of public life, should be either rejected as pernicious or at best tolerated as embodying objectives of only secondary importance. For example, if the nationalist demands as regards the schools were car-

ried out, the break-down of culture and intellectual progress
would result. The Vikings or Swecomen, as the Finnish
Scandinavians were frequently called to distinguish them
from their opponents, held furthermore that if the language
reform were effected and Swedish were ousted from its privileged position as the sole official language of Finland, the
administrative and legal machinery of the country would
break down. More than that, they insisted that any attempt
to tamper with the existing language situation would only
open the door to the introduction of Russian, and hence all
patriots who embraced the nationalist program and labored
for its success were in the last analysis advance agents of
Russification. They were thus put down as the real enemies
of the country: the Snellmanian program was pronounced
harmful not only because it tended to deepen the gulf separating Finland from Sweden but because it was bringing
the country nearer to the greatest of all possible evils, Russification.[6]

Especially during the half-dozen years following the close
of the Crimean War, the differences between the Fennoman
and Swecoman interpretations of the demands of enlightened patriotism gave rise to endless controversy. The controversy was carried on particularly in the press. It was
fought with a fury and abundance of invective and denunciation that was new in Finnish journalism and frequently
led to unrestrained calumny destined to damage rather than
aid the cause of the contestants.[7] One of its conspicuous
results was the appearance of a Swede-Finn nationalist
movement in opposition to the Finnish nationalist movement. Another was the emergence of the Young Fennomen
group, determined to carry the Finnish movement to a
speedy and complete victory.

SWEDE-FINN NATIONALISM

The definite beginnings of the Swede-Finn nationalism were closely associated with a devolopment that was approximately contemporary with the controversies mentioned. It might be called, for want of a better term, the Discovery of the Swede-Finns.

From the beginning of its formulation in the days of Arwidsson, as we have observed, the Finnish nationalist doctrine was stated in terms that made the attainment of internal unity the be-all and the end-all of enlightened and unselfish patriotic endeavor. Both the continuation of Finland's political autnomy and the existence of the Finnish people, it was held, depended upon the successful fusion of the people into one nation, separate and indivisible. From this basic conviction, expressed in innumerable variations in the writings of the patriots during the second quarter of the nineteenth century, sprang the notion that the upper classes whose language was different from that of the majority of the people and who therefore strikingly illustrated the extent to which the nation was a house divided against itself, must become Finnish in speech. Unless they became Finnish in speech as well as in interests and loyalties, the country would be denied the strength without which, the patriots maintained, it could not hope to withstand the dangers which the association with Russia would sooner or later bring forth. During the period 1820-1850 the propaganda of the nationalists was concerned with few questions that were not directly or indirectly connected with the problem of speeding up the process whereby the upper classes were to become linguistically Finnish and truly national.

In their anxiety to remove the language barrier separating the classes from the masses, the Swede-Finn intellectuals and professional men who led the nationalist movement overlooked a language problem of greater magnitude. They either forgot or paid no attention to the fact that the Swedish-speaking population in Finland extended far beyond the small handful of academicians, clergymen, government officials, large landowners and business and professional men who constituted the bourgeoisie and the gentry. In 1850, the population of Finland numbered approximately 1,532,-000 souls. The Swede-Finns represented at the time roughly one-eighth of the total. Fully ninety percent of this one-eighth was composed of farmers, fishermen and common laborers who were socially, economically and educationally as far removed from the upper classes as were their lowly Finnish-speaking fellow citizens. [In other words, the language line divided the people of the country perpendicularly as well as horizontally. This the nationalist leaders failed to perceive. They were concerned with the uplift of the Finnish-speaking common man whose idealized character had been drawn with reverent patriotism in Runeberg's *The Elk Hunters* and whose poetic endowment, it was believed, had been disclosed by the *Kalevala*. His Swedish-speaking compatriot was left to shift for himself. The nationalists' attitude toward this larger Swede-Finn population was well illustrated by Snellman, who declared, in speaking of the Swede-Finn language group as a whole, "I distinguish between an unjustifiable and a legitimate [Swede-Finn] minority. The former includes all the state and local officials. They must obey and serve their master, the people, for they are paid to do so, and they must accept the language and the national spirit of the majority of the nation. The latter . . . is composed of [the remainder of the Swede-Finns]. They may live in God's peace." [8] Nor was their peace disturbed. Least of all did they become the objects of the nationalists' solicitude for rapid progress in matters of education.[9]

However, the sponsors of the Finnish nationalists movement contributed in two ways to the discovery, which was made during the controversial years of the closing fifties, that the language problem was greater and more complex than the conventional formula indicated. Both were indirect rather than direct. In the first place, the popular as well as learned local studies and descriptions of the forties and the fifties, which did so much to spread knowledge about Finland and its people among the nationalists, deviated at times from subjects that dealt only with the Finnish-speaking parts of the country. The Swede-Finn who lived by wresting a poor living from a niggardly soil or plied the sea or the lakes in quest of their riches, was also occasionally brought to the attention of the purveyors of the new dispensation. To be sure, many of the latter were primarily absorbed in turning out watertight definitions of nationalism or engaged in scanning the pages of some English or German writer for guidance in the art of nationalist argument and took but little notice of these glimpses of the Swede-Finn common folk. But the interest in them, once aroused, grew rather than diminished, especially because they also offered interesting material for the philologist and the student of folk-ways.[10] It was probably inevitable that the appearance of the Swede-Finns on the horizon would in time project a new element into the contemplation of the nationalist leaders.

Secondly, some of the more abstract aspects of the Finnish nationalist creed contributed to the same end. One of its major articles was, as we have repeatedly noted, the idea that language is not only the primary but the only lasting criterion of nationality. For example, the slogan "one nation, one language" embodied Snellman's conception of the insoluble connection between nation and language and expressed the main tenet of his reflections on the bases of nationality. It is doubtful if Snellman would have become irrevocably committed to this notion, had it not been for the fact that his main concern was the Finnization of the upper classes. In common with the other nationalists, he paid no attention to the majority of the Swede-Finn element and appears to have been unaware of the implications of his principle if applied to the Swede-Finns as a group. Yet it is obvious that as soon as circumstances should lead — accidentally or otherwise — to the application of this principle to the Swede-Finns, they would be endowed, by the very reasoning that led Snellman and his followers to their dogmatic assertions about the connection between language and nationality, with the indelible attributes of a separate nationality. Their Swedish speech, despite its deviation in vocabulary and pronunciation from the Swedish spoken in Sweden, would stamp them with Swedish nationality and would make more or less unavoidable interests and loyalties different from those extolled by the Fennomen.

These treacherous reefs and shoals submerged under the surface of the Finnish nationalist dogma remained long undiscovered. To be sure, the thesis that the Swede-Finns constituted a group somehow separate from the majority of the population of the country was formed in a general way already before 1850, and the plea that the Swede-Finns should not be forgotten in the enthusiasm for the Fennoman cause was occasionally presented years before the Crimean War.[11] But these were only stray clouds in a clear sky and did not become ominous until the controversy, let loose by the contest over the pros and cons of Scandinavianism, had swept over the land. This controversy proved to be the catalyst which precipitated, out of the disconnected and incidental cogitations concerning the Swede-Finns' place in Finland, the substance necessary for the formulation of a second, Swede-Finn nationalist creed. Its major arguments were furnished by A. Sohlman, a seasoned Swedish Scandinavian and journalist.

Sohlman was a conspicuous participant in the discussions centering on the possibilities created by the Crimean War for a more aggressive Swedish foreign policy and the chances for recovering Finland. In a pamphlet printed in 1855 [12] and secretly but widely circulated in Finland, he assumed a severely critical attitude toward the Finnish nationalist movement and its leaders. Starting from the contention that the Swede-Finn upper classes in Finland represented a fragment of the Swedish nationality and were not Finns at all, he proceeded to the conclusion that their attempt to merge themselves with the Finnish-speaking part of the population was stupid and deplorable. He held that this attempt represented a perverted attitude toward the Swedish mother tongue of the nationalists. The Swedish language should not be sacrificed on the altar of a falsely conceived and artificially stimulated nationalism. Such a course was nothing less than "national suicide" — a crime perpetrated by men who were voluntarily abandoning their language under the stimulus of an ideal founded on the poetic fiction that Finland constituted a single nation and that the people should therefore become one in speech. In divesting themselves of their Swedish mother tongue, the Finnish nationalists were committing a tragic error that was mortifying, silly and useless. It was mortifying because Swedes usually cling tenaciously to their language; it was silly because the nationalist leaders went about the business of Finnicizing themselves in the belief that they were engaged in an enterprise involving a noble and necessary sacrifice; and it was useless because instead of helping the Finns, it spelled nothing less than irreparable damage to the whole country for whose alleged benefit the denationalization of the Swede-Finn classes was urged.

Sohlman's concern for Finland and the Finnish nationalists was fundamentally that of a Swedish nationalist who considered the country a sort of *Svecia Irredenta* and the Swede-Finn upper classes its logical redeemers. However, though he completely failed to appreciate the assumptions and fears upon which the Finnish nationalist movement rested, he made one significant contribution to the nationalist movement in Finland. He specifically raised a question which had not previously been encountered by Snellman or his followers: What is the relation between the Swede-Finn upper classes and the majority of the Swede-Finn language group? The answer was clearly suggested by the contention that the former were pure Swedes whom historical circumstances had placed outside Sweden's political boundaries. It followed that they were part and parcel of the nationality of which the Swede-Finn hewers of wood and carries of water constituted the core. Being Swedes, theirs was not the responsibility for leading the Finns to the promised land of nationalist emancipation. On the contrary, the sacred laws of true nationalism imposed on them the duty to prevent Finnization in any form and to labor for the strengthening and further development of the Swede-Finn minority. While the obligations of citizenship in the Finnish body politic required nation-wide interests in other matters, the dictates of nationalist devotion demanded unflinching allegiance to the linguistic and related interests of this minority. In other words, the people of Finland represented two separate nationalities. Only sentimental theorists suffering from faulty logic could weld them into a united whole.

Within a few years of Sohlman's analysis of Finland's language problem and its implications, his ideas were transformed into a Swede-Finn nationalist theory. Its author was A. O. Freudenthal, the son of a Swede who had settled in Finland about the turn of the century. Freudenthal considered Sweden his fatherland, the Swedish people his nation. Coming under the influence of the "Scandinavian debates" during the middle fifties, he became an enthusiastic Scandinavian, condemned the course and aims of the Finnish nationalists as pernicious — he believed they were leading the country toward Russification — and soon emerged as the outstanding opponent of the Fennomen among the younger academicians. Following the reasoning of Sohlman, most of whose contentions he unqualifiedly accepted, Freudenthal formulated the notions which, with certain modifications, have determined the nationalist Swede-Finn outlook during the past fifty years and more.

According to Freudenthal, nationality depends wholly on

language; neither laws, customs, social institutions, historical factors, nor political conditions furnish its basis. For
example, because the language of the Americans is English,
they belong to the English nationality and do not constitute
a separate national group. With reference to the situation in
Finland, he held that the Swedish-speaking inhabitants of
the country should not and could not be called Finns, for
they were nothing less than pure Swedes living in a land
that was formerly a part of the Swedish kingdom. The
Fennomen's attempt to undermine their natural, Swedish
nationality was therefore sufficiently insane to justify the
use of the word Fennomania as a fitting appellation for the
Finnish nationalist movement. A genuine national spirit, he
stated, could mean nothing more than love of one's own
nationality and enthusiasm for its continued existence and
extension. Effort and work on behalf of the Finnish-speaking part of Finland's population was commendable, and
circumstances made it more or less inevitable, despite the
fact that the Finns constituted a "foreign nation." However, this work should not be allowed to undermine the position of the Swedish language in the country, and least of
all should Swedish men labor — by advocating the Finnization of the upper classes — for the diminution of the Swede-
Finn population in the country. The two language groups
were so different and incompatible as to make their amalgamation impossible for centuries to come, and therefore no
useful national policy could be based on the expectation that
real linguistic unity would some day be attained. Finally,
the Swede in Finland must defend at all cost the supremacy
of Swedish in the country. This obligation brings him into
conflict with his duties as a citizen of the Finnish state. The

conflict is more apparent than real, however, for the real interests of Finland require that the future of the country be placed in the competent hands of the Swedish-speaking upper classes. They and they alone were able to maintain Finland's membership in the Scandinavian family of nations without which all hope of genuine advance and progress would have to be abandoned.[13]

New Influences

Roughly coincident with the appearance of these beginnings of the Swede-Finn nationalist aspirations was the growing indifference toward the nationalist and language controversy among many of the younger intellectuals who came under the influence of English Liberalism. The channel through which English Liberalism flowed to Finland was the writings of John Stuart Mill. His essay on *Representative Government*, published in 1861, was extensively discussed in Finland's press in the course of the same year and furnished most of the ideas expounded by the Finnish Liberals for some twenty years. Although Mill was more interested in the abstract principles of government than in the concrete traditions and the moving life of nations, his work yielded much that seemed pertinent to Finland in the eighteen-sixties. For instance, his notions concerning nationality appeared to many to provide a way out of the dilemma created by the stormy controversies of the time. "A portion of mankind," he declared, "may be said to constitute a Nationality if they are united among themselves by common sympathies which do not exist between them and any others. . . ." The feeling of nationality is "generated by various causes . . . But the strongest of all is the identity of political antecedents; the possession of a national history, and consequent community of recollections; collective pride and humiliation, pleasure and regret, connected with the same incidents in the past." [14] Contrary to the contentions of the Fennomen, language did not seem to be the most important element of nationality; the authoritative pronouncement of the English philosopher rather appeared to suggest a view that was closely related to the Swecomen notions in regard to the importance of the Finnish language movement on the one hand and the significance of the Swedish traditions of Finland on the other.

The Finnish Liberals' stand on the language question was by no means exclusively determined by Mill's ideas concerning the relation between nationality and language. The Liberals were of the opinion, in the main, that because of the overwhelming preponderance of the Finnish-speaking part of the population and because of the undeniable justice of the demand that the language of the majority should be placed in a position of complete equality with Swedish, the Finnish cause would win a complete victory in the near future. The very extent of the following and support it had already obtained gave the nationalist movement the weight necessary to carry it to its logical conclusion. The time for other and more vital interests had arrived; the strengthening and further development of constitutional government, the stimulation of economic advance along all lines, the eradication of social maladjustments — such problems, the Liberals believed, had become increasingly important and had usurped the place which the nationalist cause had occupied for decades. The study and speedy solution of these problems were the real prerequisites for the progress — eco-

nomic, political and intellectual — without which Finland
would fail to advance in the arts of progressive civilization.
Adam Smith and John Stuart Mill rather than the prophets
of language reform or the masters of the abstract aspects of
nationalist ideology were to furnish the necessary guidance
in this important work.[15]

While the Freudenthalian anti-Finnish tendencies and the
creed of the Liberals were slowly gaining ground, the country was approaching an important turning point in its history. After the meeting of the Porvoo Diet in 1809, when
the representatives of the four Estates participated in the
work which gave political autonomy to Finland, no Diet
had been permitted to meet for more than fifty years. Acting in accord with the Finnish Constitution which reserved
to the Tsar of Russia, in his capacity of Grand Duke of Finland, the right to convoke the Diet, both Alexander I and
Nicholas I had refused to call upon the representatives of
the nation to share in law making. From 1809 to 1863, the
country was governed by administrative decrees some of
which originated in the Finnish Senate and others in the
offices of the imperial government. Government and legislation by decree was limited, however, by certain provisions
in the Constitution. The fundamental laws of the land could
be revised or repealed only by and with the consent of both
the Diet and the Grand Duke. As long as the fundamental
laws corresponded roughly to the needs of the country, no
absolute necessity for the Diet's participation in legislation
existed, and executive decrees sufficed. But when changing
economic and other conditions made revisions of the antiquated Constitution imperative and disclosed a growing need
for new legislation of fundamental character, provision had

to be made for the coöperation of the Diet, unless the Constitution were to be discarded and the country reduced to the status of a province administered directly from the Russian capital. When Alexander II came to the throne in 1855, a situation had appeared which made one of these alternatives unavoidable. Projected railway and canal construction involving far-reaching changes in the system of taxation, wholly inadequate laws regulating industry and commerce, a deficient control of the manufacture and sale of intoxicants — these were only a few of the outstanding problems that could be solved only with the assistance of the Diet. Unless the Diet were speedily convoked, the whole administration of the country would soon grind to a standstill.

The convocation of a committee in 1862 to discuss the more important legislative and administrative needs of the day suggested a revival of the Diet in the near future. The long-expected event occurred a year later when the representatives of the four Estates assembled to act upon the manifold question which the committee of 1862 had considered particularly pressing. The work of the Diet gave a new impetus to much-needed change in economic, social and educational legislation and conditions. A monetary reform, begun some years earlier, was completed and led in 1864 to the first coinage and circulation of a separate Finnish monetary unit, the mark. The establishment of a national currency served to stabilize finances and to give added relief to Finland's separateness from Russia. The construction of railways was seriously begun. Communal government was infused with new life by a law that considerably widened the sphere of local self-government. Progressive laws affecting

the rights of women were placed on the statute books, and
the modernization of the land laws was begun. The first
legislative attempts at curbing the liquor evil were made and
a more liberal press law was enacted. The educational system was overhauled and a state-directed, national primary
school system came into being. In spite of the anachronistic
organization of the Diet and the undemocratic basis of representation on which it rested — the former dated from the
Middle Ages and the latter from the eighteenth century —
it thus began, with marked success, the task of making up
for the time lost during the fifty years that had elapsed
since the meeting of the first Finnish Diet in 1809.[16]

AGGRESSIVE FENNOMEN

By the time the Diet of 1863 convened, it was becoming
evident that the language problem was arriving at a new
stage. Owing to the play of the many factors mentioned —
the Scandinavianism of the middle and late fifties, the gradual "discovery" of the Swede-Finns and the activity of men
like Sohlman and Freudenthal — the lines separating the
Fennomen from those whose attitude toward the Finnish
cause was either indifferent or hostile were being more
sharply drawn. The tendency was accentuated by a more
aggressive spirit among the Fennomen. They began to insist upon a speedier acquiescence in their demands. While
many obstacles had been surmounted, they held that much
remained to be accomplished. They pointed to several shortcomings in the achievements during the preceding thirty
years which appeared to challenge all true patriots to more
energetic effort on behalf of the Finnish cause. A few illustrations will suffice to indicate the reasons for the continued

Fennoman discontent which made them determined con-
tenders for the complete triumph of the nationalist movement.

Although the Finnish language appeared to have gained a
secure footing in the University in the course of the fifties,
the situation was far from satisfactory from the Fennoman
point of view. The commencement exercises were conducted only in Swedish as late as 1853.[17] In 1858, a special
permit was required for the presentation of the first dissertation written in Finnish,[18] and similarly, a special permission was required for the delivering in Finnish of professorial lectures. Such a permission, embodied in a special
ordinance, was not issued until 1863.[19] Also, the observance
of some of the earlier language edicts left room for complaint. It will be recalled that an ordinance dating from
1851 required civil servants to show evidence of a satisfactory command of Finnish. In pursuance of this aim, a
professorship in Finnish had been established in the Faculty
of Law, designed to give future lawyers and judges the
familiarity with Finnish which was contemplated by the
enactment. The chair was not filled, however, because the
Faculty of Law stipulated that the incumbent should be a
full-fledged jurist as well as a competent linguist, and no
person with the proper qualifications could be found. As a
result, the law students' knowledge of Finnish was not appreciably greater, by 1865, than it had been a decade earlier.
It seemed that the ordinance of 1851 was being nullified by
the conservatism at the highest educational institution in the
country.[20]

The unwillingness of the powers that be to make voluntary concessions to the Finnish-speaking part of the popula-

tion was illustrated in many ways at the very time when the famous Language Ordinance of 1863 was placed on the statute books. When the first railway line connecting Helsinki and Hämeenlinna was completed in 1862, no real effort was made to accommodate Finnish travellers or shippers. The railway personnel was almost wholly Swedish-speaking and time tables and tickets were printed almost exclusively in Swedish. The situation led one irate observer to remark that "all that was forgotten was the appointment of a committee to investigate . . . the passengers' knowledge of Swedish. . . Probably the only honor reserved for the Finnish-speaking people is the payment of the state loan on which the railway was built." [21] Ship sailings were only infrequently advertised in the Finnish papers, and, according to one writer, it was easier to keep informed on the sailings between England and France than between Finnish and foreign ports. [22] Even in the wholly Finnish parts of the country, tavern and hotel registries were kept in Swedish and in Russian, but not in Finnish. Birth certificates and other important documents were issued only in Swedish, [23] and the same applied to government bonds. The business world — in bookkeeping, commercial paper, bills, by-laws and the like — seldom employed Finnish. [24]

The situation in the capital was such as to serve the Fennomen as a cause of constant complaint. The number of Finnish-speaking inhabitants was, in 1863, somewhat less than one-half of the total and was rapidly growing. Yet all municipal authorities employed Swedish exclusively: the minutes of the town meetings were kept in Swedish, police ordinances and all public announcements appeared in Swedish and were published in the Swedish-language papers only.

All city administrative and other offices were equally closed to Finnish. When the municipal government considered, in 1865, the matter of making provision for the use of Finnish in the city government and offices, it was decided that no change in the existing situation was demanded by the circumstances. Furthermore, the city made no provision for the founding of Finnish schools, although the number of Finnish-speaking children was considerable. They were compelled to attend Swedish-language schools or remain outside the pale. Private enterprise and funds were necessary to change this situation, and when the first Finnish school was founded in 1860, it was financed and its staff manned by interested private individuals, most of whom were young university students.[25] The Fennomen's response to this slighting of the interests of the Finnish-speaking inhabitants of the capital was: "We must win Helsinki for the Finnish language." [26]

The early application of the Language Ordinance of 1863 likewise disclosed strong resistance to the introduction of Finnish into court procedure and administrative offices. One of the clauses of the law obligated the Senate to devise ways and means for carrying into effect the provisions designed to elevate Finnish to the status of the second official language of the country. In spite of the keen interest with which the Senate's action was awaited by all friends of the Finnish cause, it remained long inactive. The delay led the leader of the Young Fennomen, Professor Y. Koskinen, to charge the Senate with deliberately nullifying the intent of the law, whereupon the Senate instituted libel proceedings against its critic. On the strength of the Language Ordinance, the defendant's brief was presented in Finnish, whereupon the court handed down a decision that has become famous in the annals of the nationalist movement. The law of 1863 "concerning the placing of the Finnish language on a footing of equality with Swedish in all matters that directly concern the Finnish population of the country," it stated, "retains Swedish as the official language of the land. . ." However, Professor Forsman [Koskinen] cannot be included among this [Finnish-speaking] group in our population, and as we must rather assume that he fully masters the Swedish language . . . he is hereby required . . . to submit a Swedish translation" of his brief to the court.[27]

This decision gave an interpretation of the Language Ordinance that was fraught with far-reaching consequences. By refusing Koskinen the privilege of using Finnish in his own case, the court was in effect holding that no person who knew Swedish could employ Finnish in law suits. If this contention were correct, it followed that the Finnish-speaking part of the population was somehow inferior to the Swede-Finn group. The language situation which separated the upper classes from the lower, it appeared, was a condition which would be indefinitely prolonged. While the Language Ordinance and the enactments that had preceded it were designed, according to popular interpretation, to break down the linguistic barrier of generations, as well as to provide for the Finns the opportunity to be served in their own language, this decision appeared to strengthen the barrier and to limit the privilege of using Finnish to those who knew no Swedish. The reasoning of the court was filled with humiliation for all who had labored long and persistently for the Finnish cause: Swedish was official and national, while Finnish was the language of an inferior class

and could be official only in legal and other matters specifically and directly pertaining to this class.[28]

Although this narrow and untenable interpretation remained an isolated instance of a type of legalistic obtuse-
ness, it was more than sufficient to convince the Fennomen
that their battle was far from won. This feeling was en-
hanced when the recommendations of the Senate for the
legislation designed to carry the Language Ordinance into
effect led to the issuance of a supplementary language enactment in 1865. While it contained extensive provisions for
the use of Finnish in the conduct of public business, it retained the distinction between the two language-groups
which had been brought to light in the Koskinen law suit.
Its clauses also disclosed that the full application of the law
of 1863 would in all probability be postponed for several
years beyond 1883, the year set by the original enactment as
the date when the two languages would be on a footing of
complete equality. Only beginning in 1872 would judges
and administrative officials be obliged to use Finnish in the
discharge of their duties — that is, in cases involving Finnish-speaking citizens — and only after January 1, 1872,
would judicial and other appointees be required to know
Finnish. All incumbents already holding office on that date
were specifically exempted from this obligation.[29] As all
appointments to public office were made for life, it was
obvious that a substantial part of the judicial and other positions would be manned, in 1883 and for many years there-
after, by persons unable to serve the people in the language
of the majority. Furthermore, Swedish remained the language used in all business within the government and administration in all their branches. In a word, the law of

1865 showed clearly that the language situation, against which the nationalists had been protesting for decades, would not be righted in a spirit of voluntary and magnanimous coöperation on the part of those who held the reins of power. Their obstinate resistance to a liberal language reform added not a little to the resentment of the Fennomen and was largely responsible for the increasing bitterness which characterized the language controversy in the closing sixties and seventies.

Such were, then, some of the conditions and circumstances that served to gear the Fennoman movement to speedier processes and carried it once for all beyond the stage of protest and supplication, to the stage of more energetic and direct action. Under the standard of the more aggressive nationalist movement which made its appearance during the sixties, rallied the Young Fennomen, led by Y. Koskinen. Koskinen was a typical representative of the Swede-Finn intellectuals who furnished, as we have seen, nearly all of the leadership and strength of the nationalist movement. Born into a Swede-Finn family where no Finnish was spoken, he learned Finnish relatively late in life, changed his name Forsman to the more national Koskinen and became the first Finnish historian of note — he was appointed professor in 1863 — who wrote and published his works in Finnish. A devoted disciple of the veteran leader Snellman, Koskinen believed nevertheless that Snellman's program and tactics had served their purpose and should be replaced by a more radical approach and procedure. The elevation of Snellman to a seat in the Senate in 1863 virtually left the active leadership of the nationalists in the hands of Koskinen and enabled him to consolidate the strength of like-minded nationalists into a semblance of a party organization.[30] While the Young Fennoman group represented much the same diversity of opinion that had characterized the supporters of Snellman, the following may be said to represent the Young Fennoman views on the language question and the general objectives they considered essential for the nationalist movement.

According to Koskinen, a progressive nation's destiny is none other than advance in the arts of civilization. For such advance, a national language is an indispensable prerequisite, for without a well developed national language a nation lacks the medium necessary for this progress. Cultural progress, if it is to affect a whole people and not only relatively few individuals, demands two other essentials. The first is the use of the language of the common man in the transaction of all public business: laws must be enacted in it, justice must be dispensed in it, and public administration must be conducted by means of it. Secondly, the speech of the upper and educated classes must not be foreign to the bulk of the nation. Both of these prerequisites, Koskinen pointed out, were lacking in Finland. They could be acquired only by preparing for Finnish a secure and uncontested place in the public life of the country and by measures necessary for the growth of a numerous, Finnish-speaking upper class. Only a rigorous application and further extension of the Language Ordinance of 1863 could lead to the former result, and the Finnization of the secondary and higher schools would produce the latter. But no mere concern in general cultural and educational advance demanded the solution of the language problem along these lines. There were other more tangible reasons that urged a speedy and complete remedy of the situation. The bulk of the nation could never be expected to take a firm stand in defense of the country's institutions and laws unless the common man could perceive in them something worth defending, and not only something redounding to the profit and benefit of his "betters." However, as long as Swedish was retained in its privileged position to the exclusion of Finnish, the majority of the nation was automatically and effectively excluded from the full enjoyment and appreciation of the institutions and conditions that made Finland an autonomous state, governed by Finnish citizens. Until Finnish should become the real national language of the Finnish people, the citizens who spoke it would be deprived of many of the advantages enjoyed by the Swede-Finns by virtue of the fact that they spoke Swedish. Both the present and the future welfare of the country demanded therefore the Finnization of the classes, the educational institutions, and the official language.[31]

These views did not appreciably differ from the principles put forth by the nationalists ever since the eighteen-twenties. But the Young Fennomen showed that new wine had been poured into the old vessels. Their predecessors had hoped that the Finnish language would some day become the master in its own house; the Young Fennomen held that no human power could prevent it from becoming master in the near future. Firmly convinced that Finland's people would have to be welded into a single united Finnish people and that the day for the continuation of the peculiar and harmful linguistic division had passed they insisted that those in power should cease opposing the Finnish cause. "It is our conviction," said Koskinen in 1869, in speaking for the

Young Fennomen, that the government measures on behalf of the Finnish language "should not be permitted to appear as forced concessions. They should be measures originating in a frank and intelligent recognition of what is necessary and reasonable . . . At the present time there is no doubt but that the Finnish movement will be carried to its goal, either by persuasion or by compulsion. We much prefer to rely on persuasion, and the powers that be could not possibly commit a more regrettable error than to show 'de mauvaise grâce' . . . when called upon to perform a patriotic duty." [32] This threat of coercion introduced a new and militant element into Fennoman propaganda. It rested on the firm belief that the sheer weight of the Finnish-speaking part of the population would furnish the momentum necessary to make it effective.

Especially since the days of Freudenthal, one of the stock arguments of the Swede-Finn nationalists has been the contention that excepting possibly its earliest stages, the Finnish movement has meant outright and deep-seated hostility toward everything Swedish, and more particularly, definite aversion to the Swede-Finn population. For more than two generations the infinite variations of this claim have furnished a good deal of the substance of the Swede-Finns' justification for their opposition to the Finnish objectives. In view of the charges and counter-charges caused by this accusation, it will not be amiss to note what the supporters of the Finnish cause had to say, at the time when Freudenthal and Koskinen were beginning to obtain a growing number of followers, concerning the "Swedish traditions" in Finland and their relation to the Finnish movement.

"We are convinced," said a writer in 1859, "that . . . the

so-called Fennoman movement is a direct product of the feeling of patriotism which inheres in the liberty and in the social, legal and institutional life of Scandinavia. It is rooted in them, and from them it draws its strength. . . ." [33] The same idea was expressed by another sympathetic observer who summarized more than half a century of the history of Finnish nationalism as follows. For the Swedish-speaking upper classes in Finland, he maintained, the separation from Sweden meant a significant turning-point.

Deprived of support from Sweden and unable to lean upon the mass of the people who spoke a language different from theirs, the Swedish-speaking upper class felt that it was a stranger in the land of its fathers. It was inevitable, under the circumstances . . . that within the nation two forces would soon be contending for supremacy. The contest between them would determine whether the nation would continue along the familiar road of Teutonic-Scandinavian civilization and cultural advance or would lapse into barbarism.[34] At this critical point the Swedish-speaking educated class stepped forth to assume a new and higher leadership of its people. They learned the language of the nation, and anxious as they were to turn the scales in favor of Scandinavian civilization, they began to write in Finnish in order to foster thereby the intellectual progress of the people. . . This was the only way, lest Scandinavian civilization disappear [from Finland] like a wave on the sea of time. This is the substance of the so-called Finnish movement which has often been . . . branded inimical toward Sweden. Far from it; it is . . . the only way whereby the upper classes can labor for the maintenance of the spirit of Scandinavian institutions among our people.[35]

Koskinen and his followers spoke and wrote in the same vein. They neither desired nor demanded that Finnish should suddenly and completely replace Swedish. They did not wish that Swedish should disappear from the country nor did they believe its disappearance possible. The Swedish language was of unique historic significance for Finland and had penetrated, in the course of centuries, deep into the nation. For example, when the Diet convened in 1863, Koskinen repudiated the idea of classifying its members — as an enthusiastic nationalist newspaper writer had done — exclusively on the basis of their stand on the language question, and pointed out that while such a classification might well be made of the members of the Finnish Literature Society, it had no place in an evaluation of the competence of the representatives of the nation. In the matter of effecting the introduction of Finnish into the law courts, it was pointed out that no responsible Fennoman urged that this objective should be at once realized or that the consequence of the introduction of Finnish should be the ousting of Swedish. Also, the Fennomen frequently stressed the great significance for Finland of the Swedish period and the manifold influences that had shaped every phase of Finland's life during the six centuries of union with Sweden. But they showed no patience with the attempts, frequently made by their opponents, to justify the opposition to the Finnish movement by holding that Finnish nationalism constituted a danger to and a negation of the cultural and political progress associated with the Swedish period. Such efforts were strongly condemned by the Fennomen, who interpreted them as nothing less than proofs of an unreasoning aversion to the Finnish movement, and maintained that they were particularly harmful because they tended to "poison the most sacred feelings that can exist" between the peoples of Finland and Sweden.[36]

As regards the Fennomen's alleged aversion to the Swede-

Finn group in Finland, it will perhaps suffice to point out once more that especially during the first fifty or sixty years of the nationalist movement, nearly all of its supporters came from this group. They were Swedish-speaking upper class individuals who spoke and wrote on behalf of the cause almost exclusively in Swedish. Indeed, not a few among them failed to learn Finnish well enough to employ it in their propaganda. Their antecedents were in most cases neither more nor less Finnish than was the case with those who found the Freudenthalian creed congenial to their tastes and interests. Yet it is obvious that when the Fenno-men were declaring that "it is our intention, by using all permissible and legal means, to seize the reins which control Finland's weal and woe, and to carry to its final conclusions the cause which alone adequately provides for the needs of the country," [37] they were thinking in terms of the linguistic majority rather than in terms of the narrower and more provincial interests that were the main concern of Freuden-thal. They considered persistent labor for the strengthening of the nationalist consciousness of the Finns absolutely necessary, for the final arbiter of Finland's destiny, they believed, was power — the power that resides in the spirit of nationalism which can be best steeled in the forges of nation-wide education. Those who lacked the imagination and perspective to perceive the necessity of placing Finnish in the position which of right belongs to the language of the majority everywhere, were considered devoid of the social altruism and political insight which alone make intelligent and truly patriotic citizenship possible. Being thus primarily interested in the majority of the people, the Fennomen in-sisted that the welfare and advance of the majority should be the concern of all patriots, but it is difficult if not impossible to find among their pronouncements any hostility toward the Swede-Finns as a group. What resentment and hostility there was, must be considered a consequence of the obdurate conservatism of the bureaucratic elements against whom it was directed.

The endless controversies to which the appearance of the Swede-Finn nationalist movement gave rise during the closing decades of the last century need not concern us here. We turn instead to a consideration of some of the more obvious consequences of the contending nationalist movements. Among them were the following: (1) a series of legislative acts which placed Finnish on a footing of equality with Swedish; (2) the establishment of a national system of free primary education, and the appearance of nationwide effort on behalf of adult education; and (3) the rise of organized labor. Out of these consequences of the nationalist agitation grew centripetal forces strong enough to hold the nation together when Russification became, at the end of the century, something more than the dreaded possibility which had spurred Arwidsson, Snellman and many others to work on behalf of the Finnish cause.

CHAPTER VI

THE OLD ORDER CHANGES

LANGUAGE LEGISLATION

"The Language Ordinance of 1863," stated the Diet Committee on Petitions in 1877, "has become a sort of Magna Carta for the Finnish-speaking part of the nation. It is a document which grants them the privilege of free access to educational opportunity and to all the other advantages of citizenship which our laws and institutions guarantee the other inhabitants of the country." [1] Concerning the ordinance of February 20, 1865, which specified the manner in which the former enactment was to be carried out, the Committee observed that in its formulation, "a good deal of caution was exercised in order that more important interests and sound and steady social progress would not be endangered by too precipitate measures, nor by too strict an insistence upon a command of Finnish" among public servants. [2]

When this evaluation was made, fourteen years had elapsed since the beginning of the process whereby Finnish was to become official and six years remained of the twenty designated by the enactment of 1863 as the period within which the equality of the two languages would be fully established. But the measures taken by 1877 for the realization of the ultimate objective of this law were few and inadequate. While communal authorities in Finnish-speaking districts obtained in 1868 a somewhat wider use of Finnish in official communications addressed to them,[3] the regulations issued in 1871 concerning the language examinations of prospective candidates for advancement in judicial or administrative positions appear to have meant a step backward rather than forward. First, the personnel of the Senate, the Governor-General's Office and the Finnish Office in the Russian capital — for the discharge of whose duties "the Finnish language is not necessary" — were totally exempted from the obligation to present evidence of an adequate knowledge of Finnish. Secondly, the examinations in Finnish required of future lawyers could henceforth be taken either before or after admission to the bar, while they had previously been required before admission.[4] The paucity of these measures led several members of the Diet to state, in 1877, that "it is not without reason that the Finnish people anxiously inquire about the steps which will bring us, within the specified time, to the great goal. Irrespective of whether existing laws demand further adjustment, or new and more effective enactments are needed, it is . . . of utmost importance that the whole question be taken up for thorough reconsideration at the earliest opportunity, for when the Diet . . . convenes for its next session [1882] its initiative will unquestionably come altogether too late."[5]

Not only were the enactments mentioned inadequate; their enforcement was far from satisfactory. According to the opinion of the Committee on Petitions, the provisions of the decree of 1865 concerning the furtherance of a command of Finnish among employees were "admittedly devoid of practical value." Furthermore, the instruction in Finnish in the elementary schools leaves much to be desired, and the number of Finnish lycées is wholly inadequate. At the University, students from Finnish homes are at a disadvantage; the Faculty of Law graduates students without examination in Finnish, and it has occasionally happened that such persons have been appointed, in direct violation of the decree of 1865, to serve in Finnish-speaking districts; the use of Finnish in the administration of law in the rural regions has not become an actuality to the degree contemplated; the Finnish-speaking population has experienced difficulties in City and Superior Courts, because of the absence of detailed specifications concerning the issuance of legal and other documents in Finnish; finally, men who lack the knowledge of Finnish which will be necessary after 1883 . . . have been appointed to the lower and higher courts and . . . administrative offices, even without any kind of test of proficiency

in that language.[6]

While these factors and circumstances served to keep the language question before the public, there were a number of minor reasons why the controversy grew hotter as the seventies wore on and the year 1883 approached.

For example [ran the summary of the Committee on Petitions], the law of 1865 specifically states that all employees of the Survey and Forestry Office, the Post Office, the [State] Bank and the Customs must serve the public in Finnish whenever requested. In many cases this provision has not been observed. It would also seem natural that the same obligation should be extended to establishments like the State railways, and that the spirit and intent of the ordinances of 1863 and 1865 ought to be interpreted to mean that at all meetings and official occasions, which have a public and patriotic purpose, the reasonable demands of the Finnish-speaking citizens should not be neglected. Reality has shown, however, that . . . the Finnish-speaking population in the country has occasionally received but little accommodation, and has even met with disrespect. The causes for dissatisfaction may often be relatively unimportant . . . But the pettier the reasons for dissatisfaction the easier should it have been to remove them. . . .

if only good will and a desire to be reasonable had been present.[7]

At the Diet of 1877-1878, no less than six separate law proposals for the effective execution of the oft-mentioned Language Ordinance of 1863 were presented and discussed.[8] Also, because the existing language enactments were administrative decrees, and in view of the failure of the government to make adequate provision for the complete realization of the language reform delineated in 1863, some of the representatives made an effort to obtain a satisfactory law enacted jointly by the Diet and the Executive. The attempt failed because of conflicting views among the legislators, some of whom opposed further measures while others considered the language question a matter reserved for decision by the Executive alone.[9] The Diet appeared to be unable or unwilling to make adequate preparation for the changes that were to take place after 1883.

An attempt to divert the attention of the public from the language controversy and to give new direction to the political life of the country was made a few years later, when a number of the leading men of the day published the so-called Liberal Program. It may be said to have represented a summary of the views of the moderate Swede-Finns [10] whose influence in the Swede-Finn camp had been the most serious obstacle to the more rapid spread of the ideas formulated by Freudenthal and actively espoused, especially during the seventies, by the radical nationalist Swede-Finn leaders. Among the objectives presented were a reorganization of the Diet and a more democratic franchise; a clearer

definition of Finland's position in the Russian empire — a
somewhat meaningless proposition in view of the obvious
impotence of the Grand Duchy to initiate or effect any
marked change in the situation; a more liberal press law;
and the acceptance of economic liberalism. The language
question was relegated to a secondary position. An effort
was made to find a golden mean between the aggressiveness
of the Fennomen and the excessively conservative resistance
of the ultra-Swecomen to the Finnish cause. The objectives of the former were accepted, in the main, but many
features of their program were condemned. The Swecomen's
objectives failed of acceptance because, according to the
sponsors of the Liberal Program, they tended to divide
rather than to unite the nation. However, "safeguarding the
position" of the Swedish language in Finland was considered indispensable by the signers of the Liberal Program.[11]

Nothing came of this attempt to rally the country around
the flag of Constitutionalism, Manchester Liberalism and
moderation in the language question. The extremists within the Swede-Finn group rejected the liberals' program
without hesitation as a wholly inadequate means for the
realization of the creed of Sohlman and Freudenthal. The
Fennomen likewise refused to accept it, but not without
hesitation. The contemplated party would have become the
leading group in the four Estates and would probably have
guaranteed the execution of the language decree of 1863.
Furthermore, through it the Fennomen would have obtained a following among the Swede-Finns hitherto unwilling to support the Finnish cause. These advantages were
outweighed, however, by the meaninglessness and imprac-
ticability of the liberal program and by its failure to appeal

for support on the basis of specific pronouncements concerning the really pressing questions of the day. That is to say, the pronouncements concerning the further development of the Constitution, for instance, were of no real value because so long as Finland remained a part of the Russian empire, the Finnish government and people would be compelled to accept the verdict of circumstances rather than follow programs of the sort formulated by the Liberals. Therefore, any attempt to construct a political party on a platform which included high-sounding references to the modernization of the Constitution and similar matters, was bound to seem more or less divorced from the realities of life. Moreover, the Fennomen had arrived at the point where victory seemed to be within reach even without commitments of the kind that membership in the liberal alignment would have entailed. Not a few of the Fennomen were convinced that, in the words of Snellman, the question was "none other than the old concrete problem: ôtez-vous-en que je m'y mette" — that, in other words, the Finnish cause had grown sufficiently strong to elbow its way even without the aid offered by the sponsors of the liberal program.[12]

The suspicion that the government was attempting to retard the reform contemplated by the ordinance of 1863 was at least partly justified by a Senate proposal submitted to the Diet in 1882. The proposal contained a frank admission of the inadequacy of the measures taken since 1863 (". . . it is probable that a considerable part of our corps of judges still lack a sufficient knowledge of Finnish to use it easily in writing. . ."), and inquired concerning "the time which the Diet deems appropriate for the beginning of the full operation" of the decree.[13] That Finnish had failed to gain ground among the jurists of the country was well known even before the submission of the proposal, but the confession of the government made plain the fact that the authorities had been resting on their oars and were now taking soundings of the current that was carrying the country ever closer to the year 1884. However, all the Estates agreed in their replies — in spite of the predominance of Swecoman views in the Burghers and the Nobles — that the application of the language ordinance should not be postponed, although minor adjustments were suggested as a remedy in exceptional instances where an inflexible insistence upon the letter of the decree might cause difficulties or work unnecessary hardships. Judging by the official replies of the Estates, it seemed that they all agreed upon one point: the reform should be carried out within the time contemplated by the ordinance of 1863.[14]

Not long after the Diet had thus gone on record in behalf of having the ordinance fully applied by 1884, certain opponents of the Finnish cause made a move which was destined to influence the language controversy for several years to come. In the summer of 1883 — a few months before the elapse of the oft-mentioned twenty year period — the claim was put forth that all the existing language laws were unconstitutional, null and void. The claim rested upon an interpretation of the Finnish Constitution which requires brief mention of Finland's fundamental laws and legislative processes.

We have noted earlier that when Finland became a part of Russia in 1808-1809, the Grand Duchy retained the constitutional and general laws and institutions of the Swedish period with only such changes as the position of the new, autonomous state required. According to the Finnish (Swedish) Constitution, the Executive could "make no new law or abolish existing law without the consent of the Diet." [15] In practice this provision meant that the participation of the Diet was guaranteed in all important legislation, and strictly speaking the word "law" referred only to enactments which had come into being as the result of joint action on the part of the Executive and the Legislative. However, the Constitution granted the Executive the right to issue decrees having the effect of law. The circumstances under which recourse could be constitutionally had to legislation by decree were nowhere clearly defined, but the generally accepted practice was that legislation by decree was proper where no existing law enacted jointly by parliament and the Executive was applicable or where the constitution specifically reserved to the latter the sole right of decision.[16] In ordinary matters of civil law Finland was subject to the common law of Sweden which was cited much as English common law is cited in the United States, and more particularly, to the Law of the Swedish Realm of 1734.

The Law of the Swedish Realm of 1734 contained among other things lengthy provisions pertaining to the procedure and decisions of law courts. One of them stated in part that in court decisions "foreign laws shall not be applied, nor shall a foreign language be employed." [17] This prohibition dated from the Middle Ages when the legislators had attempted to free Swedish legal terminology from Latin and other foreign words and expressions. In its original form, it specifically decreed the use of Swedish in the administration of justice, but when the laws of the kingdom were codified in 1734, the reference to Swedish was omitted and the words cited above substituted, presumably because the basic cause for the original prohibition had largely disappeared by the eighteenth century. However, the intent of the statement retained in the code of 1734 was unmistakable: law courts could use no language other than Swedish in the discharge of their duties.

The contention that the Finnish language decrees from 1863 on were unconstitutional rested upon the following arguments: (1) the law of 1734 was a so-called Diet law — that is to say, jointly enacted by King and Riksdag, and therefore could be amended or changed only with the consent of both the Legislative and the Executive; (2) existing law clearly provided that law courts must use the Swedish language and no other, and the constitution in no way reserved to the Executive alone the right to decree in the matter; (3) the language enactments were all executive decrees issued by the Tsar in his capacity of Grand Duke. The representatives of the nation had had no direct part in their passage. Therefore they were devoid of binding force. Until and unless the Law of the Swedish Realm of 1734 should be changed by and with the consent of the Diet and the Grand Duke, all attempts to legalize the use of Finnish in court procedure and decisions would be in vain.[18]

If these conclusions were accepted, others equally startling could not be avoided. The constitutionality of laws was decided by the courts. This meant that any court in the land might have refused to recognize the binding force of the executive language decrees since 1863 and in doing so, would have deprived the Finnish-speaking part of the population of advantages it had grown accustomed to look upon as not only necessary but indispensable. The finespun logic of jurists, it appeared, had been enlisted in an effort to block the demands of common sense and justice.

While it is not necessary here to delve into the hidden recesses of this constitutional argument, a brief evaluation of its pertinence will serve to suggest that it was inspired by a desire to prevent the Finnization of the law courts and thus to stem the advance of the Finnish movement, rather than by a genuine interest in safeguarding legislation against dangerous unconstitutional innovation.

The interpretation of the Law of the Swedish Realm of 1734 which made Finnish a "foreign language" in Finland was untenable. We have seen that when Finland was separated from Sweden, the Grand Duke remained subject to the constitutional, civil and criminal laws in operation in the Swedish kingdom at the time. However, neither the Swedish constitution nor the code of 1734 was ever strictly applied in Finland after 1809. Both became clothed, as it were, with a new meaning when they became the basis of the political and social life of the autonomous Grand Duchy. For example, the references in the constitution to the Swedish State and the King of Sweden were properly and necessarily interpreted to mean the Finnish State and the Tsar-Grand Duke. Similarly, when the Criminal Section of the code of 1734 prohibited the citizens of Finland (Sweden) from entering the service of a foreign country, the word "foreign" was naturally endowed with a different meaning after 1809 from that which it had before the separation. It is an interesting fact, worthy of note in this connection, that the basic "Law of the Swedish Realm of 1734" never became the "Law of the State of Finland" until after the Finnish declaration of independence in 1917. Thus the strict interpretation urged by the supporters of the argument that the language decrees were unconstitutional, would have led, if literally applied, to the absurd conclusion that the title of the code rendered it inapplicable in Finland.

With respect to the specific question of whether the code of 1734 effectively barred the introduction of Finnish into the administration of justice, the answer must be in the negative. The main aim of the provision, which was held to render the language decrees unconstitutional, was to make the judgments and decisions of law courts understandable to the common man. Its provisions, when applied in Finland, could not be interpreted to exclude the use of Finnish unless the same literalness was consistently observed throughout, and that such a literal interpretation of the code of 1734 would have meant a *reductio ad absurdum* of its provisions had been amply demonstrated by the actual application of the code since 1809. Both the clear intent of the contested provisions of the code, and the precedent created by the manner in which it had been observed and applied since 1809, favored an altogether different reading of the code from that offered by those who discovered in its clauses a weapon for destroying the results of two decades of legislation.[19]

The attempt to stem the tide by the constitutional argument failed completely. On December 29, 1883, an administrative decree was issued which paid no heed to the contentions advanced by the supporters of the constitutional interpretation. It stated in substance: (1) Beginning in 1884, the lower courts shall use, unless otherwise requested, the language employed by the communal authorities in the district where the court sits; (2) until January 1, 1894, the lower courts could use only Swedish in such criminal cases as would be submitted to higher courts for confirmation of the sentence; (3) as a rule, the language used by the lower courts would determine the language of the superior courts' decisions; (4) in cases going directly to superior courts, the courts were permitted a free choice in the matter of language; (5) all communications from law courts to communes should be in the language used by the local authorities; (6) the Department of Justice of the Senate could decide in each case the language it would use, but beginning in 1885, Finnish translations would have to accompany all decisions and communications involving cases in which Finnish had been originally used by an inferior court or official.[20]

The decree of 1883 touched only indirectly upon another phase of the language problem. By the early eighties, the Fennomen and their well-wishers were demanding that specific provision should also be made for the Finnization of all branches of the national government — i. e., that in all inter- and intra-administrative and related business both languages should have equal status. In response to this demand, a decree was issued on March 16, 1886. It stated in part that "with a view to the final establishment of the equality of Finnish and Swedish [it is hereby declared] that all administrative departments and officials . . . are . . . permitted to use Finnish as well as Swedish" in their correspondence and the discharge of their business.[21] The detailed provisions necessary for the application of this decree were issued in the following year. Prepared by the Senate during debates that disclosed considerable feeling between the two contending factions, they provided that (1) all local, lower authorities should use the language employed in the minutes of the local governing bodies. In bilingual communities, the authorities could decide whether Finnish or Swedish would be employed. (2) In all higher administrative offices, the officials could choose between the two, being under no specific obligation to use one to the exclusion of the other.[22]

The exceptions in favor of Swedish contained in the two decrees were completely removed in 1902 when a decree touching the language of both law courts and the administrative officials was issued. Its provisions may be said to have established the equality between the two languages for which the Fennomen had been agitating for decades: (1) in uni-lingual communities, law courts and all administrative officials shall use the language of the community; (2) if an administrative district comprises both Finnish and Swedish localities, the language used by the majority of the localities determines the language of the administrative authorities; (3) in case both languages are equally represented in such districts, a free choice in each case may be made; (4) if a party to a law suit, or one who has recourse to administrative offices, requests the use of a language other than the one ordinarily employed by the courts or the administrative offices, the request shall be granted; (5) the language of the superior courts is determined, in each case, by the language used in the lower courts. The same principle applies to administrative offices whose jurisdiction includes the whole country; (6) in inter-administrative business, the matter at hand shall be disposed of in the language of the locality concerned. In cases where this rule cannot be easily followed, a choice of the language that is more useful and appropriate is permitted.[23]

By the time the law of 1902 provided for the complete

realization of the intent of the famous Language Decree of 1863, nearly twenty years had elapsed beyond the period within which the latter decree was expected to eliminate all justifiable cause for complaint among the friends of the Finnish cause. During those twenty years, the "language fight" had served as a most fertile soil for party strife, heated newspaper polemic and general dissension and controversy among students, academicians, men of business, labor organizations, art clubs, theatres — indeed it is well-nigh impossible to name a single group of men or women, or a single walk of life which did not at one time or another illustrate the disturbing effects of the struggle between the Fennomen and the Swecomen. It would take us too far afield even to summarize the arguments of the controversialists as presented in the press, pamphlets and books. It will suffice to say that the main themes were those supplied by Freudenthal and his supporters on the one hand, and those formulated by Y. Koskinen and his followers on the other.[24] But however keen the controversy was at times, and however acrimonious the debate, it was during this score of years that some of the most conspicuous accomplishments of the nationalist movement were recorded. This was particularly true in the field of education.

EDUCATION AND THE NATIONALIST MOVEMENT

The influence of the nationalist movement upon educational progress was far-reaching. Of its manifold consequences two may be distinguished as sufficiently important and conspicuous to justify special mention. The first was the establishment of national primary education and changes effected in the existing system of secondary schools, and in

the instruction offered at the University. The second was
the appearance of rapidly growing and varied educational
enterprise for the benefit of adult citizens.

A limited amount of formal schooling had been provided
for the bulk of the nation ever since the Reformation in the
sixteenth century. The efforts of the clergy to teach the art
of reading to the lowest orders of society were only moderately successful, however. The government did little to improve the situation until the eighteenth century. A notable
step forward was taken in 1723 when a royal ordinance concerning the instruction of the children of the lowly was
issued.[25] It required all parents, on penalty of a fine, to
obtain for their children the art of reading. In case parents
were unable to instruct, they were compelled to employ a
competent school master. The main objective was to enable
the children to absorb the more important principles of religion, morals and good conduct. Before long, a number of
elementary schools appeared, but as home instruction became more efficient, parents often freed themselves from the
expenses which the employment of teachers entailed and
took over the responsibility of imparting the necessary instruction. The literacy of the people was placed on a firmer
foundation in 1740, when the clergy was instructed to conduct confirmation schools for periods ranging from three to
four months yearly. Beginning in 1763, this obligation was
made compulsory, and the leaders of the church saw to it
that the work was not neglected. In 1762, the responsibility
for employing teachers, which had hitherto rested on the
parents' shoulders, was placed upon the congregations as
corporate bodies.[26] The reform made more secure the economic position of the school masters and improved their

quality. During the remainder of the century, the art of reading made marked gains and by the time Finland was separated from Sweden, most of the people could read.[27]

This educational system was obviously neither secular, national, nor nationalistic. It was wholly under the traditional control of the clergy. The subjects taught were unpretentious in the extreme. The rudiments of reading, and occasionally of writing and of arithmetic, Bible history, singing, moral precepts and simple rules of good conduct constituted the sum total of the offerings of which the common people were required to partake. Important though this work was — it appears that the clergy faithfully superintended these beginnings of nation-wide educational effort designed to wipe out illiteracy — it fell far short of measuring up to the needs and accomplishments of a later and more progressive age.

During the first three decades of the nineteenth century, several new educational impulses indicated the approach of a new era. The Pestalozzian methods of teaching were introduced for the first time in 1812, when O. H. Gripenberg, who had become familiar with them under the guidance of the great educator a few years earlier, founded a private school. Lack of means prevented this experiment from becoming a lasting influence in the modernization of Finnish public education, but the contact thus established with the genius of Pestalozzi was destined to have significant results later. Another illustration of the gropings toward more efficient means of educating the nation was afforded by the Bell-Lancaster schools. In these schools, a monitorial system was introduced whereby the older, more advanced pupils were used in the instruction of the younger children. The first of the Finnish Bell-Lancaster schools was founded in Turku in 1820, and during the next thirty years this English system spread in town and country. Beginning in 1840, the Sunday School movement began to gain ground — still another example of the growing interest in the elevation of the masses to a higher level of educational accomplishment.[28]

During the eighteen-forties, when the nationalist doctrine assumed new importance under the guidance of Snellman and others, the whole problem of education was taken up in a more aggressive spirit. We have repeatedly noted the emphasis with which the nationalist leaders urged the importance of mass-education for their cause. Indeed, one might say that the most frequently recurring idea in the nationalist propaganda was the contention that only by means of popular education could the country be brought to a full realization of the needs of the hour and a wholehearted acceptance of the saving creed of nationalism. Not only was the basic importance of literacy pointed out and the significance of schools for the masses emphasized;[29] the larger meaning of education for intelligent citizenship was likewise stressed. "Only a high degree of educational accomplishment among the many and not only on the part of the few," said a writer in 1857, "can possibly save the people from absorption [by Russia] and secure for them a place among the nations . . . Extreme effort, work and struggle in the domain of intellectual advance is required if the Finnish nation is to enjoy continued existence."[30] "The right of a nation," declared Snellman a few years later, "never extends farther than its might. But might depends not only on material strength. Education also is power, especially in our day, not the least because it makes a nation an integral part of the civilized peoples of the world." [31] Even more emphatic were the words of A. Meurman, written in 1875: "The material strength and resources of our people are almost equal to zero . . . and we cannot possibly attain to importance among the peoples of the world, except by virtue of educational advance . . . Education is therefore not only important for us; it is the very foundation of our existence." [32] National self-preservation demanded more efficient agencies for the education of the people. Only the state could provide them.[33]

The first steps leading to the establishment of a national system of education were taken in 1856. In that year, the Finnish Senate was instructed to prepare a program for the founding of schools for the common people.[34] After a decade of discussion and debate, in which clerical conservatism and bureaucratic inertia were ranged against the proposed reforms,[35] the friends of national public schools won a signal victory in 1866 when the Act for the Organization of Elementary Schools was passed.[36] During ensuing years, elementary schools were founded throughout the land and sustained efforts were made to improve the teaching personnel by means of up-to-date seminaries or normal schools. Some slight indication of the progress during the thirty years following 1874, the year when the new system may be said to have obtained a firm hold, is given by the table below. It includes only public primary schools.

The act of 1866 did not provide for compulsory attendance,[38] and for many years the physical equipment of the new schools left much room for improvement. However, the cultivation of a strong feeling of patriotism appears not to have depended upon such inadequacies. The uniform curriculum introduced into the new schools placed a marked emphasis upon the teaching of Finnish.[39] Reading of "suitable patriotic literature" became from the beginning an inte-

PRIMARY SCHOOL TEACHERS AND ATTENDANCE, 1874-1905 [37]

SCHOOL YEAR	TEACHERS			PUPILS		
	CITY	RURAL	TOTAL	CITY	RURAL	TOTAL
1874-1875	167	272	439	5,920	9,300	15,220
1879-1880	282	432	514	9,690	16,860	26,550
1884-1885	410	650	1,060	13,400	23,430	36,830
1889-1890	523	852	1,375	17,270	32,060	49,330
1894-1895	691	1,264	1,955	23,420	51,470	74,890
1899-1900	582	2,022	2,874	27,480	76,520	104,000
1904-1905	975	2,703	3,678	30,450	95,420	125,870

gral part of the instruction given, and the stirring *Tales of Ensign Stål*, various patriotic writings of Topelius, and the *Kalevala*, sustained the generations of Finns who partook of the offerings of the primary schools. Home geography and history as well as singing of patriotic songs introduced an added nationalist element into the group of studies through which the common folk were expected to reach a more vital understanding of the meaning of love of country, and of its importance for the future of the nation.[40] The Finnish-language teachers' training schools and seminaries, for the founding of which the act of 1866 also made provision, likewise reflected a conscious effort to introduce into the field of education a larger element of patriotic appreciation of the history of the fatherland and of the language and literature of the Finnish people.[41]

While the newly established system of primary education was beginning to minister to the needs of the masses, the secondary schools were turned into a more effective instrument for the conversion of the classes. The renovation of the secondary schools was begun in the closing fifties. Its fundamental objective was the oft-mentioned transformation of the upper classes into Finnish-speaking citizens, in order that the linguistic gulf separating the few from the many might be bridged. Considerable difficulties had to be overcome before the secondary schools — which served as the main channels through which the youth of the land could enter the University — were brought to serve this aim. The outstanding drawback was the paucity of competent teachers and of adequate books written in Finnish. In spite of these obstacles, and in the face of considerable opposition, the first secondary school dedicated to the progressive orientation of the Fennomen was founded in Jyväskylä in 1858. That instruction at this school was at first given partly in Finnish and partly in Swedish, that a goodly part of the teaching staff mastered the former only in the process of teaching, and that many of the students were at the outset but poorly prepared to study in Finnish, may be mentioned by way of suggesting the circumstances under which the Finnish-language secondary schools began their work.

The real history of the Finnish-language secondary schools may be said to have begun with the founding in 1873 of the Hämeenlinnan Normaalilyseo. This institution had had its inception six years earlier as a subordinate part of a Swedish-language school in Helsinki. Largely because of the unwillingness of the conservative School Board to harbor a Finnish-language institution in the capital, the Finnish section of the Helsinki school was discontinued and provision made for a Finnish school, to be founded in some provincial city. The result was that from 1873 onwards, the friends of the Finnish cause could point to a unique result of agitation and propaganda extending over more than thirty years: a first-class secondary school where the language of instruction was exclusively Finnish. Both the Jyväskylä and the Hämeenlinna institutions were located far enough from the capital to make it inevitable that they would draw primarily upon the countryside for their students. It would be going beyond the evidence to say that the students of these schools, or of the many other Finnish-language secondary schools founded between 1880 and 1900, came primarily from families to whom the older Swedish-language schools had been more or less closed. However, within a couple of decades a rapidly growing number of *cives academici* from Finnish homes reached the University through the portals of the new institutions. In 1880, the total enrollment in Finland's *lycées* was approximately 3,500; of this number some 1,300 were classified as Finnish-speaking.[42] Ten years later the corresponding figures were 4,850 and 2,150, and at the turn of the century, 8,600 and 5,200. By that time the Finnish tide was running strong, and during the last thirty years the proportion of Finnish-speaking students in the secondary schools has constantly increased until they have come to constitute, on an average, about eighty per cent of the total.[43]

The effects of the Finnization of the secondary schools were soon reflected in the changing composition of the student body at the University of Helsinki. Perhaps the best indication of the trend since the early seventies is given by the number of Finnish-speaking and Swedish-speaking students matriculated at the University. During the two-year period 1870-1872, the number of new entrants was 516; those listed as Finnish-speaking numbered 43, or considerably less than ten percent. Half a dozen years later (1879-1881), 567 new students enrolled at the institution. By that time the Finnish-speaking element had increased to 178 or about one-third, and by the early nineties (1891-1893), they constituted more than one-half of the freshmen (496 out of 956). A decade later (1900-1902), 850 out of a total of 1,500 were of this group. The same tendency was observable in the Helsinki Polytechnic Institute, founded in 1885.[44]

The Finnization of the secondary schools and of the student body at the University was paralelled by the Finnization of instruction in higher institutions of learning. Beginning in 1863, lectures at the Helsinki University could be given in Finnish, but for several years few professors availed themselves of this right. The first Finnish-language requirement was imposed upon the university staff in the year 1872, when a decree became operative which required that all professors should understand Finnish, and that the members of the Faculties of Law and Divinity should know the language well enough to speak it. These regulations succeeded but poorly in changing the language of university instruction into Finnish, however, and another and more stringent law was passed in 1894. Its provisions stated that all professors must know Finnish as well as Swedish but gave them the right to use either in their lectures. Thus the growing numbers of graduates from the rapidly expanding Finnish secondary schools were offered increasing opportunities for advanced studies without being compelled to rely exclusively upon Swedish lectures, as had been the case before the Fennoman movement began to capture the Helsinki University.[45]

One of the most interesting examples of the persistence with which the friends of the Finnish cause were moving heaven and earth in their effort to achieve a secure victory for Finnish in all advanced instruction is given by the work of certain scientific and literary societies. In 1876 there was founded among the university students at the capital the Home Language Society whose aim was to provide opportunities for the mastery of Finnish.[46] The establishment of the Duodecim Society in 1881 brought into being an organization which has left an indelible imprint on Finnish medical science. Its purpose was to develop an adequate Finnish terminology in the field of medicine. To it goes the credit of having devised a complete medical vocabulary in Finnish — no easy accomplishment in view of the fact that prior to the eighties, all medical studies had been carried on in Swedish.[47] The National Economic Society, founded in 1885, performed the same service in the realm of economic studies. It sponsored the publication of a wide variety of works on the various phases of this subject, and likewise was active in devising the technical vocabulary necessary for the exploitation of this field of academic endeavor. The science of physics enlisted the efforts of another organization, the Vipuset, which has been active since 1893. An elaborate German-Finnish dictionary represents its most important contribution. The Vanamo Society, established in 1896, devoted itself with equal thoroughness and success to the task of bringing forth a complete technical terminology in zoology and botany, and the Society of Finnish Technologists, founded in the same year, contributed a massive dictionary of general scientific terms. Finally, the Association of Finnish Jurists, which came into being in 1898, made important contributions in law studies by sponsoring translations of basic works in the field, and by providing the necessary material for an impressive Swedish-Finnish legal dictionary.[48]

The consequences of the activities of these organizations cannot be easily measured but it seems that the following estimate of one of the results obtained, formulated by a Finnish scholar, is essentially correct. The Finnish language, he says, "which in the beginning of the last century was used only in religious writings and in popular books of the simplest kind, was formed . . . into a language of culture in which we can present Homer, Sophocles, Molière, and Shakespeare, as well as all kinds of modern fiction; which can be used as well in philosophy as in mathematics, in physics as well as in the science of law and in philology." That "this . . . development was brought about in almost as many decades as other countries required centuries for" [49] may be an exaggeration, but there is no denying its fundamental significance for every phase of Finland's intellectual and cultural history during the past generation.

The general purpose of the primary schools for which the act of 1866 made provision was ambitious. Putting it briefly, most of the sponsors of the scheme for nation-wide elementary education hoped to raise the bulk of the people to a keener and more active appreciation of the demands which the complicated business of living imposed upon a people struggling toward national consciousness.[50] This ambitious objective could be but partly attained in the public schools, however. Their function was necessarily limited to the task of imparting the three R's to the pupils, together with other instruction of an elementary sort. Although the number of schools and the attendance increased rapidly during the last three decades of the nineteenth century, only a fraction of the population was able to secure, through organized institutions of education, the fundamentals of book learning. Nor was it intended that the primary schools should shoulder the whole burden of educating the nation. The act of 1866 specifically comtemplated the participation of the family in the work, especially in instruction in reading. This instruction was to be disposed of at home before the pupil enrolled in school. In other words, the system of national education for which provision was made in 1866, was to rest upon a broader foundation than that afforded by the schools alone: the home and the schools were both to serve as cornerstones of the new edifice.

It did not take long before organized attempts were made to provide agencies dedicated to the task of supplementing the educational work of home and school. The first notable contribution was made under the auspices of the university student corporations. Their membership had engaged in various popular educational activities before the middle of the century, although they began to play an important part only after 1860. Both language groups were represented in the work, which was colored by no small rivalry between them, the Finnish-language corporations ministering to the needs of the Finnish-speaking sections, and the Swedish-language organizations addressing themselves to the Swedish-speaking parts of the country. Both sponsored lectures and established and frequently maintained reading clubs and other societies by means of which useful knowledge concerning practical life, as well as greater love of cultural and educational studies, was spread among the masses. Perhaps the most important part of this work for popular education consisted of the large amounts of appropriate literature issued and distributed by the students. "Penny Libraries" and "People's Libraries" were printed in series that offered a wide variety of reading matter. For example, one series published from 1866 to 1880 consisted of thirty-seven booklets and ranged from historical and biographical essays to non-technical treatments of law, government and natural science. Another of sixteen titles was published from 1867 to 1880.[51]

Although this type of student activity accomplished much, it suffered from a number of shortcomings. The nature of the student corporations, with their ever-changing membership, imparted to their effort an element of instability which did not ease the task of providing the kind of adult education that was deemed necessary.[52] Largely as a consequence of the defects which marred the students' work, there was founded in 1874 the Adult Education Society. The society came into being through the initiative of students at the Jyväskylä Seminary. The Adult Education Society was placed on a non-partisan basis from the beginning and resolutely steered clear of the language controversy. It soon became the center of manifold activities in its chosen field. One of its main objectives was to arouse and develop interest in reading and the spread of literature. Free lectures for this purpose were held, and hundreds of books, many of them of permanent value, were published. The Society was also active in founding public libraries and promoted the organization of great public choral and musical festivals, thus adding new variety and interest to the daily round of the common folk. While it would be an exaggeration to say that the Adult Education Society was in any sense engaged in nationalist propaganda, its enterprises grew out of the Finnish movement and gave it the broad and democratic basis without which the Finnish cause would have largely remained what it was at its inception: an upper-class movement devoid of nation-wide support.[53]

Equally dedicated to educational purposes, but ultimately more unmistakably nationalist in their program and objectives, were the Young People's Associations. The first was founded in 1881, under the leadership of S. Alkio, a writer-politician of great ability who later rose to eminence. By the close of the century the Young People's Associations had grown into a national institution, with 250 local organizations and a membership exceeding 17,000. These figures were more than doubled by 1907. Unwilling to accept any party affiliations or to recognize political party limits, these associations carried their message to high and low throughout the land. They aimed to enlist the younger generation in the effort to create an intelligent, well-informed and thoroughly patriotic citizenry. For many years they paid little heed to the language controversy, but the nature of their work placed them inevitably on the side of the champions of the Finnish language. In 1906, at the general meeting of the representatives of the Young People's Associations, a resolution was unanimously adopted which committed the organization to the Finnish cause. It stated in part:

The Young People's Associations shall endeavor to work to the end that all members shall consider themselves in duty bound to use Finnish, and shall aid in freeing it from foreign influences . . . [Also], the past intellectual and cultural accomplishments of our people shall receive full appreciation and recognition in the work of the Associations . . . The Associations shall labor further-more for the nationalization of Finnish literature, for the placing of Finnish in the position of the principal language of Finland — in other words, shall participate in the work whose aim is the strengthening of our love of country, and the elevation of the Finnish-speaking part of our population to that position and pre-ëminence which of right belongs to it. . . The meeting holds that it is the responsibility of the Young People's movement to assure the observance of . . . these resolutions.[54]

Less completely devoted to the service of the patriotic cause, but of great importance as agencies in the work of popular education, were two other types of organization. The first were the People's High Schools. Based on the principles of adult education evolved in Denmark under the guidance of N. F. S. Grundtvig, the first People's High Schools in Finland appeared in the closing eighties and the early nineties. By 1900 twenty-one such institutions were functioning. Most of them had come into being under the stimulus of university students who became very active in this form of educational effort during the closing decade of the last century. In the educational program of these insti-tutions, national history and related instruction were given a prominent place, although practical subjects, such as handi-crafts and home economics, constituted the major part of the offering. While the People's High Schools were pri-marily designed to minister to the needs of the countryside, the Workers Institutes represented an effort to render simi-lar service in urban centers. The first was established in 1899, and their number grew slowly during the ensuing years. Their importance became considerable only after the attainment of independence in 1917.[55]

Not the least conspicuous indication of the strength and advance of the Fennoman movement during the closing decades of the nineteenth century is afforded by the rapid growth of the Finnish-language newspapers. Despite the valient efforts of Snellman and his followers, newspapers printed in Finnish were outdistanced well into the seventies by papers printed in Swedish. In 1876, the two language groups were each represented by twenty-three newspapers. Ten years later, the scales had been definitely and permanently turned in favor of the Finnish press, which was represented by fifty-one newspapers while the number of Swedish-language papers was only forty-four. By 1896 the figures were one hundred for the former and seventy-two for the latter, and in 1905 the corresponding figures were one hundred and fifty-three and eighty. Among the strictly political and party sheets, those printed in Finnish were in 1905 more than twice as numerous as the Swedish language papers. The growth of the Finnish press served as evidence of the onward march of the nationalists and incidentally proved the existence of tangible rewards for journalists willing to serve the linguistic majority.[56]

LABOR AND NATIONALISM

The two decades which followed the close of the Crimean War witnessed a remarkable economic growth in Finland. A network of railways began to cut into the countryside, opening unexploited virgin forest and new farming lands to business enterprise. A rapidly growing number of steamers large and small began to ply the countless inland lakes, annihilating distance and bringing town and country into closer and more beneficial contact. Aided by a liberal policy of state loans, hundreds of industrial enterprises were founded — iron and textile factories, lumber and paper mills, leather and glass works were assisted to a promising start. The last remnants of the antiquated guild system were swept away. The era of large-scale banking and finance was ushered in, especially after the completion of the nationalization of the monetary system in 1865. Agriculture likewise underwent important changes. Dairy farming began to push aside the cultivation of the traditional crops. As a consequence of these tendencies, the position of labor also began to change. The distinction between the employer who furnished the capital for the countless new enterprises and the employee who worked for wages became more fixed. In Finland also the stage was being set for the contest between labor and capital.[57]

However, the rise of the organized wage earner was more intimately connected with the nationalist movement than with the manifold consequences of industrialization. The earliest workers' organizations were reading clubs and similar associations founded in the fifties and the sixties for the purpose of enabling the laboring man to become familiar with the trends of the time in general and the Finnish movement in particular. They were established under the auspices of middle-class nationalists genuinely interested in obtaining the broadest possible base for the nationalist movement. Organizations like the Finnish Literature Society published considerable amounts of appropriate reading matter. The cheap editions of *Readings for the People* in particular were widely read by the lower classes. Thus the nationalist movement became responsible for a devolopment probably unique in the history of organized labor: instead of being produced by a class struggle, the Finnish labor movement was brought into being by the essentially democratic policy of Snellman and his followers. The service the nationalists rendered to popular education by means of these early workers' associations was considerable. The evening and Sunday schools which often supplemented the reading and discussion clubs appreciably improved the education of the laboring man long before the national system of public schools, founded in 1866, began to produce marked results. Probably the best statement concerning the relationship between the nationalists and the earlier phases of the labor movement was made by a labor leader in 1888. "This connection," he said, "is an outgrowth of the mighty contest in which our people has been involved for decades: the Finnish movement. The Finnish movement is democratic, for its aim is the elevation of the lower classes and the raising of the whole nation to conscious political maturity. The labor movement is therefore an outgrowth of the nationalist movement." [58]

In the course of the eighteen-eighties, the educational labor clubs were replaced by Workers' Associations whose objectives were more definitely connected with the welfare of the industrial proletariat. These organizations also owed their existence to middle-class individuals moved by liberal and humanitarian considerations. Their aim was lower-class advance, within safe limits. The Workers' Associations were for, but not by and of, the common people. Partly because of the preponderance of the bourgeois nationalist elements in their leadership, and partly because of the demo-

cratic aspects of the nationalists' endeavors, the membership of the associations supported the Finnish cause. They
manifested a genuine interest in the language controversy
which at times well-nigh monopolized the political life of
the country. On occasion, the Workers' Associations became citizens' organizations for the specific furtherance of
the Finnish program. "The nationalist struggle is a contest for the protection of the rights of the poor," declared a
laborite in 1895. "The Finnish group desires to eliminate
the maladjustments which weigh down on our society";
therefore it deserves the support of the workers.[59] In some
instances, however, the concern in specific labor problems
appears to have left little time or inclination for a live interest in the language question, while in others, the existence
of bilingual associations testified to the class solidarity of
the Finnish-speaking and the Swedish-speaking laborers.[60]

Several of the Finnish nationalists were conscious of the
necessity for progressive social legislation and labored for
measures designed to prevent the appearance of the worst
evils which usually attend upon the growth of an industrial,
propertyless working class. Partly under their influence
several beneficial laws for the protection of the workers were
passed. In 1889, the employment of women and children in
factories was regulated. The minimum age for child workers was fixed at twelve years and both women and children
were excluded from certain occupations. Provision was
made for the safety of workers and the sanitation and in-
spection of industrial establishments.[61] Compulsory accident insurance for nearly all but agricultural workers was
obtained in 1895,[62] and two years later a number of supplementary laws concerning industrial accidents and the con-

trol of accident insurance companies were enacted.[63] Cities and counties supplemented these attempts to create more tolerable conditions for the workman. Municipal housing schemes, labor exchanges, public works and local insurance for relieving unemployment bore testimony to their effort.[64]

During the years when the antiquated Diet was thus slowly beginning to serve the larger ends of an enlightened social policy, the labor movement began to take on a new aspect. It was freed from its earlier middle-class tutelage and developed into a clear-cut workingmen's enterprise. The reasons for the break with the bourgeois element were inherent in the basic interests of labor, although other factors also played a part.

Of fundamental importance was the trade-union movement in the eighties. The movement came into being under the auspices of the Workers' Associations previously mentioned. Conscious of the existence of grave abuses and problems in the industrial order, the bourgeois leaders of the Workers' Associations sought to lessen the misery of the worker by organizing individual trades into unions. The trade unions, it was hoped, would become imbued with the respectable middle-class spirit of the Workers' Associations. It did not take long, however, before the latter found themselves unable to control the former. The tail began to wag the dog, and by the early nineties the Workers' Associations were increasingly absorbed by the more radical trade unions. The latter developed in many instances into outright strike organizations interested primarily in shorter hours, higher wages and more tolerable working conditions. The business crisis from which the country suffered in 1892-1893 speeded their growth. Efficient organization of the worker, it was maintained by the more aggressive labor leaders who began to emerge in the course of the nineties, would bring more and speedier concessions than the altruism of the upper and middle classes was willing to grant. It goes without saying that this radicalization of labor led to the withdrawal of most of the non-labor individuals from the movement and its capture by men who more adequately represented the hopes and ambitions of the wage-earner.[65]

The growing trade-unionism was sustained by a political issue of considerable importance. Ever since the revival of the Diet in 1863, the national parliament had retained its markedly non-democratic character. Its membership represented less than one-tenth of the population of the country. The majority of the working classes, the petty farmers and the landless agricultural laborers were excluded from representation in it. Despite periodic efforts to improve the situation, the classes in power showed no inclination to change the electoral system which preserved their predominance. An equally strong distaste for democratic innovations marked local elections, in which a graduated scale of votes, dependent on taxes paid, determined the franchise. The right to vote was a privilege reserved for the propertied classes only. Yet it was obvious that without a voice in local and national government the working class could not hope to improve its condition. Middle class leadership in the Workers' Associations having failed to produce any real change in the existing system, the standard bearers of the trade unions proceeded to agitate for a thorough liberalization of the franchise. Political democracy became the magnet that drew the worker from the Workers' Associations into the trade unions.

Many foreign lands [wrote one of the upper-class friends of
Finnish labor in 1893], where Socialists, Anarchists and other
purveyors of like destructive doctrines have agitated among the
workingmen, offer us a sad picture indeed. They are troubled by
internal disunion and conflict, and many a worker hates his fatherland and its institutions. There is no doubt, however, that Finnish
workers would stoutly resist all efforts to tempt them from the
path of responsibility and justice. They know that the Government
and the Diet . . . care for their interests. The Finnish workingman
knows that in his country, freedom founded upon law prevails
and that labor is here a badge of honor. It is this knowledge that
has awakened in him the noble spirit of patriotism. It is the feeling
of patriotism that stimulates him to prove himself worthy of
citizenship . . . By skill in his trade and dignified participation in
the affairs of his nation he is gradually preparing himself for an
increasing degree of self-government.[66]

It would be too much to say that this statement represented an altogether fair sample of the cautious conservatism that prevailed among all those who wrote and spoke
for the Finnish workers down to the middle nineties, but it
may be considered representative of the notions entertained
by a substantial part of the Finnish upper class.[67] That the
analysis fell short of establishing contact with reality was
indicated by the program of reforms adopted at the first
General Assembly of the Representatives of the Workers'
Associations, held in Helsinki in the fall of 1893. The demands put forth included a moderate democratization of
the franchise, a ten-hour day, compulsory public education,
a revision of the land laws, improvement in workers' housing, the collection of official labor statistics and the equali-
zation of men's and women's wages.[68] These objectives
constitute a complete refutation of the notion that the road
to the emancipation of the working class lay through increased vocational skill and the empty abstraction "dignified

participation in the affairs of the nation." It is worth noting that these demands were formulated by a predominantly respectable middle-class congress and not by class-conscious laborites. The discussions concerning the advisability of founding a special workers' newspaper furnish convincing evidence of the conservatism of the congress. "It was noted, and with good reason," we read in the record of the proceedings, "that a special labor paper is unnecessary because most of our newspapers — the Finnish-language newspapers especially — are friends of the Workers' Associations and discuss workingmen's problems in their columns. A labor newspaper would obtain readers only among the enthusiastic supporters of the workers' cause, while at present, when labor questions are discussed in the daily press, the general public is able to follow them. Furthermore, a labor newspaper would oust the existing larger papers from the worker's home; as a result, the worker's understanding of the questions of the day would become more limited." It was resolved not to expose the workers to these dangers.[69]

At the Diet of 1894, labor made its first concerted effort to obtain a voice in the deliberations of the national parliament. The effort was not made through labor deputies — for no attempt had been made in the election to capture seats for bona fide labor representatives — but through members belonging to the Finnish parties. The resolutions of the Helsinki meeting of the preceding year furnished them with the workers' program. The results were disappointing. Despite the support of the Finnish nationalists, the suffrage reform was blocked by the Swede-Finn conservatives who looked upon the proposal simply as a means of swelling the ranks of Finnish-speaking voters.[70] It was clearly shown that labor could expect but little from the Diet as long as the undemocratic four-estate representation prevailed and that unless the workers succeeded in getting the right to vote, they would obtain occasional minor concessions, but no unqualified recognition of their objectives as necessary and just. Well might a bourgeois friend of labor declare that "the workers' condition must be improved because the interests of the nation absolutely demand it and the example of foreign lands yields no argument in favor of the conservative view," [71] but only by means of political power could the workers hope to translate their aspirations into national laws.

In degree as the importance of suffrage reform was realized, it furnished the basic and most immediate objective of the labor groups whose activity became more conspicuous as the nineties wore on. The founding of the *Työmies* (*The Worker*) in 1895 gave the workers an organ wholly dedicated to working-class interests. When the second general meeting of Workers' Associations delegates was held in the following year, the program discussed and adopted went considerably beyond the reforms urged three years earlier — an indication of a definite swing toward the Left. That the founding of *The Worker* and the more radical labor demands were met with abuse and opposition from the conservative camp speeded rather than retarded the process.[72] In 1899, it culminated in the establishment of a separate political party, styled the Labor Party of Finland. The party platform adopted at the constituent meeting stated in part: "The Labor Party of Finland . . . attempts to further in every possible way the economic and social emancipation of Finland's workers. Cognizant of the basic importance for these aims of the maintenance and protection of Finland's national independence, the Party adopts the following program for the realization of its most immediate objectives." The program was thoroughly democratic. It included universal and equal suffrage, the eight-hour day, free and compulsory public education, progressive income and inheritance taxes, adequate labor legislation and the improvement of the condition of the landless agricultural population.[73] The new party was but four years old when it formally changed its name to the Social Democratic Party of Finland. Its Socialism was the Marxian creed formulated by the German Socialists at the Erfurt Congress in 1891. Henceforth Finnish labor proposed to stand on its own feet and to fight its own battles in the arena of politics.[74]

When the workers began to free themselves from middle-class leadership, their attitude toward the nationalist problem underwent a marked change. The earlier acceptance of the Finnish cause, for example, gave way to a more critical attitude. According to the workers' contentions, the reason for this more critical attitude was the shortsightedness of the conservatives whose unwillingness to grant economic and political concessions had brought about the consolidation of labor forces in the class-conscious trade unions. The same die-hard spirit was precipitating the working classes out of the nationalist movement. "The Finnish party," stated the annual report (in 1898) of the workers' organization in Tampere, the chief industrial center of the country, "has treated the working class as if it were a disowned child, whenever the question of obtaining a labor representative in the city government or the Diet has been raised." [75] The formation of the Labor Party, according to another labor source, was brought about by the fact that "the supporters of the Finnish movement showed clearly that they were aristocrats at heart." [76] "This business of being patriotic," declared a writer in *The Worker*, "is the mask behind which the vested interests parade on every occasion. If one accepts a view different from theirs, he is at once branded as traitor of his country." [77] While these statements undoubtedly contained an element of exaggeration, they showed that according to the worker's view, it was the uncompromising and overbearing attitude of the middle and upper classes that made labor suspicious of the nationalist argument.

The attitude of the bourgeoisie toward the labor problem, however, was not the only factor that contributed to the workers' growing distrust of the nationalist movement. When the most important objective of organized labor was defined as "the arousing of the workers to a conscious appreciation of their class interests in society," [78] it was clear that the concrete interests inherent in the contemplated emancipation of the workingman would inevitably take precedence over nationalist aims. In the face of social and economic issues which labor considered vital, the nationalist controversy receded to a position of secondary importance. Already before the Labor Party was founded in 1899, the slogan "Cut loose from the bourgeoisie" had come to stand not only for the elimination of timid middle-class leadership from the workers' organizations, but for a revaluation of the significance of the language controversy as well. [79] After 1899 the labor group left the traditional moorings of earlier days and set out on a course that deviated markedly from the nationalist channel. The markers that indicated the new course displayed colors other than the blue and the white of the nationalists.

In rejecting the language question as the mainspring of

political endeavor, organized labor did not become insensitive to the larger aspects of the nationalist movement. On the contrary, it was repeatedly stated that the workers fully appreciated the demands placed upon the individual citizen by genuine love of the fatherland. But the right to interpret what those demands were, labor reserved to itself. The result was a repudiation of much that the middle and upper class nationalists regarded as the substance of true patriotic devotion, and a marked tendency to consider the nationalist movement — in its traditional aspects at least — as primarily designed to serve the interests of the rich and well-born. "It is all right for those whose yearly incomes run into thousands and tens of thousands to talk about patriotism and to exploit the possibilities of the language question," exclaimed a labor writer in 1897. The worker cannot afford such a luxury, "for earning a living is literally the alpha and the omega of his existence." Although "love of country and nationality mean much to the worker also," he is bound fast to the realities of life and must fix his main attention upon them.[80] The workers' rejection of most of the old nationalist gods, and their revision of the nationalist dogma to suit their own needs and interests, indicated, according to the labor leaders, not less but more genuine nationalism. "Whose work is more patriotic and of greater significance," inquired a laborite in 1901, pointing an accusing finger at the bourgeoisie, "— yours, which is trying to maintain the barriers that divide the nation into classes, or ours, which attempts to destroy them in order that the *people* may become strong and powerful?" The answer was obviously in favor of the workers whose program, it was maintained, spelled national unification in a far deeper sense than could ever be attained by "language nationalism." [81]

The story of the Swede-Finn toilers, and their connection with the nationalist movement, was different in more than one respect from that of the organization and nationalist tendencies among the Finnish-speaking workers. The Swede-Finn workers' organizations began to appear in the eighteen-eighties. They were affiliated in a national association in the early nineties. In general, their growth and development were similar to the rise of the Finnish labor organizations before the swing of the latter to the Left in the closing decade of the century. The leadership in the Swede-Finn Friends of Labor — as the associations were styled — was furnished by the bourgeoisie whose views came to dominate the whole Swede-Finn labor movement. The membership of the Friends of Labor was largely composed of men of business, professional men, bookkeepers, clerks and an occasional representative of hard toil. Unlike corresponding organizations of the Finnish-speaking workers, the Friends of Labor did not pass through the stage of trade unions to the status of a clear-cut labor party. The Swede-Finn organizations were not called forth nor was their growth conditioned by the processes that were effecting new and strange transformations in the field of economic enterprise, and their members were no industrial workers drawn together by a common need to evolve means of defense and aggression. Associations of the petty bourgeoisie, they acquired only limited influence over Swede-Finn labor as a group.

The Friends of Labor subscribed to a markedly conservative doctrine of workingmen's emancipation. According to one of its annual publications, friendly and helpful coöperation between employers and employees was desirable, "for only thereby . . . can the worker acquire self-reliance and the ability to take into his own hands his higher, more general interests. But before this great objective can be realized, it is necessary that the workingman fix his attention primarily upon developing himself and his faculties — his comprehension, feelings and will-power — because intellectual and moral advance must of necessity precede material progress." [82] The most important specific reform approved by the Friends of Labor was the collection of official labor statistics. The following statement from 1899 will serve as an illustration of the association's attitude toward industrial conflicts: ". . . a strike breaker is one who urges others to strike, or participates without protesting in a decision to strike and then goes to work." Those who refuse to strike "must be protected by law . . . for the right to labor is sacred." [83] A simple faith in the immutability of existing political institutions and a naïve interpretation of the significance of the industrialization which was bringing capital and labor into sharper conflict were at the basis of these and related doctrines offered by the Friends of Labor.

While the Friends of Labor thus stopped far short of accepting a vital creed of social and economic betterment, the attitude of the organization toward the nationalist controversy was more positive. During the early years of the Swede-Finn organizations their membership consisted at times of individuals of both language groups, but by the eighteen-nineties they had become representative of the Swede-Finns only. By that time, they had been definitely drawn into the main current of the language problem. The familiar arguments of the Swecoman group began to appear with increasing frequency in the Friends' annual reports.

We read about new local branches being founded in order
to combat the Finnization of the Swedish-speaking workers,[84] and learn about the harmful effects of the process:
". . . this Finnization can in no way help in the advancement
of the Swedish-speaking laborers, because the Finnish language, having been recently developed, represents a lower
level of cultural accomplishment than does Swedish which
has been used a thousand years and more."[85] That both
logic and facts were sorely bruised by this type of reasoning is less important than the fact that it reflects clearly the
success with which the Swede-Finn nationalist ideas had
been instilled into the membership of the Friends of Labor.

Upon their attitude toward the means of improving the
conditions under which labor existed, this surrender to the
traditional Swecoman views had an effect that appears to
have been decisive. No sustained effort was made by the
Friends of Labor to throw bridges across the chasms that
separated rich and poor. To the criticism that the Swede-
Finn organizations were too much tinged with the interests
of the upper classes, and that their failure to achieve social
and economic betterment was a consequence of this liaison,[86]
replies were made disclosing a greater interest in the language question than in the elimination of industrial and
urban misery. Statements concerning suffrage reform —
the most important problem among the many that had to be
solved before labor could hope to inject a new spirit into
social and economic practice and institutions — serve as
illustrations of the manner in which the language problem
was permitted to arrest the evolution of a liberal, critical
diagnosis of the ills of society. The question of reforming
the franchise, it was held, involved nothing but "a party

controversy, brought into being by the Finnish party. The demand that the requirements for voting should be lowered is not based on any unwholesome or disadvantageous condition of the workers which can be eliminated by means of the proposed reform." [87] In 1895, when the scaling down of the existing property qualifications for voting was much discussed, the proposals were condemned. "It is obvious," stated the official publication of the Friends of Labor, "that the changes now demanded are not at all democratic and least of all are they formulated in a spirit friendly toward labor . . . The only difference between the existing requirements and those now proposed is that by the latter artisans and others with defective education and sense of judgment would acquire more influence in elections. . . Among this class of citizens . . . we find a considerable number of voters whose sympathies are Finnish, and it is no secret that the present franchise reform is nothing more than an effort on the part of the Fennomen leaders" to strengthen their position in the Diet. An increase of the Finnish representation in the national parliament "must be considered a misfortune for the country" and hence the existing franchise should be retained without change.[88]

One result of the process that was placing the Friends of Labor in the tow of the Swede-Finn nationalist movement [89] was the well-nigh complete disappearance of bona fide workers from the organization.[90] Another was the trend among a minority of Swede-Finn labor toward Socialism. While the class was by no means carried *en masse* over to the Socialist camp, the conversions were sufficiently numerous to constitute a welcome addition to the Social Democracy of the country and to call forth a separate

Swede-Finn labor newspaper. Along with this radicalization went a refusal on the part of Swede-Finn Socialists to accept the extreme Swede-Finn nationalist views.

"The friends of the Finnish movement," wrote a Swede-Finn laborite a few years after this approach toward the Left had begun, "in their exertions for the advance of their cause, have addressed themselves to the masses and have thus obtained a broad foundation for their work. Although it pretends to further the interests of the whole Swedish-speaking element, the so-called Swedish party has been concerned only with the maintenance of unjust class rule founded on property and sustained by property. Because of its objectives, the Swedish party has aroused, among the friends of the Finnish cause, a lively and justifiable hate which has been often extended, unfortunately, to the Swede-Finns in general. Instead of promoting the interests of the Swede-Finns, the Swedish party has actually harmed them to a terrifying degree. Our workers have been left to go their own way. The Swede-Finn bourgeoisie should therefore not be surprised if they discover, upon approaching us with the claim that they labor for our linguistic interests, that we regard their objectives only as means whereby the power of this very bourgeoisie will be strengthened." [91] In common with their Finnish-speaking fellow Socialists, the more radically inclined Swede-Finn workers were primarily concerned with adequate adjustments in the body politic and were wholeheartedly in favor of eliminating the language controversy from its position as the most prominent issue in national politics.[92]

In the early stages of Russification, discussed in the next section, organized labor — using the term to include both language groups — placed itself on the whole outside the conflict and assumed the position of a more or less disinterested spectator. The main reason for this laissez faire attitude must probably be sought in the intolerant and shortsighted attitude of the bourgeoisie which had prepared an unfavorable soil for the kind of coöperation between labor and capital which Russification seemed urgently to demand. The workers' stand was changed, however, when the Russian policy of assimilation became more aggressive. The inroads made upon the constitutional rights of Finnish citizens carried a sinister meaning to the men of heavy toil as well as to the classes. Also, when the growing pressure compelled the bourgeoisie to abandon their hostile stand toward the workers' party, the road leading to labor's participation in the opposition to Russia's policy was freed from its most serious obstacle. During the years when the country attempted to stave off the attack by means of passive resistance to the illegal measures, passive resistance was given the unqualified support of organized labor. Later when the patriots resorted to the policy of active and at times violent resistance, the workers responded to the call. Not a few of the outstanding labor agitators worked hand-in-glove with the advocates of direct action and from the ranks of class-conscious workingmen came some of the most daring opponents of the Russian dictatorship. The group as a whole was inflexibly opposed to a policy of truckling and concession. At least one labor newspaper went so far as to declare openly that passive resistance was inadequate and that new and more effective means for combatting the enemy had to be found. Despite their avowed class interests, the workers were thus amply demonstrating their fidelity to the national cause. "The workers' love for our national institutions has proved to be strong and vigorous and this will be . . . undoubtedly admitted even by the staunchest of patriots," wrote a laborite.[93] This was indeed no empty boast.[94]

RUSSIFICATION — THE TEST OF STRENGTH

When the language law of 1902 established equality between Finnish and Swedish, the general situation in the country was sufficiently serious to give pause to Fennoman and Swecoman alike. Russification, the fear of which had been one of the mainsprings of the Finnish movement since the days of Arwidsson, was now becoming a reality. Russian imperial policy was beginning to challenge Finnish constitutional rights and prerogatives, and the Russian language was gradually being introduced into the administration of the country, to the exclusion of both Finnish and Swedish.

Omitting some earlier and minor attempts to abridge Finland's autonomy, the attack upon the constitution of the country may be dated from the eighteen-seventies. The establishment of national conscription in Russia in 1873 inaugurated a policy which, during the ensuing thirty years, resulted in a systematic undermining of the status of the Grand Duchy as established in 1808-1809. An effort was made to compel the Finns to perform military service equally with the other peoples of the Empire and to amalgamate them with the other Russian forces. Yet this could hardly have been done except by forcing upon the people a law contrary to their constitution and wishes. The constitution was observed, however, and the problem was solved in accordance with its provisions. The Finnish Diet was advised concerning the necessity of introducing conscription into the Grand Duchy, and in 1877 it passed a bill, promulgated in the following year, which accorded with the desires of the Russian authorities. It provided for the establishment of the Finnish army on the basis of universal conscription; stated that the object of the army should be the defense of Finland; and that the officers should be Finnish citizens. Fourteen clauses of the enactment were clothed with the sanctity of fundamental laws and could therefore be changed only with the consent of the Diet and the Emperor-Grand Duke.[95]

For some ten years after the passage of the military law, no further attempts were made to dislocate the constitution. On the contrary, and in spite of the increasing and disturbing attention which the nationalist, Pan-Slav press in Russia was paying to Finland, at least two important additions were made to the mechanism of Finland's self-government. The first was the establishment, in 1882, of three-year Diets in the place of the five-year legislature which had met regularly since 1863.[96] The second was accomplished by a decree of June 25, 1886, whereby the Diet obtained the right of legislation by bill, to supersede the inadequate and antiquated procedure of legislation by petition.[97] Before the end of the decade of the eighties, however, it was becoming evident that the change toward reaction in Russia, which became marked after the accession of Alexander III in 1881, would also make itself felt in the relations between Finland and the Empire. More particularly, it appeared that the earlier respect for the constitution of the Grand Duchy was being replaced by a policy based on the claim that Finland's autonomy should not be permitted to stand in the way of a closer union between the Grand Duchy and the Empire.[98]

The first definite indication of trouble came in 1889 when the Finnish criminal law reform, which had already obtained the customary sanction of the Tsar and was to go into effect in 1891, was annulled by Imperial decree on the grounds that it contained a number of provisions of allegedly separatist nature. In the early part of the following year, several Russian committees were appointed to investigate ways and means whereby the Finnish Post Office, customs service and monetary system could be brought to conform more closely to the corresponding institutions in Russia. The first result of the work of the committees was the manifesto of June 12, 1890. It stated in part: "Because it is deemed advisable to introduce uniformity into the postal system within the entire Russian empire . . . the direction and administration of the Finnish Post Office shall be concentrated in the Imperial Ministry of the Interior and the Directory of the Post and Telegraph," and made a knowledge of Russian obligatory for future appointees to positions within the postal system. Without the consent of the Diet, an important public institution was thus arbitrarily placed under the supervision of non-Finnish citizens. The feeling of uneasiness and consternation created by this disregard of the constitution found clear expression in the Diet of 1891, but led to no change in the application of the manifesto.[99]

Especially down to 1894, when the accession of Nicholas II to the Russian throne brought a few years' respite, the attack upon Finland's autonomy and laws continued unabated. The Committee for Finnish Affairs in St. Petersburg, established in 1857 to serve as a connecting link between the Finnish Senate in Helsinki and the Minister-Secretary of State for Finland, was discontinued in 1891.[100] An important part of the administrative machinery through which the affairs of the self-governing Grand Duchy were transacted was thus eliminated. In the same year, the use of the Russian language was introduced into certain branches of the Finnish government, and more specific requirements concerning a knowledge of Russian among railway employees, the customs personnel and the police were formulated.[101] A new press law was issued which went considerably beyond the earlier enactments in establishing a detailed control over the newspapers.[102] Russian postage stamps were introduced, although their use was not made obligatory until 1900, and even after that date Finnish stamps could be used in domestic mail.[103] Instruction in Russian was increased in secondary schools as well as at the University and civil servants and teachers were given added opportunities for studying Russian by the creation of fellowships.[104] These innovations, however, were but an introduction to the wholesale attack that followed. The real process of Russification began in 1899, when an imperial manifesto, dated February 15, 1899, was issued. It stated in part as follows:

The Grand Duchy of Finland possesses . . . by . . . consent of Emperor Alexander I . . . and of his . . . Heirs, special institutions with regard to internal administration and legislation . . . But in addition to the local legislative matters in Finland, which arise from the peculiar conditions of society in the country, there also arise, in the administration of the Empire, other legislative problems in regard to Finland which, on account of their intimate connection with the general interests of the Empire, cannot be exclusively treated and disposed of by the institutions of the Grand Duchy. In regard to the manner in which questions of this kind are to be decided, the laws now in force contain no definite stipulations. Their absence has brought about considerable difficulties.

In order to remedy these difficulties, We . . . have seen fit, with a view to completing the ordinances now in force, to establish a fixed and unchangeable order for the work of the respective authorities in the Empire and the Grand Duchy, in the elaboration and the issuance of laws of general interest and importance for the Empire.

While maintaining in full force the prevailing statutes concerning the promulgation of local laws which relate exclusively to the internal affairs of Finland, We have found it necessary to reserve to Ourselves the final decision as to which laws come within the scope of general Imperial legislation. With this in view, We have . . . confirmed the Fundamental Statutes, proclaimed herewith, concerning the preparation, revision and promulgation of laws . . . for the Empire, including . . . Finland. . . . [105]

The Fundamental Statutes mentioned in the manifesto were issued separately and laid down the general rules which were henceforth to be observed. (1) Whenever changes in existing laws or the enactment of new legislation were necessary, "gracious Imperial consent" was first to be obtained. This provision pertained "to the laws applicable throughout the whole Empire, including Finland," as well as to laws "which are applied only within the limits of the Grand Duchy, in case they touch the common interest of the Empire, or are connected with the legislation of the Empire." (2) The "gracious Imperial consent" was to be obtained by petition addressed to the Tsar, all petitions for consent to be handled by the proper Russian Minister and the Minister-Secretary of State for Finland. (3) Consent having been obtained, the Finnish Senate, the Finnish Diet and the Governor-General of Finland were to be approached, "in order to get their opinion in regard to the wording of the proposed law." (4) The opinions having been obtained, the proper Russian Minister was to place the legislative proposals, accompanied by the opinions of Finland's Senate and

Diet, before the Imperial Council at St. Petersburg. (5) The legislative proposal would then be examined by the Finnish Minister-Secretary of State and by certain members of the Finnish Senate. After such scrutiny, the decision of the Imperial Council was to be "promulgated in the duly ordained manner both in the Empire and . . . in Finland." [106]

These provisions constituted a revolutionary deviation from the fundamental laws of the land. No precise definition of the matters which fell within the provisions of the Fundamental Statutes was attempted. That they might be interpreted in a way that would deprive Finland of all real opportunity for making her own laws was obvious. The manifesto expressly reserved to the Emperor the "final decision as to which laws come within the scope of general Imperial legislation." By reserving to the Finnish Senate and Diet only the right of expressing an opinion in such legislative questions, the Fundamental Statutes in effect abolished the constitution and substituted only meaningless and ineffective forms of participation in the transaction of public business for the real substance of self-government. If the policy outlined in the Fundamental Statutes were carried out, the Finnish constitutional would be dead.

The manifesto and the statutes created general consternation and restlessness in Finland. Uneasiness and indecision prevailed in the Senate, which finally decided to promulgate the manifesto only after the vote of the vice-president had given a bare majority to the group which felt that failure to promulgate would entail greater dangers than promulgation. The Diet resolved to enter a protest, but failed to obtain a hearing in St. Petersburg, as did a Senate deputation dispatched to the Emperor to emphasize the illegal and uncon-

stitutional aspects of the contemplated policy toward Finland. The most that was obtained was an assurance that the
Tsar considered that "he had given the country the best
guaranty for the undisturbed preservation of its internal
legislation when he personally undertook to decide, in each
separate instance, whether a matter ought to be classified as
pertaining to imperial legislation. . . ." [107] It goes without
saying that a guaranty of this sort was far from satisfactory,
especially in view of the fact that the scope of the legislation
which might be considered imperial was in no way indicated,
but might be extended to any and all legislative matters.

Supplication and protest were by no means limited to the
Finnish executive and legislative. The first steps leading to
a truly national protest were taken within a few days of the
issuance of the February manifesto. The decision to enlist
the whole nation in a weighty expression of disapproval of
the Russification policy was made by patriots in Helsinki,
and early in March the movement was well under way.
Acting in complete secrecy — neither the post office, the
telephone nor the telegraph could be used, for fear that the
enterprise would be discovered by the Russian authorities —
the necessary funds were obtained and the organization developed. An address to be signed by the people was drafted,
and copies dispatched to all parts of the country. On March
5, citizens' meetings were held throughout the land where
the contents of the address were read, the signatures of the
protestants were affixed, and the representatives — one from
every parish — chosen to constitute a Committee of Five
Hundred which was to present the protest to the Tsar in the
Russian capital. The work was completed a week later. It
was found that 522,931 adult men and women had affixed

their names to the address. The figure represented approximately one-sixth of the total population — a mighty result obtained in little more than a week of feverish effort. Not the least interesting feature of it all was the fact that only after the thousands of copies of the address had been bound, and the five hundred deputies entrained (on March 16) upon their errand to St. Petersburg, was the enterprise brought to the attention of the Russian Governor-General Bobrikoff.[108]

This impressive demonstration brought no relief, however. The national address, which declared that the February manifesto had undermined the foundations of Finland's body politic and expressed the hope that the Emperor would remove this threat to the peaceful and orderly development of the country, was never permitted to be presented to the Tsar, and the deputation returned without having accomplished its purpose. The same fate awaited the international committee of distinguished European statesmen and scholars who made an effort to reach the Tsar in June of the same year. It intended to present a plea for the recognition of the unconstitutional character of the recent Russian policy toward Finland. The address was signed by more than one thousand prominent citizens of England, France, Germany, Italy and seven other countries. Among the outstanding names were those of Herbert Spencer, Florence Nightingale, J. Westlake, Émile Zola, Anatole France, Gaston Paris, the Count de Broglie, ex-Minister of Justice L. Trarieux, Rudolf Eucken, Theodore Mommsen, Hans Delbrück, Hendrick Ibsen, Björnstierne-Björnson, Frithiof Nansen, Verner von Heidenstam, Mittag-Leffler, Georg Brandes, W. van der Vlugt and Senator E. Brusa, the then president of the

Institut de Droit International. However, the voice of the thousand was no more effective than the plea of the five hundred thousand in stemming the tide of Russification.[109]

In the meantime, the press of the country was beginning to feel the effects of the new policy. The newspapers and periodicals, almost without exception, had raised their voices against the Russian menace. As a consequence, they soon became the objects of the special attention of the Russian authorities in Finland. The existing press laws placed only inadequate obstacles in the way of the persecution of the newspapers. No constitutional provisions guaranteeing the freedom of the press existed, for the regulation of the press was one of the matters left to imperial initiative. In the absence of adequate legislation the newspapers were peculiarly open to the arbitrariness of the Governor-General's policies. In the course of 1899, a score of newspapers were discontinued, some permanently and others for periods ranging from one to three months. During the year 1900, this type of duress increased in severity. Heavy fines, tightening of the existing censorship regulations and forced changes of editors — that is to say, making the continuation of a newspaper contingent upon the appointment of a new editorial staff — were other means of putting down opposition. Measures of this kind were probably effective in preventing the publication of objectionable matter, but they contributed but little to the disappearance of the opposition which they were designed to eliminate. The public subscribed to the papers hit by the edicts decreeing discontinuation, thus helping to tide them over the periods of forced silence. Furthermore, as the screws were increasingly tightened, pamphlets and other forms of uncensored reading matter printed secretly at home or smuggled from abroad, began to serve as means of anti-Russian propaganda. While the censored press was muted, the uncensored literature of pamphlet and tract sounded a resonant note of criticism and protest.[110]

Undeterred by Finnish opposition or foreign opinion, the work of Russification was carried on under the energetic guidance of N. Bobrikoff, the Governor-General.[111] An unconstitutional conscription act was forced upon the country in 1901 (July 12). It disbanded the Finnish troops and provided that Finnish recruits were to perform their military service with the Russian troops, subject to Russian regulations, although it was intimated that they would serve in separate contingents "consisting mainly of persons of Finnish birth." [112] The act led to the first real trial of strength between the Russian authorities and the Finnish opposition. When the enrollment of conscripts took place in the spring of 1902, it was found that more than half of the conscripts absented themselves from the levy — this in spite of the fact that out of approximately 25,000 men of military age, only 500 would be called to the colors.[113] Also, the use of Russian was considerably extended: it was made obligatory in the Finnish State Secretariat, the Governor-General's Office and the Finnish Passport Bureau; and it was decreed that beginning in 1905, Russian should be exclusively employed by all civil servants responsible to the Senate or the provincial governors. The Collection of Finland's Laws, which had hitherto appeared in Finnish and Swedish, was printed in Russian as well, and the Russian text was made official, to the exclusion of the Finnish and Swedish versions. After 1908, Russian was to be used even in the oral transaction of business in the Finnish Senate. The teaching of Russian in the secondary schools was materially increased. Recalcitrant governors, judges, mayors, city and town councillors and other civil servants were dismissed by the hundreds, and their places filled either by Russians or by Finns unwilling or unable to resist the pressure from St. Petersburg. Government by law had become government by arbitrary decree.[114]

The acute constitutional conflict begun by the February manifesto of 1899 and continuing down to the Russian Revolution of 1905, had a profound effect upon the Finnish and the Swede-Finn nationalist movements. The earlier clear-cut lines which had separated them began to disappear. The ill-wind that blew from Russia was sufficiently strong to wear down or to eliminate class and party barriers. It brought forth new sympathies and changed the meaning of old allegiances. Nationalist allegiance in particular became charged with new and exceptional responsibilities.

When more than half a million adult citizens signed the great protest against the February manifesto, it was obvious that the nation had been aroused to action in defense of the constitution and laws of the country. It did not take long, however, before opinions began to differ as regards the course of action demanded by the policy of Russification. Some believed that salvation lay in an inflexible insistence upon the full recognition of Finland's rights and an uncompromising refusal to yield to any measures that the Russian government might undertake in violation of the fundamental laws. "Passive resistance" became the slogan of the Constitutionalists who subscribed to this view. Others were of the opinion that while resistance to Russification was absolutely necessary, the best interests of the country counseled against too pointed an opposition, for resistance compounded of little more than impotence and a confidence in the ultimate triumph of right over might, would be more likely to intensify the attack than to serve as a stout bulwark against it. Therefore, everything that might serve the Finnophobe Russians as an excuse for the complete destruction of Finland's autonomy should be carefully avoided. The corps of civil servants in particular should remain at their posts instead of resigning in protest against the lawlessness of the Russian régime, for such resignations would only hasten the process whereby the administration would fall into the hands of Russians. "Concede a little in order that we may save the remainder" may perhaps be accepted as a characterization of the so-called Retreaters' attitude. Finally, a secret organization was formed (in 1901) for the purpose of directing the opposition to Russian policy. This organization, called the Kagaali, was in close coöperation with the Constitutionalists but may be considered as representing a third and independent effort to save the country from Russification.

Under the stress and strain of the struggle, earlier party alignments were erased. The Constitutionalists, the Retreaters and the Kagaali drew their strength from all political parties and from both language groups. However, some of the old groups contributed more than others to the new parties. Speaking in general terms, the followers of Y. Koskinen, known since the late eighties as the Old Finns, furnished the majority of the Retreaters. The liberal Young Finns, a party that had come into being some twelve years earlier largely through the efforts of Eero Erkko, the emi-

nent journalist and statesman, gave the Constitutionalists a
source of strength without which the party would have remained wholly ineffectual. The Swede-Finns added conspicuously to the resources of the Constitutionalists, and as
regards the Social Democrats, it may be said that many of
their leaders were heart and soul for the national cause, and
the Socialist party contributed some of the most successful
and active agents of the Kagaali. The latter organization
took part in the propaganda against the illegal military
levies of 1902 and 1903, printed or imported and distributed
large amounts of forbidden literature, and served as a sort
of general bureau for the dissemination of all manner of
information, advice and leadership necessary for upholding
the morale of the nation during the particularly trying years
of 1902-1905. Women as well as men were found in its
ranks and rendered invaluable service in the work of anti-
Russian agitation.[115]

In degree as passive resistance proved inadequate to
stem the tide of Russification, a more radical, revolutionary
movement made its appearance. It centered in a group
styled the Finnish Activist Opposition Party which came
into being in 1903. Its leading spirit was K. Zilliacus, an
energetic and able patriot. The outbreak of the Russo-
Japanese war in 1904 gave this direct-action group added
strength and opportunities. Secret negotiations with Japanese agents, purchases abroad of arms and munitions which
were smuggled into Finland, meetings and subterranean co-
operation with Russian revolutionaries and Polish and other
non-Russian independence enthusiasts, the engineering of
acts of violence and preparations for an armed uprising in
Finland, plots and counterplots — such activities occupied

Zilliacus and his small band of followers who placed their faith in the efficacy of force where protest and peaceful opposition seemed to be of no avail. As an indirect result of the undertakings of this group, Governor-General Bobrikoff was assassinated in July, 1904, and Attorney-General Johnsson-Soisalon-Soininen met with the same fate in the following year. The former fell a victim of his energetic effort in behalf of Russification, and the latter lost his life because he had lent the authority of his high office to acts designed to speed the work of Bobrikoff.[116]

When Russian discontent with the reactionary and inefficient imperial government was brought to a head in the Revolution of 1905, Finland's position was considerably eased. The disturbances in the Empire were reflected in Finland also, notably during the closing week of October, 1905, when the nation went on strike. The national strike was an impressive demonstration involving all classes and nearly all phases of the economic life of the country. On November 4, the Tsar signed a manifesto which reestablished law and order in the Grand Duchy. All the illegal measures of the preceding half-dozen years were rescinded, and the constitution was restored. The Diet was summoned to meet in extra session for the purpose of resuming the work which for several years it had been unable to perform. The most important among the many reforms which it effected was the modernization of the national legislature and of the existing franchise laws. A new Senate was appointed. Its members were drawn from the Constitutionalists and included one Social Democrat. The Retreaters, who had been in control of the national executive, thus found themselves ousted from the government. The appointment

of a new Governor-General who at once proceeded to remove
the old causes of friction between the Finns and the Russian
government likewise illustrated the extent to which the authorities in St. Petersburg repudiated the unconstitutional
régime of the preceding years.[117]

In spite of the hesitancy and indecision which characterized many phases of the Finnish opposition during the
period 1899-1905, the nation may be said to have been fairly
united in denouncing the illegality of Russia's policy and in
maintaining that only by concerted action could the people
hope to save Finland's autonomy from destruction. While
this unanimity of opinion was by no means sufficiently
strong to eliminate all instances of obsequious acceptance of
the program which Bobrikoff was considered to personify,
it was strong enough to make possible the truly nation-wide
Great Protest against the February manifesto of 1899, as
well as the equally nation-wide demonstration during
the strike in October, 1905. Considered as a whole, the
six years that separated these impressive mobilizations of the
opinion of the people constituted the first real test of
the strength of the nationalist movement.

We have seen that especially since the appearance of
Snellman in the forties, the objective of the Finnish cause
had been in the last analysis the creation of a nationalist-
conscious citizenry mindful of the necessity of internal union
and appreciative of the importance of safeguarding the institutions and laws of the country against Russification. The
emphasis placed by the Fennomen upon the Finnization of
the Swede-Finn upper classes, the conservative inclinations
of those most effected by the onward march of the Finnish
language in the transaction of public business and the ad-

ministration of law, and other factors that we have noted, had served to bring forth the Swecoman nationalist movement. Two mutually antagonistic nationalist movements had thus come into being. From the sixties down to the closing nineties, controversy, debate and denunciation had characterized the relations between the leaders and articulate followers of the two persuasions. By the time of the February manifesto, it seemed that instead of having made for internal union, the Snellmanian nationalist movement had divided the country into two contending camps, and that instead of having furnished the nation with the strength necessary for the combat that was about to begin, it had created internal discord which would make resistance both hopeless and ineffective.

The superficial character of this internal division was soon disclosed, however. Brought face to face with the Russian attack, even the ardent "language nationalists" of both groups joined hands, at least temporarily. More important than the rapprochement between these nationalists, however, was the response of the broad masses to the appeals for participation in the unequal struggle. That the men and women of the farm and the factory rallied against Russification is to be explained, it appears, more in terms of the extensive educational work, described in another connection, than in terms of a clear understanding and appreciation of the more abstract phases of the nationalist argument which had served for decades to fix the gulf between the Fennoman and Swecoman leaders. Without the support of the masses, the nationalist leaders would have been lost from the beginning. It was the common people who furnished most of the half million signatures for the Great Protest; it was the common people who defied the authorities by absenting themselves from the levies in 1902, and it was the common people who made the national strike of 1905 a success. It is probably no exaggeration to say that the Finnish nationalist movement brought forth its most abundant fruit during these years primarily because of the extensive work in the field of popular education from, say, 1870 to 1900. While the Russian Revolution of 1905 was responsible for the restoration of the Finnish constitution, it was this educational effort and its consequences that had prevented Finland from being reduced by that time to a state where constitutions and self-government meant, for the average citizen, only empty words devoid of substance and meaning.

CHAPTER VII

THE LAST TWENTY-FIVE YEARS

THE LANGUAGE PROBLEM AND POLITICS, 1906-1916

Among the manifold consequences of the restoration of lawful order in 1905, probably the most important was the drafting of a new constitution and a new electoral law. The Parliament Bill and the Franchise Law, promulgated on July 20, 1906, revolutionized the national legislature. The antiquated Diet of four Estates was scrapped and a unicameral legislature of 200 members took its place. The 200 representatives were chosen by direct and proportional election; all men and women — with a few minor exceptions — of twenty-four years of age or over were entitled to vote. No distinction was drawn between the right to vote and eligibility for seats in the Diet; women and men were placed on a footing of complete equality in all political matters. When the old Diet adjourned on September 18, 1906, the incident brought to a close representation by classes that had outlived its usefulness, and ushered in a period when the vote of the common man would determine the composition of parliamentary majorities and the course of legislative effort — and the fate, consequently, of nationalist programs.[1]

The demise of representation by Estates served as the signal for the opening of a keen contest for control of the Diet.

Old party alignments were dissolved and new political parties came into being. The Agrarian Union was formed to marshal the strength of the farming population. The Young Finns and the Old Finns — the latter having been badly damaged by the policy of Retreatism during the years 1899-1905 — underwent a process of reconstruction. The Social Democrats tightened their organization with a view to capturing the recently enfranchised masses. The Swede-Finns likewise found themselves compelled to prepare for the onward march of political democracy.

For the Swede-Finn group in particular, or to be more exact, for the leading Swede-Finn nationalists, the reform of the national legislature meant considerable difficulties. By this reform the politically articulate Swede-Finns who had exercised no small influence in the days of the Estate Diet — they had, as a matter of fact, constituted a sufficiently large element in the Burghers and the Nobles to block many a bill — were placed in a position markedly different from the one formerly held by them. The coming of a popular franchise, especially when coupled with the other innovation, a uni-cameral legislature, at once reduced them to a permanent minority. On this point the verdict of the national census was disconcertingly final. It disclosed that out of a total population approximating (in 1900) 2,350,000 only some 349,000 were Swede-Finns.[2] The figure amounted to a fraction less than thirteen percent and rather definitely set the limits for possible Swede-Finn mandates in the national legislature. It was obvious that unless the political leaders succeeded in obtaining the support of the Swedish-speaking farmers, laborers and common folk in general, it would be impossible to reach even the unpretentious representation that a full utilization of the numerical strength of the Swede-Finn population might assure. Whether they liked it or not, the Swede-Finn nationalists found themselves compelled to race with democracy or stand idly by while "one man, one vote" was giving the prizes to the numerically strong.

Confronted by this dilemma, the leaders proceeded to organize the Swede-Finn citizens in a political party. Old lines were drawn in and re-baited and new lines thrown out for a bigger catch. Largely under the leadership of Dr. A. Lille, one of the most active and militant Swecomen since the early eighties, a constituent party conference was convened in May, 1906. The conference was attended by some 300 representatives. They agreed to the establishment of a new party, to be known as the Swedish People's Party, and accepted a lengthy program designed to furnish the broad platform upon which the Swede-Finn intellectual, farmer, fisherman and financier could stand shoulder to shoulder with the Swede-Finn butcher, baker and candlestick-maker. The program stated, under the heading "Language and Educational Problems" that (1) the language enactment of 1902 should be replaced by a Diet law providing that every citizen should be permitted to use his own language in all dealings with public authorities, and should be served in it by them, and that in all but uni-lingual localities, judicial and civil authorities should have a free choice as regards the language employed by them; (2) that localities having a minority language population which constituted one-fifth of the total, or exceeded 2,000 souls, should be considered bilingual and the language situation within their confines solved in accordance with the demands of equality and justice; (3) that all persons in State employ should know both Swedish and Finnish; (4) that the "Swedish-speaking part of the population must inflexibly insist that instruction in lower and higher educational institutions shall be given, for all time to come, in the student's mother tongue. . ."; and (5) that Swede-Finn educational institutions should receive State aid in accordance with the principles that apply to Finnish institutions.[3]

While the Swede-Finns were thus girding their loins for the electoral campaign of 1906 which would determine the composition of the first uni-cameral legislature, scheduled to meet in January, 1907, the other contestants were likewise marshalling forces and raising alluring standards. The Agrarians, though new comers in the arena of politics, went into the fray under a flag designed to attract farmers far and near. Determined not to lose sight of the nationalist significance of the occasion, they declared that (1) Finnish should be the predominant language in Finland, and educational and cultural accomplishment in that language should be elevated to the position which ninety percent of the population consider proper; (2) the requirement that civil servants must know Swedish should apply only to government employees appointed to serve in Swedish-language localities, and to such central administrative and other officers as deal with Swede-Finn districts; (3) Finnish should be the official language in the transaction of all public business; but the inhabitants of Swede-Finn districts should have the right to demand that their language be used in all dealings they might have with central offices, etc.; (4) the official language of the University of Helsinki should be Finnish, and all permanent members of its staff should lecture in Finnish;

and (5) the State should not maintain Swedish-language schools in the Finnish parts of the country.[4]

The veteran Old Finns, the doughty champions of the Finnish movement ever since the days when Y. Koskinen began to sound a more insistent note in the Fennoman demands, took the field in new attire. Having suffered heavy losses in power and prestige during the preceding half-dozen years, they now went forth to battle as the National Finnish Party. Mindful of the importance of standing guard over the gains already made by the Finnish cause, and of the necessity of capturing new laurels for it, the leaders of the National Finnish Party drew up a party program which gave prominence to the language question. It stated in part that (1) Finnish should be the official language of the country; (2) that Finnish should become official by means of a constitutional provision, which should also fix the right of all citizens to use either Finnish or Swedish in law courts, administrative offices, etc.; (3) that a complete command of Finnish should be required of all appointees to public office, and that those appointed to posts in Swedish-language localities should know Swedish; adequate provision should also be made by central authorities for the discharge in Swedish of business pertaining to such localities; (4) that the State should maintain and support only Finnish-language schools in Finnish-language districts; (5) that instruction in all subjects at the University should be given in Finnish; and (6) that in Finnish-language schools, instruction in Swedish should be designed only to enable the students to understand that language. The time saved should be primarily used for adequate instruction in English, French or German. In the higher Swede-Finn schools, instruction in Finnish should be made more effective than hitherto.[5]

The Young Finnish Party could look forward to the election with considerable confidence, for its supporters had furnished the backbone of the opposition to Russification whose consequences, one might have urged with some reason, had made possible the democratic reform of the Diet. Being largely interested in liberal social and economic reforms, the Young Finnish Party — it was also called the Constitutional Finnish Party — paid relatively less attention to the language question than did the other Finnish parties mentioned. However, that it was genuinely concerned with the fundamentals of the Fennoman creed was clearly shown by its platform. It held that the aim of the party was "the elevation of Finnish to a leading position" as the medium of art, letters, science and all phases of higher intellectual endeavor, and "as the official language of the country." The former objective, it was stated, could not be attained by means of legislative enactments; it required further cultural and intellectual advance. With regard to the second, its realization should come naturally, without forcible Finnization of the Swede-Finn population in schools or by other means. Swedish should be assured "a just position" as the language of the minority; it should be recognized as the second national language in Finland. However, Finnish should become the language mainly used by the central authorities, and an adequate command of Finnish should be required of all public servants. Nor should the State be expected artificially to maintain — by means of grants and the like — Swedish-language schools in localities where the Swede-Finn population was very small or non-existent. Finally, it was urged that the language situation at the University should be so arranged as to meet fully the needs of Finnish-speaking students.[6]

During the campaign, the language question became a rich source of argument and invective. The Swede-Finn party was frankly founded on a language-nationalist issue. The National Finnish Party likewise coined currency out of the same metal, and as regards the Young Finns and the Agrarians, they showed no inclination to accept or use baser alloys, although the former disclosed considerable moderation in their use of the language argument. Against the exploitation of the language problem, the Social Democrats protested in words that left no doubt as to their stand in the matter: "Throughout the land the National Finnish Party fans the fires of the language controversy in a most audacious and shameless manner." The Swede-Finn party, "in past years, has ever been fundamentally a language party. Now, however, it has stepped forth as a rabid language party pure and simple — for it knows that its power in this country has gone the way of all earthly things — and has but one real plank in its platform: the preaching of hatred against their Finnish 'oppressors.' For this purpose it has christened itself the Swedish 'People's' (!) party and pretends to work for cultural objectives. . . ." True patriotism, the Socialists held, required something more than meaningless wrangling over the language question. "The national cause will be really promoted only if we set our house in order in a manner that makes possible the intellectual and material advance of all our citizens. The greatest danger to our nationality threatens from our neighbor to the east, as everyone knows." The best way to meet the danger is by safeguarding Finland's self-government. Yet the bourgeoisie have shown no real inclination to strengthen it. The lower classes "promote the nationalist cause by insisting that the people be given *rights*. For where is the fatherland of the cotter whose rights are practically limited to the obligation to pay taxes? Where is the fatherland of the unemployed laborer wandering in search of work. . . ? Justice alone will kindle in the hearts of the proletariat that love of the fatherland on which the bourgeoisie prate so prettily — obligations alone will never awaken it.[8]

The Social Democrat views on the language question and all it implied was formulated at the Annual Party Conference in 1906 in the following manner:

(1) The development of Finnish into a fully satisfactory literary and educational medium, and its elevation to the position of an official language, has ever been and still is important for the educational, moral and material progress of the Finnish-speaking workers. The advance of the Finnish language must therefore . . . be still further promoted. (2) Swedish is indispensable for the advance of the Swede-Finn people in Finland. It is also an important channel through which educational influences and Social Democratic ideas may be brought to us . . . For these reasons, the Party Congress favors the retention and further cultivation of Swedish. (3) The Russian language has been and still is hated among our people because [of] bloody wars [in the past]. This hatred has been sustained by the bureaucratic tyranny imposed on our country by Russia. The Finnish people have not always succeeded in distinguishing between the Russian language on the one hand and Russian oppressors on the other. In order to aid them in overcoming this common fault and with a view to lessening the national hatred between the two people, the Social Democratic Party declares that the Russian language should not be despised because there are Russian tyrants; that the use . . . of Russian should be permitted in Finland; and that modern Russian literature dealing with the ideal of liberty should be spread in Finland. . . .[9]

It is impossible to say how far the "language planks" in

the platforms of the major parties mentioned determined the outcome of the heated campaign. There is no doubt, however, that they were of fundamental importance in the case of the Swede-Finn party, and that the National Finnish party, the Young Finns and the Agrarians obtained a substantial part of their support on the strength of their pronouncements concernng the language situation. The outcome of the election is indicated by the following table. In view of the fact that the language programs drafted in 1906 remained virtually unchanged during the following ten years, the results of later elections, down to the year 1916, are also given.

While the language controversy and related issues played a part in all elections between 1906 and 1916, the relative strength of the "language parties," as disclosed by the campaign of 1906, did not materially change during the decade. Several factors contributed to this end. In the first place, the steady growth of Socialist strength meant increasing political influence in the hands of a party disinclined to exploit the possibilities of "language nationalism." Secondly, the Swede-Finn group was unable to escape the handicaps which its position as a minority group placed in the way of a realization of the demands formulated by the Swede-Finn leaders. Thirdly, the National Finnish party steadily lost in power, and while the Agrarians were by no means insensitive to the language situation, their growth was too slow to place them in anything like an important position. More important than any of these circumstances, however, was the renewed policy of Russification which appeared within a couple of years of the restoration of Finland's constitution in 1905.

STRENGTH OF PARTIES AND COMPOSITION OF THE DIET, 1907-1916 [10]

	Socialists		Finnish Party		Young Finns		Swede-Finns		Agrarians		Others		Total	
	Votes	Rep.	Votes	Rep.	Votes	Rep.	Votes	Rep.	Votes	Rep.	Votes	Rep.	Votes	Rep.
1907	329,946	80	243,573	58	121,604	26	112,267	25	51,242	9	32,358	2	890,990	200
1908	310,826	83	205,892	54	115,201	27	103,146	25	51,756	9	22,620	2	809,441	200
1909	337,685	84	199,920	48	122,770	29	104,191	25	56,943	13	24,963	1	846,471	200
1910	316,951	86	174,661	42	114,291	28	107,121	26	60,157	17	18,378	1	791,559	200
1911	321,201	86	174,177	43	119,361	28	106,810	26	62,885	16	17,953	1	802,387	200
1913	312,214	90	143,982	38	102,313	29	94,672	25	56,977	18	14,146	—	724,304	200
1916	376,030	103	139,111	33	99,419	23	93,555	21	71,608	19	15,486	1	795,209	200

RUSSIFICATION, THE WORLD WAR AND INDEPENDENCE

The respite ushered in by the Russian Revolution of 1905 was brought to an end before long. The policy delineated in the famous February manifesto (1899) and the spirit of arbitrariness in evidence during the Bobrikoff period, were soon permitted to dominate once more the Finnish policy of the imperial authorities. A series of measures was introduced, beginning in 1908, which gave the lie to the solemn statements of the manifesto of November 4, 1905. All legislative and other matters which in any way concerned the empire were withdrawn from the competence of the Diet and reserved to the Council of Ministers and the Russian Duma. The Finnish Senate was bent to the will of the friends of Russification. Beginning in 1912, native-born Russians were increasingly appointed to seats in it. In degree as its membership became Russian, the Senate became a more pliable instrument in the hands of the Finnophobe Russian nationalists. Arbitrary financial levies were imposed upon the country; the Civil Service was gradually Russified; Russian became the sole official language of the Senate; instruction in Russian was given a more prominent place in the schools; the important national pilot service was subordinated to the Ministry of Marine and to Russian law; Russian subjects were placed on a footing of equality in the matter of civil rights with Finnish citizens; judges and other public servants who refused to apply or recognize laws that had been illegally imposed on the country were frequently imprisoned or expelled, and on occasion exiled to the interior of Russia or Siberia; and funds appropriated for educational and related purposes were arbitrarily assigned to other ends. When the World War broke out, orderly processes of government had largely disappeared.[11]

During the World War, Russification continued unabated. The proclamation of a state of war in the early days of the conflict gave new opportunities for further violations of the constitutional and other laws of the land. Freedom of assembly was restricted; the printed word was subjected to stricter control; citizens were frequently apprehended and subjected to Russian laws. Military necessity became almost an everyday excuse for violations of private property; special war taxes were illegally levied; renewed efforts were made to prepare the ground for a linguistic Russification of the students in the secondary and higher schools, and of the broad masses as well; provision was made for the introduction of Russian law courts, and for the abolition of Finnish citizenship; and Russian gendarmes became ever more numerous, as visible symbols of the policy which was rapidly breaking down all obstacles. The Diet's appeals to the constitution and its frequent protests against the illegalities committed during the years 1914-1917 seemed only to hasten the process which was dissolving what little remained of the foundations upon which the government and institutions of the country rested. By the time the Russian Revolution broke out in March, 1917, it appeared that the day was drawing nigh when a formal abrogation of the constitution would lead to a complete political amalgamation of the Grand Duchy with the Empire. Self-government had become for all practical purposes an empty abstraction.

Meanwhile, consternation, indecision and apprehension gripped the leading men of the country. Most of the promi-

nent leaders of both language groups seemed unable to cope
with the mounting difficulties. Many of them were strongly
committed to passive resistance which seemed to have been
successful in staving off the attack of 1899-1905. Also, the
issues involved in the World War served to confuse rather
than to clarify the prevailing situation. In spite of Russian
propaganda which was more or less forcibly fed to the press,
public opinion tended toward pro-Germanism from the outset. While the liberal elements considered Germany and
Russia the greatest enemies of the rights of small nations
and maintained that Germany had in fact served as Russia's
guide in the arts of imperialism, militarism and intolerable
bureaucracy, the conviction that only a defeat of Russia
would ease the situation in Finland was enough to swing
public opinion to the side of the Central Powers. To be
sure, those unwilling to abandon completely their Entente
sympathies hoped for an Allied victory in the west and a
German victory in the east. However, when the March
Revolution in Russia served to bring such an outcome of
the war within the limits of possibility, pro-German sentiment had already carried the day. Germany appeared to
be the only power capable of "defeating our deadly enemy,
Russia." [12]

Pro-German views gained ground most rapidly in University circles. Not a few of the students and younger instructors believed that the war offered a solution for the
problems of the preceding half-dozen years. The solution
was political independence. Already before 1914, a small
group of independence enthusiasts had been busily at work
for the realization of this objective, and after August, 1914,
they began to draft plans for the overthrow of the Russian

régime in Finland. The movement was well under way by the close of November of that year. The friends of independence at first proceeded on the assumption that Sweden would sooner or later be drawn into the struggle on the side of Germany. The outcome of Sweden's participation in the war, they believed, would be the creation of an independent Finland to serve as a buffer state between Sweden and Russia. These hopes were laid low, however, when the Swedish government assumed early in the conflict a policy of strict neutrality, maintained throughout the war. Unsuccessful in Sweden, the patriots turned to Germany. By January, 1915, secret agents dispatched to Berlin had succeeded in obtaining the ear and support of the General Staff. Provision was made for the military training of a handful of university students who would later become, it was hoped, the kernel of a national fighting force. In the course of 1915-1917, a considerable number of prospective officers were smuggled out of Finland and dispatched to the Lockstedt training camp in Schleswig which became the center of the work. Ultimately some 2,000 men were included in the Lockstedt group. Meanwhile the nation was being prepared by means of secret organizations and literature for the contest the patriots saw ahead.[18]

The preparations for a military uprising to take place as soon as Russia's reverses should assume sufficient proportions to assure a fair chance of success, had the effect of eliminating most internal language jealousies and party squabbles. The story of the eventful years from 1899 to 1905 was thus repeated. The patriots responsible for the extensive underground organization whereby the independence idea was popularized and volunteers dispatched to

Germany, or those who contributed to the enterprise by enlisting in the Lockstedt troop, or participated in other ways in the revolutionary labors, represented no single party or language group. Conservatives, liberals, Socialists, Swede-Finns and Finns were found in the long list of independence men whose names independent Finland has come to look upon as a national roll of honor. Also, while university students and younger instructors constituted a substantial part of the Lockstedt volunteers, not a few clerks, farmers and workers gave the "Jaeger movement" the complexion of a truly national movement.[14]

When the March Revolution began in Russia, it was looked upon in Finland as the beginning of civil war and anarchy which would speedily dissolve the empire and thereby provide an opportunity for Finnish independence. The relatively peaceful situation which characterized the beginning of the Revolution, however, appeared to disclose democratic strength sufficient to permit the transformation of the former autocracy into a state founded on popular rights. The provisional government headed by Lvov held the reins of power, and to it the Finns were compelled to look for deliverance when the expected chaos failed to materialize.

The autocratic régime in Finland collapsed almost simultaneously with the abdication of Nicholas II. The Russian naval forces stationed in Helsinki began to square their accounts with their officers on March 15; considerable blood was spilled in the process. The Governor-General and the higher officials were incarcerated by the soldiery on March 16 and political prisoners freed. Beginning on the seventeenth, the press censorship was abolished, except in the case of military news. Three days later, the Russian Provisional Government hastened to deliver a blow at the whole system of arbitrary, unconstitutional government which had held Finland in its grip for nearly ten years. The manifesto issued on March 20 — it had been drafted by a Finnish Parliamentary committee — declared null and void all the ordinances and decrees which had been forced upon the country since 1890, granted amnesty to all political prisoners, solemnly assured the people of Finland their right to self-government, provided that Senators would in the future be appointed from among parliament members, and promised a reorganization of the Senate Department of Justice. Within a week of the collapse of the monarchy, Finland was thus able to point to a complete recapture of the self-rule which had all but disappeared during the years 1908-1916.[15]

During the spring and summer of 1917, Finland drifted slowly but surely toward complete independence. The Russian Provisional Government convened the Finnish Diet on April 4,[16] and within a few weeks several of its members were beginning to urge that the connection with Russia be severed for good. The Socialists in particular advocated such a course, although supporters of independence were found among all parties. Indecision created by the continuation in office of the Provisional Government postponed action till July 18, when an abortive attempt was made to vest all legislative and executive power in the Finnish Diet. This revolutionary action prompted the Provisional Government to dissolve the Diet, and new elections were proclaimed for October 1-2.[17] After considerable hesitation, the authority of the Russian government was recognized, and the country

proceeded to the electoral contest which would determine
the composition of the Diet scheduled to meet on November
1, 1917. That the Diet might then be called upon to face a
situation markedly different from that which obtained when
the July coup d'état was frustrated, was intimated by an
"Open Letter" issued by Kerensky on September 12. It
attempted to take the wind out of the sails of the supporters
of independence by providing that the Finnish Senate would
henceforth be the final authority in all matters which had
hitherto been the personal prerogative of the Tsar, except
(1) the convocation and dissolution of the Diet; (2) new
elections; (3) confirmation of the budget; (4) certain par-
dons; (5) the appointment of the Governor-General, the
Finnish Secretary of State and other higher officers of
state; and (6) the final decision in matters involving Russian citizens in Finland, or the relations between Finland
and Russia.[18]

The October election became a keen contest between the
Socialists and the bourgeois groups. The former, who contemplated not only political independence but far-reaching
social and economic legislation, had commanded an absolute majority in the last Diet [19] and attempted to obtain a
preponderance in the new that would assure a victory for
their program. These hopes were frustrated, however, for
the Socialists captured only ninety-two seats. The remainder
were divided as follows: The National Finnish party, thirty-
two; the Agrarians, twenty-six; the Young Finns, twenty-
four; the Swede-Finns, twenty-one; and a new party, the
Finnish People's Party, five.[20] Within two weeks of the
meeting of the Diet on November 1, the legislators voted to
put into effect the law of July 18 and thereby effected the

coup d'état which the provisional government had prevented four months earlier. A new Senate was also formed; the choice of members was made without the consent or confirmation of the Russian government which was being ousted at this very time by Lenin and his followers. A formal declaration of independence was issued on December 6, 1917.[21]

Independence declared did not mean independence achieved, however. During the preceding six months the country had experienced internal disturbances that boded ill for the future. Partly because of the presence of tens of thousands of revolutionary Russian soldiers, and partly because of defective leadership, a considerable part of the Socialists were swinging toward the position held in Russia by the Bolsheviks. The increasing radicalization of the masses became conspicuous during the summer and appears to have been primarily responsible for the strikes and acts of violence which became frequent beginning in July. For example, the non-Socialist press was silenced by a printers' strike between June 1 and July 9. Red Guards were being formed all over the country and frequently indulged in looting, murder, "expropriation" of private and public property and the like. While some of the Socialist leaders made strenuous efforts to check the movement, they were unable to breast the tide that was carrying the radical elements closer to a test of strength with the non-radical farmers and other bourgeois elements. The latter were busy preparing for the contest which could be clearly foreseen by the time the declaration of independence was issued. Defense Guards were being formed in feverish haste, but their organization was seriously handicapped by the fact that arms and munitions could be obtained only in limited quantities. The Red

Guards, on the other hand, fraternized with the Russian soldiery and obtained adequate equipment as well as leadership from the soldiers' and sailors' soviets.

The Red elements broke out in open rebellion on January 27, 1918. Assisted by the Russian troops, they attempted to overthrow the government and establish a workers' republic on the Russian model. The war lasted some three months and resulted in a complete victory for the White forces, who profited by the return of the Jaeger batallion from Germany and the assistance of some 12,000 German troops. The defeat of the Red forces secured the independence of the country, and when the legal Svinhufvud Senate took up its tasks in the capital on May 4, it was able to commence its work unhampered by the presence of elements desirous of effecting a union with Bolshevist Russia.[22]

RECONSTRUCTION

Independence created several problems of pressing import: the economic reconstruction necessitated by the ravages of the war, the enormous difficulties caused by an alarming food shortage, the complicated business of establishing satisfactory foreign relations, and the difficulties to be overcome before public finances could be placed on a sound basis. These problems need not concern us here, however. It will suffice for our purposes to observe the manner in which the language situation was affected by the circumstances under which Finland's existence as a sovereign state was begun.

Shortly after the declaration of independence on December 6, 1917, the Senate had introduced a bill providing for a republican form of government. The outbreak of the War of Independence postponed action on the contemplated constitution, and when the matter was taken up again after the establishment of peace, the situation was not favorable for a republican constitution. The aid received from Germany, and the events leading to the War of Independence, placed a temporary premium upon the monarchical form of government. Parliament went on record (in August) in favor of the election of a king, and in October Prince Frederick of Hesse, a brother-in-law of the German Kaiser, was chosen. However, the gradual collapse of the Central Powers postponed the arrival of the chosen candidate, and ultimately the armistice put an end to German ascendancy in Finland. The monarchical form of government was thus never put to the test, and the country found itself able to set its political house in order without outside pressure.

Under the influence of the conflicting opinions created by constitutional and other problems, the old political parties underwent a transformation during 1918 reminiscent of the changes that had taken place in 1906 when the unicameral Diet came into being. The National Coalition Party succeeded the National Finnish Party, most of whose members it was able to capture. The Young Finns were reorganized as the National Progressive Party. While the National Coalition Party supported a monarchy, the National Progressive Party was whole-heartedly in favor of a republic, as were the Agrarians and the Socialists. The Swede-Finn party remained unchanged and joined hands with the National Coalition Party in demanding a monarchy. The fate of the constitutional issue was decided by the election held in March, 1919. The Social Democrats obtained eighty seats, the Agrarians forty-two, the Coalition group twenty-eight, the Progressives twenty-six, the Swede-Finns twenty-two, and the Christian Workers two. When parliament met in April, it thus contained a republican group able to carry through a republican constitution. The new constitution was put into effect in July, 1919.[23]

SWEDE-FINN DEMANDS AND NEW LANGUAGE LEGISLATION

While the country was getting back on an even keel after the War of Independence, the Swede-Finn leaders attempted to secure for the linguistic minority the exercise of the rights and prerogatives which they considered indispensable for the welfare of the Swede-Finn population.

During the decade following 1906, the Swede-Finn party had labored persistently for its objectives. Speaking in general terms, the result had been a progressively isolationist policy which tended to draw ever more sharply the lines behind which, it was hoped, a strong Swede-Finn front could be maintained. A Swede-Finn choral society, the Brage, was established in 1906; a Swede-Finn journalists' association came into being in 1907; the temperance movement was split along linguistic lines; beginning in 1908, a special "Swedish Day" was set aside as a sort of Swede-Finn national holiday, and November 6 — the day of Gustavus Adolphus' death — was chosen for the purpose; a Swede-Finn People's Academy was founded in the same year and began its work in November, 1908. In 1908, steps were taken for the founding of an organization designed to prevent land purchases in Swede-Finn districts by Finnish-speaking buyers; a Swede-Finn farmers' association appeared in 1910, and in the same year the annual Party Conference proclaimed the necessity of Swede-Finn withdrawals from all cultural and educational enterprises which did not serve purely Swede-Finn interests. Largely at the instance of Swede-Finn university students, a movement was begun in 1910 to discard the use of the word "Finn," as designation of the inhabitants of the country, and substitute "Finlander" in its stead.[24] Also, funds were collected for educational and other purposes and a movement for the establishment of a separate Swede-Finn university was begun.[25]

While the Swede-Finns rallied around the patriot's cause during the trying months of January-May, 1918, and rendered invaluable service to the newly established independence of the country, the anxiety of some of their leaders to obtain adequate guarantees for the linguistic privileges of the minority led them to follow a course of action colored by separatist aspirations. The executive committee of the Swede-Finn party resolved on May 20, 1918, that parliament should effect such a reorganization of the provincial governments as would lead to the creation of purely unilingual administrative and judicial districts, the inhabitants of such districts to enjoy extensive rights of self-government. In June, a Swede-Finn meeting in Vaasa accepted similar resolutions and added to them the demand that in the organization of the army, care should be taken to enable Swede-Finns to serve only in Swedish-speaking units in which the language of instruction and command should be Swedish. Also, the conference gave expression to the threat that unless these demands were accepted by the government, the Swede-Finn parts of Ostrobothnia (a province in western Finland) might attempt secession. The same general objectives were embraced by another Swede-Finn provincial conference held in Porvoo on July 14.[26]

These developments seemed to suggest that the time was propitious for united effort on behalf of the Swede-Finn objectives. In the early part of 1919, the executive committee of the party issued a call for the election of members to a "Folkting of Swedish Finland," scheduled to meet in May of that year. The call was issued to Swedish-speaking citizens throughout the land excepting the Swede-Finn Socialists whose attitude toward "language nationalism" had branded them as poor material for the pending enterprise. Some 110,000 persons participated in the election [27] — the figure represented more than the average number of votes polled by the Swede-Finns in the general elections between 1906 and 1918 — and thus appear to have placed their stamp of approval on the undertaking. The main demands formulated by the congress were: (1) the position of the two language groups should be safeguarded by constitutional provision; (2) administrative and judicial districts should follow the lines separating the nation into Finnish and Swedish localities; (3) all civil servants and other state employees should know Swedish; and (4) the Swede-Finns considered it an "indispensable condition" for the future welfare of the nation that "instruction in schools shall be given, for all time to come, in the mother tongue of the pupils," and that the educational needs of the two groups be satisfied in accordance with common principles. The establishment of a separate Swede-Finn Department of Education, and the maintenance of as many Swede-Finn battalions in the army as the number of Swede-Finn recruits would necessitate, were also urged.[28]

When the constitution was drafted, room was made for provisions designed to eliminate justifiable cause for Swede-

Finn complaint. The degree to which Swede-Finn demands were embodied in the fundamental law of the land is indicated by the following paragraphs of the constitution:

Finnish and Swedish shall be the national languages of the Republic. The right of Finnish citizens to use their mother tongue, whether Finnish or Swedish, before law courts and administrative authorities, and to obtain from them records and documents in their mother tongue, shall be guaranteed by law, so as to safeguard the rights of both language groups in accordance with identical principles.

The State shall provide for the intellectual and economic needs of the two groups in accordance with identical principles.

Every conscript, unless he desires otherwise, shall if possible be enrolled in a unit whose members speak his own mother tongue . . . and shall in such unit receive instruction in that language. Finnish shall be the language of command of the armed forces.[29]

Legislation elaborating these sections of the constitution was enacted in April, 1921, and June, 1922. The more important provisions of these laws may be summarized as follows: (1) "When re-arranging the limits of administrative districts, care should be taken to create, as far as possible, unilingual districts. . . ." (2) A district is considered unilingual if the minority-language group amounts to less than ten percent of the population, and bilingual if the minority exceeds this amount. However, three cities, Helsinki, Turku and Vaasa are bilingual even if the minority group is less than ten percent. (3) In bilingual localities, the language of all public authorities shall be, whenever they deal with a private citizen, that of the individual citizen. (4) In all criminal cases, the language of the defendant shall be used. (5) Subject to the conditions mentioned, the public authorities of unilingual localities shall use the language of the district. (6) The linguistic classification of districts shall take place once every ten years, on the basis of official statistics. Bilingual districts can be changed into unilingual, however, only if the minority has decreased, during the preceding ten-year period, to eight percent or less. Similarly, a unilingual district may be classified as bilingual only if the minority has grown to at least twelve percent. (7) State employees are required to know both Swedish and Finnish. Also, the Swede-Finn churches were organized in a separate bishopric in 1924, and provision was made for a separate Swede-Finn department of education within the national Ministry of Education.[30]

THE OUTLOOK

It is improbable that the language provisions of the constitution, or the subsequent legislation designed to guarantee to both language groups their rights, will permanently dispose of the nationalist controversy. The newspapers of the past decade offer abundant justification for the contention that the legislative enactments mentioned have not eliminated the conflict. There seems to be good reason for maintaining that, in so far as the two nationalist movements free themselves from the type of controversy that has been more or less in evidence ever since the middle decades of the nineteenth century, the improvement will come as the result of tendencies which are independent of the actions of law makers. The most important of such tendencies is at least partly disclosed by statistics showing the changes that the two linguistic groups have undergone since 1880.

The Swede-Finns decreased, relative to the Finnish-language group, by twenty-three per cent. The same trend is disclosed by the changing representation of the two groups at the University of Helsinki, especially during the past decade.

NUMERICAL STRENGTH OF THE LANGUAGE GROUPS,
1880-1920 [31]

POPULATION TOTAL	FINNISH-SPEAKING			SWEDISH-SPEAKING		
	CITY	RURAL	PERCENTAGE OF TOTAL	CITY	RURAL	PERCENTAGE OF TOTAL
1880	2,060,782	100,300	1,656,081	85.2	65,725	229,151	14.3
1890	2,380,140	150,883	1,897,662	86.0	78,491	244,113	13.6
1900	2,712,562	236,388	2,116,602	86.7	97,226	252,466	12.9
1910	2,921,197	314,884	2,256,261	88.0	107,955	231,006	11.6
1920	3,105,103	373,413	2,380,815	88.7	114,049	226,914	11.0

During the ten-year period, the number of Swede-Finn students decreased, relative to Finnish-speaking students, by approximately twenty-two per cent.

ATTENDANCE AT THE UNIVERSITY OF HELSINKI,
1920-1930 [32]

ENROLLMENT TOTAL	FINNISH-SPEAKING STUDENTS		SWEDISH-SPEAKING STUDENTS	
	TOTAL	PERCENTAGE OF TOTAL	TOTAL	PERCENTAGE OF TOTAL
1920	2,712	2,014	74.3	698	25.7
1930	5,893	4,765	80.9	1,128	19.1

That a part of the population of Finland has been bilingual for generations is natural in view of the fact that Finnish and Swedish have existed side by side since time immemorial. During the past thirty years, the degree to which Finnish and Swedish are spoken by the nation has attracted the attention of statisticians, and more or less systematic surveys of bilingualism have been made since 1900. The surveys

include urban centers only, and only four of the larger cities
— Helsinki, Turku, Tampere and Viipuri — have been investigated since the turn of the century. Because of the fact
that their combined population amounts to roughly two-
thirds of the total city population in the country, the available figures may be used to indicate, in a general way, the
degree to which bilingualism has been influenced by the
changes suggested by the tables above.

GROWTH OF BILINGUALISM, 1900-1920 [33]

City		FINNISH-SPEAKING		SWEDISH-SPEAKING	
POPULATION SURVEYED		WHO SPOKE ONLY FINNISH	WHO SPOKE SWEDISH ALSO	WHO SPOKE ONLY SWEDISH	WHO SPOKE FINNISH ALSO
1900	196,293	116,245	23,607	30,076	26,365
1910	269,418	171,312	32,877	30,955	34,274
1920	338,313	199,298	58,732	22,084	58,199

Briefly stated, the evidence suggests that the number of
bilingual persons has grown considerably. In the four cities
mentioned, bilingualism was more than doubled during the
twenty-year period. However, it is worth noting that on
the whole the change was in favor of the Finnish-speaking
part of the population. Not only did the number of persons
who knew only Finnish grow, but the number of Swede-
Finns who knew no Finnish was cut down by more than
one-fourth. It seems therefore that the numerical preponderance of the Finnish-speaking element was great enough
to compel the minority to become more familiar with the
language of the majority. That the Finnization of the
Swede-Finns has proceeded without the aid of artificial or
forced "denationalization" — for example, no Finnish is
taught in the Swedish-language primary schools, and in the

secondary schools of both language groups, instruction in
the other national language is equally obligatory — is significant and invites the surmise that the demands of everyday life are sufficient in themselves to eliminate the language
line which separates, at least superficially, the Swede-Finns
from the Finnish-speaking citizens of the country.

The Finnization process has also been speeded by voluntary acceptance of the Finnish language by an increasing
number of Swede-Finns. The process was begun, as we have
seen, nearly a century ago when the Snellmanian agitation
obtained an increasing number of adherents, and has continued down to our day. On occasion, it has produced impressive results. For example, some 16,000 families changed
their Swedish names into Finnish on May 12, 1906, when
the centenary of the birth of Snellman was celebrated.[34]
While it would be an exaggeration to say that those who
commemorated the birth of the nationalist leader by changing their names were predominantly Swede-Finns — most
of them were, in all probability, persons already Finnish in
speech whose action should be interpreted as a public acceptance of the Finnish cause rather than as an open renuncia-
tion of the Swedish language — it is nevertheless true that
the Swede-Finn ranks have been depleted by the loss of
individuals who for one reason or another have found it
advisable to join the linguistic majority. The development
of the past twenty-five years suggests rather strongly that
this type of defection will grow rather than diminish.

In the realm of organized politics, the Swede-Finns have
been able to hold their ground with relatively greater success. The trend since 1919 is indicated by the following
table.

STRENGTH OF PARTIES AND REPRESENTATION IN PARLIAMENT, 1919-1930 [35]

	SOCIALIST		AGRARIAN		COALITION		PROGRESSIVE		SWEDE-FINN		COMMUNIST		TOTAL	
	VOTES	REP.	VOTES	REP.	VOTES	REP.	VOTES	REP.	VOTES	REP.	VOTES	REP.	VOTES	REP.
1919	365,046	80	189,297	42	151,018	28	123,090	26	116,582	22	—	—	961,101	200
1922	216,861	53	175,401	45	157,116	35	79,676	15	107,414	25	128,181	27	865,421	200
1924	255,068	60	177,982	44	166,880	38	79,937	17	105,733	23	91,839	18	878,941	200
1927	257,572	60	205,313	52	161,450	34	61,613	10	111,005	24	109,939	20	910,191	200
1929	260,254	59	248,762	60	138,008	28	53,301	7	108,886	23	128,164	23	951,270	200
1930	385,820	66	308,003	59	208,090	42	64,914	11	122,579	21	—	—	1,120,828	200

While the Swede-Finn party has been able to retain a sufficient number of mandates to guarantee representation commensurate with the numerical strength of the Swedish-speaking part of the population, it is obvious that the party must remain a minority party. That its representation in parliament will exceed the number of seats held during the past half a dozen years appears to be unlikely.

During the past ten or twelve years, the language situation has been influenced by two domestic problems of nation-wide significance. The first is prohibition, and the second, anti-Communism. Ever since prohibition went into effect in 1919, public opinion has been conspicuously divided on the merits of the experiment. While the debates on prohibition have not as yet assumed proportions sufficient to lead to a reconsideration of the whole question of liquor legislation, the controversy has been a fertile source of propaganda in which wets and drys have been equally active. In national politics, prohibition has become, in fact, the issue that probably divides the country more definitely than any other. Both language groups have contributed to the strength of the wet as well as of the dry cause. Among the opponents and violators of the law, and among its observers and friends, Finn and Swede-Finn stand amicably shoulder to shoulder.[36] The anti-Communist movement of the past few years has likewise led the Finns and the Swede-Finns to join hands in a common effort. When the anti-Communist Lapua movement resulted in 1930 in outlawing the entire Communist party, one of its consequences was the formation of a new Swede-Finn group in Parliament. After the October 1930 elections, eight out of the twenty-one Swede-Finn representatives in the national legislature organized

themselves into a Group for Coöperation with the Bourgeois Parties. The Group's relegation of the language question to a secondary position seems to indicate that more
than one-third of the Swede-Finn representatives in the
present Parliament should be considered as something more
than inflexible defenders of the traditional Swede-Finn
nationalist program.[37]

The Nature of the Problem

One cannot study the development of the nationalist
movements in Finland and escape a desire to interpret,
however broadly, the nature of the problem which has been
surveyed in these pages. To be sure, many of its aspects
have been clarified in the course of the narrative, but there
are others that seem to invite summary statement.

The extreme "language nationalists" in Finland to the
contrary notwithstanding, the problem is not racial. No
respectable evidence exists indicating that the two language
groups represent distinct physical types. With regard to
stature, cranial index, color of eyes, hair or skin, both
groups contain pretty much the same types, and any attempt
to classify the population of Finland according to physical
measurements at once obliterates the language line. Whatever the racial antecedents of Finnish-speaking and Swedish-
speaking Finns may be, age-long intermixture has produced
a result which renders all attempts at racial interpretation
foolish and useless. This applies particularly to the upper
classes, and in general to those who illustrate the onward
march of the Finnish language. For example, when in
1906 some 16,000 families changed their Swedish names to
Finnish, and thereby publicly testified to their acceptance of

the Finnish cause, the racial composition of the two language groups could hardly be said to have changed.[38]

Secondly, the problem is not, and never has been, religious. Both the Finnish and the Swedish groups are overwhelmingly Lutheran. Approximately ninety-eight per cent of the population of the country at least nominally profess the Lutheran creed. Consequently the nationalist movements have at no time involved a struggle between religious beliefs or a contest between antagonistic clerics.

Thirdly, the problem is not one involving competition between provinces, or between two sets of political institutions. The Swede-Finns are not localized in a sharply demarcated geographical region. They live in the western, southern and south-western part of the country and are divided by an intervening Finnish-language population into three general localities. It is interesting to note in this connection that in 1920, about 62 per cent of the Swede-Finns lived in bilingual localities. And with regard to political institutions, both language groups have the same background, and neither has been subject or inferior to the other.[39] Nor can it be said that the nationalist movements involve fidelity to Sweden on the one hand, and aversion or hostility to Sweden on the other. Excepting the Åland Islanders, the Swedish-language group has never made an effort to become united with Sweden.

Fourthly, it cannot be maintained that the nationalist controversy is a contest between two economic systems. Farming, industry, commerce, shipping and the professions all contribute to the strength of the Finnish-speaking and of the Swedish-speaking elements. Nor is it a struggle between social classes. Strictly speaking, it has never been a struggle between classes, for Snellman and his followers represented the upper classes no less than did Freudenthal, Lille and their followers. While it is true that the Finnish movement broadened so as to include the masses somewhat earlier than was the case with the Swede-Finn movement, each has represented for decades a motley crew which includes all the gradations from the lowly man of toil to those who sit in high places.[40]

It seems safe to conclude, then, that the two nationalist movements in present-day Finland are not consequences of racial, religious or economic factors. They do not rest upon political particularism, and they do not draw sustenance from the antagonism of social classes. The reason for their persistence must be sought elsewhere.

Even a superficial consideration of the course of the Snellmanian agitation, or of the early stages of the Swecoman efforts, will bring to mind the fact that both nationalist creeds were formulated by a handful of zealous patriots, and that both nationalist creeds obtained converts among the common folk only decades after their tenets had taken form at the hands of the early leaders. The articulate few gained supporters only after they had succeeded in capturing the eye and ear of the inarticulate many. By means of newspapers, pamphlets, books, and the spoken word, the bulk of the nation was made familiar with the objectives of the nationalists, and by the close of the nineteenth century, the Finnish and the Swede-Finn cause had obtained a substantial following. It was propaganda fed by the existence of various grievances and sustained by the threat of Russification that produced this result. It is propaganda that seems to be most responsible for the fact that occasionally Finn and Swede-Finn still find it difficult to see eye to eye on the language question. That much of this propaganda is garbled history; that flattering pretensions are often permitted to take precedence over reason and logic; that slogans expressing prejudices rather than frank statements of truth are often offered; and that, in general, scientific detachment seldom presides over the labors of the formulators of the nationalist dogma of our day, need surprise no one acquainted with the strong and vital interests aroused and kept alive by nationalist convictions and attachments.

What the nationalist controversy has meant in the everyday life of the ordinary citizen, cannot be easily measured. On this point statistics yield no clue, and newspapers, periodicals and the like can hardly be considered reliable evidence. It may be asserted, however, that the contest between the political parties that have stood ready, and still stand ready, to do battle for "language-nationalist" issues, or the controversial intemperance of the organs of the extremist elements within the two groups, give an altogether exaggerated impression of the manner in which the average individual regards his fellow citizens of the other language group. The division of the nation into two linguistic groups may be in our day occasionally a source of inconvenience, but seldom if ever is it in itself the cause of trouble. Despite the impression created by the arguments and demonstrations of those who keep alive the language conflict, it is the partisan newspapers and periodicals rather than the personal contacts and experiences of the average man, that serve to remind him of the existence of the conflict. If he were to justify his particular nationalist faith in terms of the workaday world as he knows it, he could hardly vindicate his allegiance or explain his prejudices. Instead, he would probably turn to the pronouncements of the leaders for the necessary justification. In a word, the agitation of the one hundred percenters is, it appears, much more important in perpetuating the nationalist movements than are those realities of the business of living that touch Finns and Swede-Finns alike.

CHAPTER I

NOTES

1. It will be well to dispose of two essential definitions at this point. The words "nationality" and "nationalism" occur necessarily throughout this study. As regards their meaning the author has accepted the following definitions. " 'Nationality' . . . is most commonly and can be most properly used to designate a group of people who speak either the same language or closely related dialects, who cherish common historical traditions, and who constitute or think they constitute a distinct cultural society." Hayes, Carlton J. H., *Essays on Nationalism*, p. 5. In regard to "nationalism," Professor Hayes states that it "stands in the first place for an actual historical process, that of establishing nationalities as political units. . . . Secondly, the term indicates the theory, principle or ideal implicit in the actual historical process. In this sense it signifies both an intensification of the consciousness of nationality and a political philosophy of the national state. Thirdly, it may mean . . . the activities of a particular political party. . . . A fourth and final use . . . is to denote a condition of mind among members of a nationality . . . in which loyalty to the ideal or to the fact of one's national state is superior to all other loyalties and of which pride in one's nationality and belief in its intrinsic excellence and in its 'mission' are integral parts." *Ibid.*, pp. 5-6, and cf. pp. 25-26. Professor Hayes also says that "Nationalism is a modern emotional fusion of two very old phenomena — nationality and patriotism" (p. 5). This succint statement of the essence of modern nationalism will be particularly useful for an understanding of the story which forms the subject matter of the present study.

2. Nordström, J. J., *Bidrag till den Svenska Samhällsförfattningens Historia*, vol. I, Introduction and Chaps. I-VI. The ninety years that have elapsed since the appearance of this work have not deprived it of the authority which it gained upon its publication.

3. Ruuth, J. W., *Åbo Stads Historia*, III, 9-10.

4. The reader will find a good account of Sweden's development from the early part of the sixteenth century down to the middle of the seven-

teenth in Hallendorff, C. and Schück, A., *History of Sweden*, Chaps. V-VIII.

5. Nordström, J. J., *op. cit.*, pp. ix-xviii.

6. Printed in Schybergson, M. G., *Finlands Historia*, I, 92-93.

7. See Hallendorff, C., and Schück, A., *op. cit.*, Chap. IV.

8. Schybergson, M. G., "Finlands statsrättsliga ställning under medeltiden," *Finsk Tidskrift* (1876), I, 67-80.

9. Palmén, E. G., *Suomen Valtiopäiväin Historia*, part I, and cf. Bondsdorff, Carl von, "De finska städernas representation intill frihetstiden," *Historiallinen Arkisto*, XIII (1894), 1-79. The author points out that in actual fact this equality of representation was imperfect, and estimates that the Finnish towns, for example, contributed but one out of every seven burghers at the Riksdags before 1720. Strictly speaking, considerable diversity in the manner of election existed in the various localities on both sides of the Gulf of Bothnia.

10. Speaking in general terms, the traders of Gottland probably profited most by the economic opportunities offered by Finland down to the middle of the thirteenth century. They were replaced by the Hansa merchants who enjoyed a well nigh complete commercial monopoly within the Swedish Kingdom well into the sixteenth century. See Ruuth, J. W., *op. cit.*, III, 13-14, 15-19, 21-42, 46-49, 60-97.

11. Hallendorff and Schück, *op. cit.*, pp. 318-22. From the point of view of the king aspiring to greater power these abbreviated Riksdags were quite acceptable. They could be assembled with greater ease, and popular discontent with governmental policy was given but a limited chance for censure in them. As a rule, they were more subservient to his will than the larger assembly. However, for the same reasons the so-called "Committee Riksdags" were disliked by the people as a whole. The minority of Charles XI (1660-1697) provided the opportunity for prohibiting by law the holding of any but full parliaments. This prohibition was observed only during the minority, and in the closing decades of the century the rump parliaments again became the rule. During the disastrous reign of Charles XII (1697-1718) the Riksdag was reduced to complete impotence, and during the middle decades of the eighteenth century the national parliament was under the control of scheming politicians. The last forty years of Finland's union with Sweden were characterized by a trend toward absolutism and a corresponding diminution of the powers of the Riksdag. *See* Schybergson, M. G., *op. cit.*, II, Chaps. I-IV, VI-VIII; Vessberg, G. V., *Om svenska Riksdagen, des Sammansättning och Verkamhetsformer, 1772-1809.*

12. Quoted in Suolahti, G., *Vuosisatain Takaa*, pp. 176-77.

13. *Ibid.*, p. 177.

14. *Ibid.*, pp. 181-82.

15. The Resolution is found in Modée, K. G. (Ed.), *Utdrag Utur Publique Handlingar, 1730-1739*, II 1396-1417. The statement pertaining to office holding in Finland is contained in par. 42.

16. It is printed in *Historiallinen Arkisto*, VI (1878), 164-72.

17. Danielson-Kalmari, J. R., *Kustavilainen Aika*, I, 17-23.

18. The document is dated Oct. 22, 1756, and is found in the *Academica Abo* MSS in the Swedish State Archives in Stockholm. *Inkomna Handlingar. Skrifvelser från prokanslärn m. fl. 1725-1787.* In 1759 a Swedish traveller in Finland observed the petty rivalry between the Finns and natives of Sweden proper in the matter of university appointments. See Hjelt, A., "Anmärkningar på en Resa infrån Stockholm till Finland år 1759. Af C. Gjörvell." *Historiallinen Arkisto*, IX (1886), 62-77.

19. Brahe to Gezelius, Aug. 17, 1666. Printed in *ibid.*, V (1876), 103-5. The word "nation" refers obviously to the inhabitants of Finland as a whole. The word was commonly used in this sense until well past the middle of the nineteenth century.

20. Suolahti, G., *Elämää Suomessa 1700-luvulla*, pp. 111-21.

21. Tessin's letter bears the date Feb. 19, 1757. It is published in *Historiallinen Arkisto*, X (1889), 449-54. The king also wrote the university authorities in a similar vein. Hjelt, A. " 'Fennomanin' och svenska regeringen i förra seklet," *ibid.* pp. 445-48.

22. Suolahti, G., *Vuosisatain Takaa*, pp. 188-89. That wire-pulling and jealousy often entered into the question of appointments is clearly shown by Palander, G., in "Daniel Jusleniuksen Johannes Gezelius nuorimmalle kirjoittamia kirjeitä," *Historiallinen Arkisto*, XVIII (1903), 236-44. In "Anteckningar ur inrikes rådsprotokollen om finske tjenstemäns tillsättande på 1740-talet," *ibid.* VI (1878), 185-206, E. G. Palmén presents documents dealing with eighteen appointments to vacancies in Finland during the seventeen-forties. One is conscious of a definite effort made to observe the letter and the spirit of the Royal Resolution of 1739. However, favoritism and other intangible factors could not be wholly eliminated. Carl von Bonsdorff has shown that as early as 1653, the peasants in Finland were protesting against the appointment of officials who did not know Finnish. "Blad ur Nykarlebys historia," *ibid.*, X (1889), 68.

It is probable that the reason for the disappearance of the difficulties, in the closing decades of the century, is that the reconstruction policies of the government had begun to produce results which eliminated the causes of friction. *Ibid.*, VI, 158-59.

23. I have used E. Ahlman's translation *Vanha ja Uusi Turku*, published in 1929 in connection with the Septcentenary Celebration of the Turku Cathedral. Chaps. II-III contain the best illustrations of Juslenius' credulity.

24. Pietilä, A. J., *Daniel Juslenius. Hänen Elämänsä ja Vaikutuksensa*, I, 59-66. Strictly speaking, the absurdities of Juslenius were not new. Many of them had been put forth, in less pretentious form, during the closing decades of the seventeenth century. The excellencies of the students' native province or town was at that time a subject often chosen by the students in their first effort at scholarly production. Many of these paeons of praise of the student's place of birth were printed and have been preserved. The spirit in which this work was carried on is suggested by the author of one of these essays, published in 1694. "If nature itself urges us to love our parents who gave us life," he wrote, "how much greater must be our gratitude to our fatherland which has been called, with good reason, the common parent of us all. We must thank her and praise her everywhere and if necessary, give our lives for her." These essays may probably be considered as something more than exercises in rhetoric. They appear to have reflected a patriotic attachment to Finland among the students at her university and form, properly speaking, the background of Juslenius' attempts to blend fact and fancy into an inspiring account of Finnish history. *Ibid.*, pp. 32-38.

25. Hultin, A., *Det Ekonomiska Tidevarvet i Finlands Litteraturhistoria*, pp. 1-13, 151-87, 285-325; *Finlands Litteratur under Frihetstiden*, I, 218-51.

26. *Ibid.*, pp. 131-75; Schybergson, M. G., *Historiens Studium vid Åbo Universitet*, pp. 33-107.

27. Pietilä, A. J., *op. cit.*, II, 177-90.

28. Söderhjelm, W., *Åboromantiken och dess samband med utländska idesströmningar*, Chap. II; Schybergson, M. G., *op. cit.*, pt. III; Niemi, A. R., *Kalevalan Kokoonpano*, pp. 1-25.

29. Palander, G., *Henrik Gabriel Porthan historianopettajana; Henrik Gabriel Porthan; Henrik Gabriel Porthan Yliopiston Opettajana*, Vol. III of Danielson-Kalmari, J. R., (Ed.), *Suomen Uudemmasta Historiasta*, pp. 59-179; Söderhjelm, W., *op. cit.*, Chap. II; Suolahti, G., "Suomen historian synty," *Historiallinen Arkisto*, XXXIII (1925), 4-6; "Henrik Gabriel Porthan," in Palmén, E. G., (Ed.), *Oma Maa* (2d ed.), VI, 156-64; Danielson-Kalmari, J. R., *Kustavilainen Aika*, III, 174.

30. Hjelt, A. J., "Några bidrag till Aurora-förbundets historia," *Historiallinen Arkisto*, IX (1886), 113-82; Lagus, W., *Strödda Blad*, III, 44-59.

31. Söderhjelm, W., *op. cit.*, p. 62.

32. "Puhe Porthanin haudalla," *Tähti*, Sept. 1, 1864.

33. Estlander, B., *Elva Årtionden ur Finlands Historia*, I, 11.

34. Among the men involved in the conspiracy were several associates of one G. M. Sprengtporten. Sprengtporten had been interested in the question of Finland's independence for several years. Together with his brother, he had rendered valuable service to Gustavus III in engineering the coup d'état of 1772. Some years later he became dissatisfied with what he considered inadequate recognition of his importance, resigned his commission (1778) and went abroad, travelling in Russia, Prussia, France and Holland. Returning to Sweden in 1781, he settled in Finland. His home became the meeting place for dissatisfied, scheming military men and it was there that the later conspiracy was planned. It was held that Finland would sooner or later fall into the hands of Russia, and that the interests of Finland would be best served if independence under Russia's protection could be obtained before military conquest had united the country to Russia. This idea was based, in a sense, upon an attempt which had been made during the Russo-Swedish war of 1741-1743 to detach Finland from Sweden. During the war, Empress Elizabeth issued a manifesto, dated March 18, 1742, which urged that the inhabitants of Finland should declare themselves independent. Their independence was to be guaranteed by Russia. The manifesto was ineffective, and the people remained loyal to Sweden. Sprengtporten and his associates based their speculations of an independent Finland upon the idea that Finland was too distant from Sweden to be properly protected, and so close to Russia as to endanger her peace, and that Finland's hope lay in the advantages which would accrue from an arrangement of the kind suggested in the manifesto of 1742.

Sprengtporten left Finland in 1786 and entered the service of Russia with the rank of Major-General. He continued to work for his pet scheme and when the war between Sweden and Russia broke out two years later, he submitted to the Empress "A Proposal for the Establishment of the Balance of Power in the North by the creation of an Independent Finland" in which he advised the formation of "The Republic of the United Provinces of Finland." Sweden's consent to the contemplated transaction was to be obtained by the acquisition of Norway, which Russia would make possible.

Nothing came of the proposal. Nor was Sprengtporten successful in his attempts to galvanize the discontent within the Swedish army in Finland into a separatist movement. — The complicated story of the conspiracy is told in detail in Danielson-Kalmari, J. R., *op. cit.*, Vol. I, Chaps. I-II; Vol. II, Chaps. II-V.

35. This is clearly shown by the hundreds of complaints and petitions in the manuscript collection of the Swedish State Archives in Stockholm. The folder labelled *Allmogens Besvär. Finland 1* contains a large number of petitions from the middle of the sixteenth century to the close of the eighteenth. The content of most of them deals with economic grievances of one kind or other. Cf. *Allmogens Besvär. Österbotten* (Nos. 1, 2, 3); *Österbotten 2, Södra Österbotten* — 1731; *Egentliga Finland 1*; Lindeqvist K. O., "Suomen talonpoikien valituksia 1600-luvun keskivaiheilla," *Historiallinen Arkisto*, Vol. XXI, 2 (1910), 1-30; Mickwitz, A., *De Finska Deputationerna till Riksdagen 1742-43 och Finska Ekonomikommissionen*, pp. 83-84; Schybergson, M. G., *Bidrag till Finlands inre historia 1721-1731*, pp. 66-68.

36. Pietilä, A. J., *op. cit.*, chaps. IX-XIV.

37. Palander, G., *op. cit.*, p. 128.

38. *Ibid.*, pp. 68-128.

39. *Ibid.*, p. 127.

40. *Historiallinen Arkisto*, X (1889), 173-74; Vol. XXII, 1, (1911), 4.

41. For example, see Pietilä, A. J., *op. cit.*, I, 268-73; II, 304; Koskinen, Y., *Finnische Geschichte von den frühesten Zeiten bis auf die Gegenwart*, pp. 471-72; Ignatius, H., Theslöf, G. *et al.* (Ed.), *Suomen vapaussota vuonna 1918*, I, 15-19; *Historiallinen Arkisto*, X (1889), 448; A. I. W., "Muistelmia suomalaisuuden suhteista ja seikoista," *Kirjallinen Kuukauslehti*, 1871, No. 9, pp. 218-20.

CHAPTER II

1. *Suomen Tilastollinen Vuosikirja*, 1922, pp. 6, 7, 9.

2. Brander, V., "Agriculture," in Donner, A., *et al.* (Ed.), *Finland, the Country, Its People and Institutions*, pp. 307-22; Snellman, K., "Communications," *ibid.*, pp. 364-75.

3. Kovero, M., *Suomen Vientiteollisuus*, pp. 27-45.

4. Fisher, J. R., *Finland and the Tsars*, Chaps. III-VI, contain a good treatment on the constitutional and administrative phrases of the settlement of 1809. J. R. Danielson's *Finland's Union with the Russian*

Empire, gives a more detailed account and contains the more important documents pertaining to the Porvoo Diet, Alexander I's proclamations, etc.

5. By an enactment promulgated in 1827 Finnish citizens belonging to the Orthodox faith were placed on a footing of equality with those of Lutheran affiliations. The measure benefited the relatively small number of Orthodox Finns in those sections of south-eastern Finland which had been united to the Grand Duchy in 1811. Palmén, E. G., *Suomen Valtiopäiväin Historia*, p. 52.

6. Quoted in Bonsdorff, Carl von, *Opinioner och Stämningar i Finland 1804-1814*, p. 59.

7. *Ibid.*, pp. 60-77.

8. *Ibid.*, pp. 79-80; Cf. Danielson-Kalmari, J. R. *Aleksanteri I:n Aika,* III, 108-18.

9. *Ibid.*, III, 78-86, 153-55, 161-69. However, it should not be over-looked that indecision and opportunism were by no means wanting in the attitudes of the leading men. G. M. Armfelt, for instance, at one time planned for an independent Finland. In 1810 he was working for Finnish independence under English protection. Finland was to become England's depot for her trade with Russia, while Russia's consent to the project was to be obtained by the grant of satisfactory commercial privileges. The arrangement would free Russia from the necessity of keeping troops in Finland and would thereby enable Alexander to concentrate upon the impending conflict with Napoleon. Needless to say, nothing came of this interesting scheme. *Ibid.*, II, 4-26.

10. C. S. F., "Brev till en vän," *Mnemosyne*, Mar., 1823, pp. 63-64.

11. An interesting illustration of a viewpoint which seems to have been fairly common during these years is given by the following words, written during Napoleon's Russian campaign by R. H. Rehbinder, the then Finnish Minister-Secretary of State: "May the righteous God bless our [sic] arms and may we then know enough to appreciate our good fortune in being able to vegetate in peace under Alexander's protection." Quoted in Bonsdorff, Carl von, *op. cit.*, p. 176. A good discussion of the manner in which Russian rule was accepted, without too much protest, is given in Bonsdorff, L. G. von, *Den ryska pacificeringen i Finland 1808-09*, Chap. XI.

12. Stichaeus, J. F. (Ed.), *Samling af Bref, Förklaringar och Föreskrifter*, I (1809-1820), 64-65.

13. Leinberg, K. G., *Handlingar Rörande Finska Skolväsendets Historia*, IV, 357, 369-70.

14. *Mnemosyne*, Jan., 1822, pp 9-17; Danielson-Kalmari, J. R. *op. cit.*, II, 507-09.

15. Törnqvist, P. (Ed), *Samling af Bref, Förklaringar och Före-skrifter*, II (1821-1828), 107-08; III (1829-1834), 318.

16. *Mnemosyne*, Mar., 1822, Sup., p. 6.

17. Danielson-Kalmari, J. R., *op. cit.*, II, 86, 511.

18. Quoted in *ibid.*, II, 513.

19. *Ibid.*, I, 272-76.

20. Quoted in Kallio, O. A., *Viipurin Läänin järjestämisestä muun Suomen yhteyteen*, p. 142.

21. Ehrström, E. G., "Öfversigt af Ryska Språkets studium i Finland," *Mnemosyne*, Mar., 1822, Supplement, p. 4. An unknown reader of a later and more nationalistic period has inserted the word "swinish" in the margin of p. 11 of this article, thereby obviously registering a protest against the submissive pro-Russianism of the author.

22. Bonsdorff, Carl von, *op. cit.*, pp. 9-42.

23. Quoted in *ibid.*, p. 141.

24. *Ibid.*, pp. 143-44.

25. Hallendorff and Schück state that at the time when Napoleon's "invasion appeared most menacing, Alexander was probably prepared to pay for the coöperation of Sweden by the restoration of Finland. . . . But Charles John regarded Finland as an obstacle to a real and lasting peace with Russia, and contemplated instead the conquest of Norway." *Op. cit.*, p. 365. By 1814, Bernadotte could point to the inclusion of Norway within his domain as adequate compensation for the loss of Finland.

26. See Donner, A., *et al.* (Ed.), *op. cit.*, pp. 89-93, 67-71.

27. Quoted in Suolahti, G., *Vuosisatain Takaa*, p. 145.

28. Leinberg, K. G., in his *Handlingar*, II, 239, 331-32, 422-25, mentions several cases in which school authorities specifically stressed the advisability of requiring a knowledge of Swedish.

29. Quoted in *ibid.*, I, 124.

30. *Ibid.*, II, 331-32.

31. Rein, Th., *Johan Vilhelm Snellman*, I, 27-28, note.

32. Leinberg, K. G., *op. cit.*, I, 146-47.

33. Suolahti, G., *op. cit.*, pp. 147-48.

34. *Ibid.*, p. 149.

35. *Åbo Tidningar*, March 25, 1793, No. 13, note 3.

36. Suolahti, G., *op. cit.*, pp. 145-49. Leinberg, K. G., *op. cit.*, II, 135, 322, 329, 333, 339; IV, 309-10, 312, 313 contain reports on the students' social status in eight schools during the period 1771-1802. Roughly one-

half of the students in these schools came from artisan or farmer homes.

37. The *Alcenius MSS* in the Library of the University of Helsinki contain a number of reports from the seventeen-seventies relative to the landed gentry. The reports were written by the clergy in seventeen parishes and show incidentally that a considerable number of the landed gentry still knew and used Finnish at that time. See III, 353, 354-55, 356-59, 360-62; Schybergson, M. G., *Bidrag till Finlands inre historia 1721-1723*, pp. 150-51; Danielson-Kalmari, J. R., *Kustavilainen Aika*, III, 37-38; Suolahti, G., *op. cit.*, pp. 154-60, 196-97; *Elämää Suomessa 1700-luvulla*, II, 503-18, 489-93; cf. Leinberg, K. G., *op. cit.*, III, 220-60; Wirilander, E. O. J., "Demologisia havaintoja Suomen aatelistosta suuren Pohjan sodan aikana," *Historiallinen Aikakauskirja*, 1930, No. 4, pp. 300-12.

38. G. Suolahti's exhaustive study of the clergy in Finland during the seventeenth and eighteenth centuries, *Suomen Papisto 1600- ja 1700-luvuilla*, Chap. I, shows that the clergy was overwhelmingly of Finnish extraction. See also *ibid.*, Chap. II, and *Elämää Suomessa 1700-luvulla*, Vol. II, Chap. VII; *Vuosisatain Takaa*, pp. 169-70, 189-94; Koskinen, Y., *Klubbekriget* (Trans. by E. O. Edlund), pp. 20-24, 60-63; *Historiallisia Tutkimuksia*, (Ed. by the Historical Association of Finland), 1864, pp. 111-23; Gummerus, J., *Mikael Agricola*, Chap. III.

39. The Alcenius manuscript collection contains over seventy items concerning the relations of the two language groups. The items cover roughly the period 1699-1804 and consist of reports from various ministers and ecclesiastical authorities. See III, 114, 162, 355-56, 360-62; IV, 7, 57-48, 87-88, 98, 170-72, 177-79, 216-17, 223, 234-35, 238-39, 258-61, 275-78, 281-82, 313-15; V, 67-68, 104-08, 203-04; VII, 2a-3, 6-6a, 7, 8a-9, 10-11a, 12-13, 15-15a, 16a, 21-21a, 35a-36, 39-53a, 58a-59, 63-64a, 66a, 75a-76, 80, 81-81a, 87, 88-88a, 95a, 115-15a, 150-51, 160a, 161a. Cf. Kovero, M., "Olavi Wibelius' en taistelu virkamiesturmelusta vastaan Kuopion läänissä," *Aika* (1910), 761-76.

It is worth noting that in south-eastern Finland, which had been united to Russia partly during the reign of Peter the Great and partly in 1743, German and not Swedish was the language spoken by the upper classes. In this part of the country, German held its own well into the nineteenth century. An interesting view of the situation is presented in L. Purgold's *Über die Wichtigkeit der Deutschen Sprache für gründliche Bildung, insbesondere in Finnland* (St. Petersburg, 1813). The title-page informs us that the author was "Oberlehrer am Gymnasium zu Wiburg." Purgold predicted that German would become, in no distant future, the sole language of education in Finland. This view was more or less natural for one familiar with the conditions which prevailed in the Viipuri province. In 1813, all of the twenty schools in the province were German, as far as the language of instruction is concerned. See *Wiborgs Tidning,* Feb. 27, 1864.

40. Estlander, C. G., *Arwidsson som vitter författare,* pp. 5-6, 18, 41-46.

41. Arwidsson, A. I., *Min Lefnads-Händelser.* This MS account of his life was written by Arwidsson between Oct. 10, 1821 and Feb. 1, 1823. It is found in the Royal Library in Stockholm and discusses in considerable detail the years 1817-1823. The spirit in which Arwidsson penned his account is perhaps suggested by the following statement on the second page of the manuscript: "My science is history. Out of respect for this loved field of study, I shall try my best to lie and misrepresent as little as human frailty permits."

42. *Ibid.,* p. 8.

43. Estlander, C. G., "Arwidsson som publicist i Åbo," Svenska Litteratursällskapet i Finland, *Förhandlingar och Uppsattser,* VIII (1894), 109-110; cf. Arwidsson *MS.* p. 24.

44. They were published under the heading "Bref ifrån Finland af en resande Svensk." in three installments in *Nya Extra Posten,* Sept. 18, 21, 28, 1820.

45. Arwidsson *MS.* The pagination of the manuscript is complete only for the first twenty-odd pages.

46. *Nya Extra Posten,* Sept. 21, 1820.

47. *Ibid.,* Sept. 28, 1820. That Arwidsson's assertions were not without foundation, and that an unblushing concern with personal advancement was by no means uncommon, and that furthermore incompetence and lack of leadership were not rare, is shown by Ahrenberg, Jarl, "Landt-dagsplaner under Alexander I's regering," in Svenska Litteratursällskapet i Finland, *Historiska och kulturhistoriska studier,* 4, 151-56.

48. "En blick på vårt Fosterland," *Åbo Morgonblad,* Jan. 13, 1821.

49. *Loc. cit.,* and "Om Nationalitet och National Anda," *ibid.* Feb. 17, 1821, p. 54. This article ran through the issues from Feb. 17 to Mar. 24, 1821, and appeared under the following quotation from Madame de Staël: "La gloire de chaque pays consiste toujours dans le caractère et l'esprit national."

50. "Betraktelser," *Mnemosyne,* Feb. 1822, pp. 39-41.

51. *Åbo Morgonblad,* Jan. 13, 1821, pp. 13-16.

52. *Loc. cit.*; Kekäläinen, Olli (A. I. Arwidsson), *Finlands Nuvarande*

Stats-Författning, pp. 50-51; cf. Arwidsson, A. I. (Ed.), *Svenska Forn-sånger,* I, iii-iv.

53. "Betraktelser," *Mnemosyne,* Feb. 1822, pp. 32-52. It was in this article that Arwidsson presented a summary of his ideas concerning nationality and related questions. His delineation of the position and functions of nationalities in the progress of humanity is of interest. Only through nationalities does humanity advance toward its goal of increasing perfectibility and only by developing its individuality to the highest possible degree can a nationality contribute toward the attainment of this goal — this is the core of Arwidsson's reasoning. It bears a striking resemblance to the Mazzinian theory of nationality, as the student familiar with the writings of the Italian patriot will observe.

Fundamentally, Arwidsson was a Romanticist and appears to have received most of his Romanticist impulses from German writers. His dissertation — *Ingenii romantici, aevo medio orti, expositio historica,* published in 1817 — was largely based on Schlegel's *Geschichte der Lit-teratur* and contains numerous references to Schelling, Heeren and espe-cially to Herder's *Ideen zur Geschichte der Menschkeit* and *Samtliche Werke. Zum Schönen Litteratur und Kunst.* See Söderhjelm,, W., *Åboromantiken och dess samband med utländska idéströmningar,* Chaps. V, VI; Danielson-Kalmari, J. R., *Tien Varrelta Kansalliseen Itsenäisyy-teen,* Chap. III; Estlander, C. G., "Arwidsson som publicist i Åbo," Svenska Litteratursällskapet i Finland, *Förhandlingar och Uppsattser* (1894), pp. 90-180.

54. Danielson-Kalmari, J. R., *op. cit.,* Chaps. IV, V, and see note 1, Chap. III.

55. Tengström, J. J., "Om Några Hinder för Finlands Litteratur och Cultur," *Aura* (1817-1818), I, 67-90; II, 93-129; *Mnemosyne,* Jan. 2, 1819, p. 3; Älskare af human polemik (pseud.), "Ett ord om Critic af de i Finland Utkommande Skrifter, och om Litterär Polemik," *ibid.,* Jan. 1821, pp. 16-26; "Finska Språket, Betraktat såsom Nationalspråk," *Åbo Morgonblad,* Mar. 24, Apr. 7, June 2, Sept. 1, 15, 1821; Söderhjelm, W., *op. cit.,* pp. 105-08, 152-71.

CHAPTER III

1. Estlander, B., *Elva Årtionden,* I, 61. Arwidsson's writings included discussions of several questions which probably caused more uneasiness among the conservative elements of the time than did his pronouncements relative to nationality, national language and the like. He argued in favor

of a free press, protested against the contemporary guild system and mercantilist policies — much of his argument was drawn from Adam Smith's *Wealth of Nations* — and urged the advisability of a more democratic educational system. See "Tryckfrihet och Offentlighet," *Åbo Morgonblad*, June 16, 23, 1821; "Om Finland's Landthandel," *ibid.*, Aug. 4, 1821; "Skråinrättningar och Näringsfrihet," *ibid.*, Aug. 11, 25, 1821. It is probable that this line of attack was no less responsible for the suppression of the paper and the later difficulties Arwidsson experienced than the articles mentioned in the preceding Chapter.

2. Schauman, A., *Från Sex Årtionden i Finland*, I, 22.

3. *Ibid.*, I, 20-21, and Cf. 12-19; A. M., "Neljännes vuosisataa takaperin," *Kirjallinen Kuukauslehti*, 1869, No. 1; Furuhjelm, E., *Ur Finlands Kulturhistoria*, I, 33-34. Schybergson, M. G., *Finlands Historia*, II, 393.

4. Quoted in Estlander, B., *loc. cit.*

5. The decree is dated Sept. 21, 1810 and is printed in Stichaeus, J. E., (Ed.), *op. cit.*, p. 14.

6. *Ibid.*, p. 86.

7. Schybergson, M. G., *op. cit.*, II, 416.

8. Törnqvist, P. (Ed.), *op. cit.*, p. 319. Even books on medicine were subjected to rigorous censorship, in 1837. *Ibid.* (1835-1842), pp. 87-88. Of course, the press was far from free before 1809. It was regulated by a law dating from 1774 and 1792. Its original provisions pertained primarily to religious matters and imposed no great hardships on the editors or publishers. However, a special supplementary decree in 1802 gave the Royal Chancellor an almost unlimited control over the press. The arbitrary system thus introduced was in force when Finland was annexed by Russia — a point worthy of notice lest we give undue prominence to the developments during the twenties and early thirties. See Estlander, C. G., "Arwidsson som publicist i Åbo," *Förhandlingar och Uppsattser* (1894), VIII, 115-18; cf. Lagus, W., *Strödda Blad*, III, 39-40, note.

9. Schauman, A., *op. cit.*, I, 19-20.

10. *Ibid.*, p. 9.

11. *Ibid.*, p. 22. It is a fact worth noting that Arwidsson published in 1827 a summary of the history of Finland during the years 1809-1826 without once mentioning the nationalist agitation of 1819-1822. Rühs, F., *Finland och Dess Invånare*, trans. and ed. by A. I. Arwidsson, I, 162-80.

12. Rein, Th., *Muistelmia Elämän Varrelta*, pp. 49-50.

13. "Betraktelser," *Mnemosyne*, Feb. 22, 1822, p. 33.

14. *Ibid.*, Supplement No. 6, June, 1819, pp. 21-22.

15. Schybergson, M. G., *Historiens Studium vid Åbo Universitet,*

pp. 147 *et seq.; Historiallinen Arkisto* (1900), XVI, 1-11, 20-21; Schauman, A., *op. cit.*, I, 58 *et seq.*

16. "Finsk Literatur," *Tidningar ifrån Helsingfors*, Sept. 3, 1830.

17. *Historiallinen Arkisto. Juhlajulkaisu, 1875-1925*, p. 7.

18. Pärssinen, J., *Kasvatusopilliset Virtaukset ja Koululaitoksen Kehitys Suomessa vuosina 1801-1843*, pp. 155, note; 210, 358.

19. Schauman, A., *op. cit.*, I, 7-9.

20. Source cited in note 17, pp. 6-7.

21. However, some emphasis appears to have been placed on the love of fatherland and patriotic virtues. This seems to be suggested by the J. P. Palmén MS (*Allmän Inledning till Historiens Studium öfverhufvud*), in the Library of the University of Helsinki. It consists of notes taken at lectures on general history, delivered in 1828. The 77-page MS contains the following statement (on p. 39) : "Among the noble sentiments which history calls forth and sustains . . . there are two which . . . form the basis of most other virtues; the love of the *fatherland* and the love of *liberty*. . . . He who is not acquainted with history can love his fatherland only by instinct, for he knows not his country; and the courage to attain to freedom can often be found only in history which shows us that liberty is possible, and *how* it is possible."

22. *Mnemosyne*, Mar., 1823.

23. *Åbo Morgonblad*, Sept. 1, 1821.

24. *Cf. supra*, Chap. II, pp. 000.

25. Leinberg, K. G., *Handlingar*, IV, 416. The survey covers pp. 413-63.

26. Alsenius *MS.*, III, 106a-7.

27. *Ibid.*, V, 86-87, 431. The authorities in Helsinki strongly protested against this practice.

28. The communication is printed in Leinberg, *op. cit.*, IV, 407-10.

29. Schauman, A., *op. cit.*, I, 22, 71-74.

30. Rein, Th., *Johan Vilhelm Snellman*, I, 403-04; *Muistelmia elämän varrelta*, pp. 14-15, 72.

31. Gylden, N. A., *Till åhörande af det offentliga föredrag, hvarmed Professoren i Finska Språket och litteraturen D:r Elias Lönnrot kommer att tillträda sitt ämbete.*

32. Törnquist, P. (Ed.), *op. cit.*, II, 107; Setälä, E. N., *The Language Fight in Finland*, p. 14.

33. *Helsingfors Tidningar*, June 27, 1832.

34. *Ibid.*, Aug. 7, 1830, May 7, 1831, Sept. 9, 13, 16, 20, 1837.

35. See Hayes, Carlton J. H., *op. cit.*, pp. 52-55, and Essay III; and *ibid., Historical Evolution of Modern Nationalism*, Chaps. IV and V.

36. "Contributions of Herder to the Doctrine of Nationalism," *American Historical Review*, July, 1927, XXXII, 719-36, by Professor Carlton J. H. Hayes, contains an exposition of those aspects of Herder's work which concern us here.

37. Quoted in Söderhjelm, W., *op. cit.*, pp. 139-40.

38. Among them were Arwidsson, A. Poppius, G. F. Aminoff, C. A. Gottlund and J. J. Pippingsköld.

39. Quoted in Niemi, A. R., *Kalevalan Kokoonpano*, p. 42.

40. Quoted in Söderhjelm, W., *op. cit.*, p. 144; and cf. p. 147.

41. *Finnische Runen.* Finnisch und Deutsch von Dr. H. R. von Schröter.

42. Söderhjelm, W., *op. cit.*, p. 167. He spent the summer vacation in 1819 collecting folklore in Savo and Karjala. *Mnemosyne*, Nov. 1819, Supplement No. 11, p. 42.

43. Niemi, A. R., *op. cit.*, pp. 45-58.

44. It was entitled *De Väinämöine priscorum fennorum numine.*

45. Niemi, A. R., *op. cit.*, pp. 63-70.

46. This suggestion had been made as early as 1810, on the basis of the folk poems that were known at that time. In 1817, C. A. Gottlund had declared with regard to the importance of folklore collection and studies: "If the young Finnish writers . . . cared more for the products of their fatherland, and tried to develop the literature of their country, what a field would be opened to their efforts! . . . [I] go so far as to maintain that if we were desirous of collecting our old folk-songs and made of them an organized whole . . . we might produce a new Homer, Ossian or Niebelungen Lied; and adorned by its originality and the honor of its unique development . . . the Finnish nation would arouse the admiration of the present and of the future." Quoted in *ibid.*, p. 35.

47. *Ibid.*, Chaps. II-V contain an excellent account of Lönnrot's work.

48. Lönnrot produced a second edition containing fifty runes of nearly 23,000 stanzas, in 1849. This edition has been translated in full or in part into fourteen languages — French, German, English, Swedish, Norwegian, Danish, Italian, Dutch, Hungarian, Russian, Estonian, Polish, Serbian and Czech. Ten of these are complete translations. The most recent English translation is that by W. F. Kirby (Everyman's Library, 1907) in two volumes. It is perhaps worth noting that the work of rune collecting has continued down to our day. By 1922 roughly 500,000 items of folk songs, poems, riddles, etc., had been collected in Finland. *Oma Maa*, III, 387.

49. See Niemi, A. R., *op. cit.*, pp. 99, 139-43, 145-46, 229-41, 250. Niemi presents a line-by-line analysis of the composition of the *Kalevala* on pp. 101-33; 146-223; 251-410.

Perhaps the clearest statement concerning Lönnrot's relation to the *Kalevala* is contained in the following words which he wrote in 1849: "The order in which the rune-singers sing their poems cannot be left out of account, although I paid no great attention to it because they differ greatly from one another in this respect. . . . It was impossible for me to consider the arrangement of one superior to that of another. . . . Finally, when no rune-singer could any longer compare with me in his knowledge of songs, I assumed that I had the same right which, in my opinion, most of the other singers freely reserved to themselves, namely the right to arrange the songs according as they seemed to fit best; or, in the words of the folk song,

> I myself began to conjure
> I myself commenced to sing;

that is, I considered myself to be as good a rune-singer as they were." Quoted in *ibid.*, p. 248.

50. *Helsingfors Tidningar*, Feb. 25, 1843, Feb. 28, 1846. Schauman, A., *op. cit.*, I, 23-24; Setälä, E. N., "Kalevala suomalaisena kansalliseepoksena," *Kalevalavihko* (Valvoja, 1909), pp. 3-7.

51. *Ibid.*, pp. 32-35, 68-76, 102-56; *Oma Maa*, I, 1045-46.

52. The *Kalevala* has never become a popular book in the sense that it is read generally by the common people. However, it is included in courses given in the schools — especially courses in Finnish literature — and has colored even popular literature and art to a degree which justifies the statement that it has become a rather tangible part of certain aspects of the cultural milieu in which the Finns of the last two generations have been brought up. See Estlander, B., *op. cit.*, vol. I, p. 104; *Kalevalavihko*, pp. 157-165; *Oma Maa*, I, 1045-46.

53. Ojansuu, H., "Suomen Kirjakieli," *Oma Maa*, III, 934-40; Niemi, A. R., *op. cit.*, pp. 75-76, 82-84, 245-47.

54. Rein, Th., *op. cit.*, I, 54-57, 77-83; Söderhjelm, W., *Johan Ludwig Runeberg*, I, 199 *et seq.*

55. Elmgren, S., "Berättelse on Finska Litteratursällskapet i Helsingfors under de första 17 åren," *Suomi*, 1847, pp. 1-45; Juvelius, J. W., "Suomalaisen kirjallisuuden seura," *Oma Maa*, II, 265-69.

56. Schauman, A., *op. cit.*, I, 24, 55-56; Estlander, B., *op. cit.*, I 79-83.

57. See Söderhjelm, W., "Runebergs betydelse som skald," *Förhandlingar och Uppsatser*, XVIII, 1-21.

58. "Muistelmia Suomen sanomalehdistä," *Suometar*, May 21, 1858;

Krohn, J., "Katsaus suomenkielisen sanomalehdistön vaiheisiin," *Kirjallinen Kuukauslehti*, 1871, No. 2, 25 *et seq.*; Palmén, E. G., "Suomen sanomalehdistöstä," *Oma Maa*, I, 262-85.

59. Soikkeli, K., *Suomen Sanomalehdistö 1771-1900*, pp. 7-8; *Helsingfors Tidningar*, Dec. 14, 1836; *Kirjallinen Kuukauslehti*, 1871, No. 2, pp. 24, 31; *Valvoja*, 1883, No. 1, pp. 32-35.

60. For example, lengthy patriotic novels of stirring content were printed in many an issue of the *Helsingfors Morgonblad*, founded by Runeberg in 1832 and edited by him till 1837, and in the *Helsingfors Tidningar*, with which Z. Topelius was associated for nearly twenty years.

61. "Tidningar på Finska Språket," *Helsingfors Tidningar*, Dec. 6, 1856.

62. *Ibid.*, Dec. 2, 5, 9, 16, 19, 1835; May 25, 1831; Jan. 7, 10, 17, 1835; *Tidningar ifrån Helsingfors*, Jan. 2, 5, 9, 12, 23, 26, 1829.

63. News from St. Petersburg was thus reported, and an account of the Polish revolt in 1831 was described in the domestic news column. See *Helsingfors Tidningar*, 1831, Nos. 3-6 and cf. *ibid.* March 5, 1832. A couple of decades later this procedure would have been unthinkable.

64. *Ibid.*, Mar. 13, 1830; July 13, Aug. 20, 1831; Sept. 9, 13, 16, 20, 1837; Jan. 24, July 25, 1838.

65. *Ibid.*, July 2, 6 and Oct. 8, 1836; June 12, 15, 1839.

CHAPTER IV

1. Tradition assigns this phrase to Arwidsson, but it is unlikely that he is its author. I have not found it in any of his unpublished or published writings, and Professor J. R. Danielson-Kalmari has likewise failed to discover it. See his *Tien varrelta kansalliseen ja valtiolliseen itsenäisyyteen*, I, 230-31.

2. See *Fosterländskt Album*, II, 58 *et seq.*

3. Cf.Rein, Th., *op. cit.*, I, 426 et seq.

4. *Helsingfors Tidningar*, Nov. 30, 1844.

5. *Ibid.*, Dec. 31, 1844, and cf. *ibid.*, March 20, 1844, and Castrén, G., "Robert Tengström," *Förhandlingar och Uppsattser*, XVII, 39, 57-58.

6. See *Johan Vilhelm Snellmans Samlade Arbeten*, II, 57 *et seq.*

7. The substance of these generalizations was understood at the time. "Tidningar i Finland," *Helsingfors Tidningar*, Aug. 17, 21, 1844, Dec. 31, 1844; "Ett ord i dagens frågor," *Saima*, Dec. 24, 1845. See also "Tidningar på Finska språket," *ibid.*, Dec. 6, 1856; "Muistelmia Suoma-

laisista sanomalehdistä," *Suometar*, May 21, 1858; Krohn, J., "Katsaus suomenkielisen sanomalehdistön vaiheisiin," *Kirjallinen Kuukauslehti*, 1871, No. 2, pp. 25 *et seq.*; Schauman, A., *Nu och förr*, pp. 357-89; Rein, Th., *op. cit.*, I, 442-43.

8. Rein, Th., *op. cit.*, Vol. I, Chaps. I-IV.

9. *Ibid.*, Chap. V. The *Spanish Fly* appeared in only three issues. The second was released in 1840 and the third in 1841. The delay was due to the carelessness of Snellman's friends whom he had entrusted with the task of seeing the second and third issues through the press.

10. Refers to the danger of Russification.

11. The letter is printed in full in Rein, Th., *op. cit.*, I, 245-51. Elsewhere in the letter Snellman stated that only if the educational system were overhauled in such a way as to provide adequately for the Finnish-speaking element, would it be useful. "An artificial tie, even though it be of the noble color of education, will not be strong enough if no strand of nationality is found in it."

12. Rein, Th., *op. cit.*, I, 409-16; *Oma Maa*, III, 203-13. An amateurish and in many respects misleading account in English of Snellman's nationalist agitation is given by Arthur Reade in his *Finland and the Finns*, Chap. II.

13. Snellman had presented these Hegelian views in his *Läran om Staten* (*Theory of the State*), published in 1842. They were fundamental in his conception of the only true course that a patriot could follow, and remained basic in his work. See Rein, Th., *op. cit.*, I, 336-49.

14. See *Saima*, Jan. 4, 11, Apr. 4, June 6, 13, Aug. 1 (Supplement) 1844; Jan. 9, Feb. 6, Dec. 24, 1845; Jan. 8, Aug. 29, 1846 and cf. "Den Finska literaturen och dess Framtid," *Helsingfors Tidningar*, May 1, 4, 1844; Rein, Th., *op. cit.*, I, 417-69.

15. Representative samples of the *Literary News*' message are found in the following issues: 1847, No. 1, pp. 3-8, 11-14; "Tidnings Revy," 1847, No. 2; No. 4, pp. 98, 100; No. 11, pp. 320-21, 326; "Finnes en Finsk Prosa?" 1848, No. 12, pp. 376-82; 1849, No. 1, pp. 3, 282, 361-71.

16. In translating the anthem, the author has made use of *Finnish Songs*, selected and translated by Anna Krook.

17. For the celebration and its nationalist significance see "Studenternas Majfest," *Helsingfors Tidningar*, May 17, 1848; "Från Helsingfors," *ibid.*, May 31, 1848; Schauman, A., *op. cit.*, I, 45, 46, 368-74; Pinello, N. H., *Små Berättelser och Tidsbilder af Kapten Puff*, II, 29-32; *Historiallinen Arkisto*, VIII, 199-202.

18. Schauman, A., *op. cit.*, I, 385.

19. The first poem in the series was "Our Country," already mentioned. The collection was augmented in 1860 by seventeen additional poems. They dealt with the same subject and were written with the same skill and in the same spirit as the first. I have used C. R. Nyblom's edition, *Johan Ludvig Runebergs Samlade Skrifter*, I, 168-265. In speaking of the poems, an English writer has said, "Even a foreigner can hardly read them without being moved to tears by their naive simplicity, by the sheer beauty they shed on noble human striving and suffering . . . by the fiery, self-sacrificing patriotism through which human clay is transformed into something greater than itself. . . ." Reade, A., *op. cit.*, p. 38.

20. "Att gråta åt," *Helsingfors Tidningar*, Feb. 10, 1864.

21. The letter was dated Oct. 18, 1844. It is found in the manuscript collection of the University of Helsinki. *Brev till Joh. Vilh. Snellman*, II.

22. See *Encyclopaedia Britannica* (14th ed.), IX, 258.

23. Ripley, W. Z., *The Races of Europe*, pp. 359, 358, 365.

24. Only in recent years have Finnish scholars begun to modify the notions concerning the racial antecedents of the Finns which Castrén bequeathed to posterity. For example, one cautiously confesses that "It is true that Castrén's conclusions . . . have been accepted by a later age only in modified form. . . ." (*Oma Maa*, III, 133). Another says it is "by no means" proved that the Finno-Ugrian language group represents a common racial background. Setälä, E. N., *The Language Fight in Finland*, p. 5. Not long ago a Finnish philologist and former follower of the Castrén interpretation maintained that the earlier view is untenable and that in so far as anything can be concluded about the Finns' antecedents, they must be sought in the Baltic basin and not in the more distant regions where Castrén thought he had found the cradle of the Finns. Mikkola, J. J., "Oikea Suomensuku," *Historiallinen Aikakauskirja*, 1929, No. 2, pp. 81-85. However, in popular thinking and writing "Our Hungarian brothers," "the Finnish race"— in the inflated, Castrénian sense — meet one on every hand. To select one instance, we find a fervid peroration on the wonder-working potency of the primordial "Ugric strength" among the orations delivered at the Turku Finnish University celebration in 1920. See Koskelainen, Y., "Ugrin Voima," *Turun Suomalaisen Yliopistoseuran Wuosikirja, 1920*, pp. 100-3.

25. *Joukkahainen*, I (1843), and *Joukahainen*, II (1845).

26. In going through the offerings of the *Readings*, one is impressed by the fact that most of the patriotic material appeared under the heading Geography, presumably to pull wool over the eyes of the censor. See especially part 2 of vol. I.

27. "Från Helsingfors," *Helsingfors Tidningar*, Apr. 2, 1845; Tigerstedt, Karl K., "Savolax-Karelska afdelningens historia," Svenska Litteratursällskapet i Finland, *Förhandlingar och Uppsatser*, XVII, 351-66; Schauman, A., *op. cit.*, I, 224-46, 208-12.

28. "En Akademisk Läseförening," *Helsingfors Tidningar*, June 10, and Nov. 4, 1846. Among the newspapers it offered its members were *Journal des debats, Revue des deux mondes, Augsburger allgemeine Zeitung* and the Danish *Faedrelandet*. The Club also subscribed to several Swedish papers and all periodicals and newspapers printed in Finland. Schauman, A., *op. cit.*, I, 336-39. By 1850 it had aroused the suspicion of the authorities who practically closed it in that year.

29. *Helsingfors Tidningar*, Feb. 11, 1846.

30. Koskinen, Y., "Pohjanmaasta," *Suometar*, Oct. 24, 1856.

31. Estlander, C. G., *Barndomsminnen*, pp. 119-20.

32. "The interest in the Finnish language continues to gain strength and ground," wrote *Helsingfors Tidningar* on Apr. 2, 1845. This pronouncement appears to be an understatement rather than an exaggeration, in view of the response of the students to the exhortations of Snellman and his immediate followers. The same paper stated on another occasion: "The new interest in the Finnish language continues to express itself in a way that shows clearly that it is no passing fad. Several of the university students intend to make it their major study; others who master it less well are competing at taking private instruction in it." *Ibid.*, March 1, 1845.

33. Rein, Th., *op. cit.*, Vol. II, Chaps. XI-XII; Schauman, A., *op. cit.*, I, 339-47, 380-83; Schybergson, M. G., *op. cit.*, II, 416-17.

34. Törnqvist, A. (Ed.), *op. cit.*, V, 139-40.

35. *Ibid.*, V, 175.

36. *Ibid.*, V, 348.

37. Schybergson, M. G., *op. cit.*, II, 418, note 1.

38. Schauman, A., *op. cit.*, I, 385-87; II, 14-15, 29-30.

39. *Ibid.*, II, 69-77, 91, 222-23.

40. Rein, Th., *op. cit.*, II, 48-55, 58-61.

41. Estlander, B., *op. cit.*, I, 165-66.

42. *Ibid.*, I, 185-88; Schybergson, M. G., *op. cit.*, II, 451 *et seq.*

43. The Finnish collection of laws, *Suomen Asetuskokoelma*, 1863, No. 26, pp. 1-2. (This source will be cited as *S.A.*) While the measure constituted the culmination of efforts which the Finnish government had been dilatorily making since 1850, the credit for it goes to the champion of the Finnish cause, Snellman. He was appointed Senator in the early part of 1863 and became the head of the Finance Department, a position

in which he remained till 1867. His first important achievement was the language ordinance which was promulgated as an executive decree by Alexander II. The Finnish government as a whole had no direct part in its drafting. See Rein, Th., *op. cit.*, Vol. II, Chap. IX.

CHAPTER V

1. *Åbo Tidningar*, 1844, No. 83; "Från Helsingfors," *Helsingfors Tidningar*, Oct. 30, 1844; "Ännu Något om Finsk Nationalitet," *Borgå Tidning*, 1844, No. 100; Lille, A., *Svenska Nationalitetens i Finland Samlingsrörelse*, pp. 1-2, 19-22, 24; Schauman, A., *op. cit.*, I, 219-20, 235, 238-39, 240-44.

2. Peder Särkilax (E. von Qvanten), *Fennomani och Skandinavism*, I, II. The Scandinavian movement is described in J. Clausen's *Skandinavismen*.

3. Rein, Th., *op. cit.*, II, 28-40; Johansson, R., "Skandinavismen i Finland," Svenska Literatursällskapet i Finland, *Historiska och Literaturhistoriska studier*, Vol. CCXIV, 6, pp. 252, 256-70; Schauman, A., *op. cit.*, II, 188-208; Pipping, H. E., "Finlands ställning till skandinavismen," Svenska Literatursällskapet i Finland, *Handlingar och Uppsatser*, Vol. CLVII, 6, pp. 130-95. Among them was A. Nordenskiöld, who later emigrated to Sweden, became a Swedish citizen and attained to international fame as the discoverer of the Northeast passage.

4. Castrén to Snellman, Oct. 1, 1844. *Brev till Joh. Vilh, Snellman*, II.

5. Quoted in Suolahti, G., *op. cit.*, p. 138; *Uusi Päivä*, Oct. 26, 1917.

6. Mörne, A., *Axel Olof Freudenthal och den finlandssvenska nationalitetstanken*, pp. 59-91. Johansson, R., *op. cit.*, pp. 270-300. It must be noted here that by no means all of the Finnish nationalists who were dazzled by the Scandinavianism of 1854-1856 proceeded to these extremes. On the contrary, the number of the Scandinavians who came to these conclusions was small, and they were important primarily because they marked, one might say, the starting point of the Swede-Finn nationalist movement. See Suolahti, G., "Vanhempi Fennomania ja Suomen itsenäisyyden aate," *Turun Suomalaisen Yliopistoseuran Vuosikirja*, 1921, pp. 132-39.

7. The controversies during 1856-1860 are discussed in Rein, Th., *op. cit.*, Vol. II, Chaps. IV-V; Schauman, A., *op. cit.*, II, 266-72, 274-76, 305-06, 313-21; Lille, A. *op. cit.*, pp. 35-55.

8. *Johan Vilhelm Snellmans Samlade Arbeten*, IX, 381-82.

9. Mörne, A., *op. cit.*, pp. 1-6.

10. Cf. "Till Fosterlandsvänner," *Ilmarinen*, Apr. 5, 1848.

11. Mörne, A., *op. cit.*, pp. 14-24.

12. Sohlman, A., *Det Unga Finland*. I have used the edition of 1880, printed in Helsinki.

13. Mörne, A., *op. cit.*, pp. 65-91; Lille, A., *op. cit.*, pp. 47, 49, 32-33; Rein, Th., *op. cit.*, II, 28-34. Excellent illustrations of a full-grown Freudenthalian creed are found in the *Vikingen*, a strongly Swecoman newspaper which appeared during the years 1870-1874. Its editor was A. Lille, who played an important part in the Swede-Finn movement for approximately fifty years. See *Vikingen*, Nov. 28, 1870; March 20, Apr. 11, May 1, June 12, July 10, Sept. 25, Oct. 16, Oct. 30, Nov. 13, 1871; Jan. 27, 1872; Dec. 31, 1874.

14. Mill, John Stuart, *Utiliarianism, Liberty and Representative Government* (Everyman's Library), pp. 359-60. Arvid Mörne in his "Liberalismens genombrott i den finländska pressen," Svenska Litteratursällskapet i Finland, Vol. CCXIV, *Historiska och Litteraturhistoriska Studier*, 6, pp. 121-84, presents an extensive survey of this phase of Finnish intellectual history in the nineteenth century.

15. See Mörne, A., in *op. cit.*, pp. 121-42; Lille, A., *op. cit.*, pp. 53-58.

16. *Protokoller förda i det Utskott af Finlands fyra stånd, som till följd af Hans Kejserliga Majestets Nådiga Manifest af den 29 Mars (10 April) 1861 sammanträdde i Helsingfors, den 20 Januari-6 Mars 1862; S.A.*, 1861, No. 9, pp. 1-4 No. 10, 1-3; 1865, No. 4, p. 1-30.

17. "Promotionen," *Helsingfors Tidningar*, June 22, 1850; "Filosofie Doktors och Magisterpromotionen i Helsingfors den 30 Mai 1853," *ibid.*, June 1, 1853. Cf. "Universitetets fester år 1857," note, in *ibid.*, May 30, 1857.

18. *Suomalaisen Tiedeakatemian Esitelmät ja Pöytäkirjat*, I (1909), 53-54.

19. "Wecko-Krönika," *Helsingfors Tidningar*, May 11, 1863.

20. "De nya fordringarne på finska Språkets införande vid domstolarne," *ibid.*, Feb. 11, 1862; "Den nya extraordinarie professuren i juridiska fakulteten," *ibid.*, Oct. 14, 1865; "Uudesta opettajavirasta yliopiston lakitiedekunnassa," *Suometar*, May 9, 1865.

21. "Kirje Toukokuulta," *Mehiläinen*, 1862, No. 5, pp. 123-24. "Hallituksen ruotsikiihkoisuus," *Helsingin Uutiset*, June 15, 1863.

22. "Paha tuosta on vaiti olla," *Tähti*, Aug. 13, 1867.

23. S., "Suomen-Kieli," *Suometar*, Aug. 3, 1860.

24. "Kuukauskirje," *Kirjallinen Kuukauslehti*, 1868, No. 9, pp. 240-42.

25. *Suometar*, Oct. 12, 1860. A.E.A., "Finska skolan i Helsingfors," *Helsingfors Tidningar*, Apr. 25, 1861. Cf. "Suomalaisuudesta Turussa," *Tähti*, Aug. 21, 1863.

26. "Kirje Toukokuulta," *Mehiläinen*, 1862, No. 5, p. 124; "Suomalaisuus Suomen pääkaupungissa," *Helsingin Uutiset*, Nov. 26, 1863; "Helsingin Suomalaisen Seurakunnan eroittamisesta," *ibid.*, Dec. 3, 1863; "Finskan vid embetsverken," *Helsingfors Tidningar*, May 11, 1865; "Om regleringen af språkförhållandena vid Helsingfors embetsmyndigheter," *ibid.*, May 15, 1865. An interesting illustration of the efforts made to win the capital for Finnish is given by an association founded in 1862 for the purpose of promoting the use of Finnish among the upper classes. Its members agreed to speak only Finnish on all occasions. It soon obtained some 350 members who included academicians, physicians, government officials and business men. "Suomenkielinen yhteys," *Helsingin Uutiset*, Mar. 5, 1863.

27. This celebrated law suit is reviewed and the decision printed in -e-, "Om rättighet att till domstol inlemna finsk skrift," *Helsingfors Tidningar*, June 12, 1864.

28. "Pressmålet mot professoren G. Z. Forsman," *ibid.*, Dec. 22, 1864, Sept. 11, 1865.

29. *S.A.*, 1865, No. 5, pp. 1-7.

30. In *Historiallinen Aikakauskirja*, 1930, No. 4, pp. 257-99, are found three articles on Y. Koskinen and his work for the Fennoman cause. One is by Professor G. Suolahti who has been engaged for some years in writing an authoritative biography of Koskinen.

31. Koskinen, Y., *Kansallisia ja Yhteiskunnallisia Kirjoituksia*, I, 565-69; "Mennyt vuosi ja Suomalaisuus," *Mehiläinen*, 1862, No. 1, pp. 1-8; "Uusi Vuosi 1863," *Helsingin Uutiset*, Jan. 2, 5, 1863; "Suomenkieli oppineissa Kouluissa," *Suometar*, Jan. 23, 1865; and cf. "Keskustelmus Viipurin ruotsinkielisen sanomalehden kanssa Suomen Teollisuudesta," *ibid.*, Apr. 4, 1856.

32. "Kuukauskirje," *Kirjallinen Kuukauslehti*, 1869, No. 2; "Koulujen Suomentamisesta," *ibid.*, 1867, No. 10, p. 247; "Mennyt vuosi ja Suomalaisuus," *Mehiläinen*, 1862, No. 2, pp. 1-8; "Kieliasia yhteiskunnalliselta ja kansalliselta kannalta," *Suometar*, Jan. 20, 1865; *ibid.*, Apr. 1, 1859, and cf. *Wiborgs Tidning*, Dec. 15, 1864; "Suomikiihkoisuus valtiollisena puolueena," *Helsingin Uutiset*, Feb. 19, 1863.

33. -er-, "Nationalkänsla och patriotism," *Helsingfors Tidningar*, July 30, 1859.

34. There appears to be no doubt but that "barbarism" refers to Russification.

35. r-Rr-, "Walfrid Alftan," *Lännetär*, X (1874), 173-74; cf. Koskinen, Y., *op. cit.*, I, 479.

36. Y. K., "Kansallisuus ja Kieli," *Suometar* May 9, 16, 1856; "J. V. Snellman ja 'Nuori Suomi'," *ibid.*, Apr. 16, 23, 1858; " 'Helsingfors Dagblad' ja suomenkielen asia," *Kirjallinen Kuukauslehti*, 1869, No. 9; "Valtiopäivä-vaalit ja pyrkijä-listat," *Helsingin Uutiset*, July 7, 1863; "Moskovalaisen lehden tuimistelemiset," *ibid.*, Dec. 21, 1863; "Hr E- och den finska språkfrågan," *Helsingfors Tidningar*, Oct. 3, 1864, and cf. -1-n, "Den finska språkfrågan," *ibid.*, Oct. 15, 1864; "Skandinavilaisista ajatuksista Ruotsissa ja Suomessa," *Suometar*, May 31, 1865.

37. "Suomikiihkoisuus valtiollisena puolueena," *Helsingin Uutiset*, Feb. 19, 1863.

CHAPTER VI

1. *Handlingar tillkomna vid Landtdagen i Helsingfors åren 1877-1878*, Vol. V, No. 25, p. 11

2. *Ibid.*, pp. 12-13.

3. *S.A.*, 1868, No. 36, pp. 1-2 (Dec. 7, 1868).

4. Dated May 30, 1871. *S.A.*, 1871, No. 17, pp. 8-11.

5. *Handlingar tillkomna vid Landtdagen i Helsingfors åren 1877-1878*, V, 19.

6. *Ibid.*, pp. 20-21.

7. *Ibid.*, p. 18.

8. *Ibid.*, pp. 1-10.

9. *Ibid.*, pp. 21-22; Rein, Th., *op. cit.*, II, 684-89.

10. See above, pp. 210 ff.

11. *Liberalisen puolueen ohjelma.* The program appeared in both languages in Dec. 1880 and was given wide circulation by the press. Cf. Mechelin, Leo "De politiska partierna," *Finsk Tidskrift*, Vol. VI (1879), 1, p. 129; Snellman, J. K., *Dagbladspartiets program.*

12. "Liberaalisen puolueen ohjelma," *Valvoja*, No. 1, Jan. 1, 1881, pp. 1-11, and cf. *ibid.*, V (1885), 281-82; Rein, Th., *op. cit.*, II, 687-92; Koskinen, Y., *Kansallisia ja Yhteiskunnallisia Kirjoituksia*, I, 12-13, and cf. Järnefelt, A., *Isänmaa*, pp. 30 *et seq.*; Estlander, B., *op. cit.*, II, 64-71.

13. *Handlingar tillkomna vid Landtdagen i Helsingfors år 1882*, Vol. I, No. 6, pp. 1-2.

14. *Ibid.*, S.S., pp. 1-14 and cf. *ibid.*, U.B., pp. 1-21.

15. Fisher, J. R., *op cit.*, p. 121.

16. For example, according to the Constitution the executive enjoyed the right to convene the Diet at will. By the Law of Parliament of 1877 it was decreed that the Diet should be convened "at least every five

years," and beginning in 1882, triennial sessions were introduced. See Wrede, R. A., *Grunddragen af Finlands rätts — och samhällsordning*, I, 113-19.

17. *Sveriges Rikes Lag Gillad och Antagen på Riksdagen åhr 1734. Jemte Bihang, innehållande i sammandrag, under lagtexten, de intill år 1855 utkomne, i Storfurstendömet Finland gällande Stadgar och författningar som ändra eller förklara lagen eller utvidga och närmare bestämma föreskrifterne i de ämnen densamma omfattar*, p. 865.

18. The author of this constitutional argument was A. A. Brunou, a member of the Senate Department of Justice and an avowed Swecoman who was determined to block the onward march of the Finnish cause. See Estlander, B., *op. cit.*, II, 108-11.

19. *The Law of the Realm of Sweden, Approved and Accepted by the Riksdag in 1734, and a Summary of the Additions Made before 1855 of the Laws in Force in Finland, Which Change, Explain, Extend or More Definitely Specify the Provisions Included Therein. Edited and Published by Imperial Command by the Law Commission for Finland Appointed by His Imperial Majesty*, (the full title in English of the work mentioned in note 17) which appeared in 1856, bears out these contentions. The very expression *Law of the Realm of Sweden* furnishes an interesting illustration of the points made. This compilation, edited for Finnish needs decades after the separation from Sweden, contains innumerable references to the King of Sweden, which obviously were read to mean the Grand-Duke of Finland. Its provisions relative to punishment for treason, the acceptance of favors from foreign sovereigns, etc., if strictly and literally interpreted, would have become meaningless in Finland after 1809. (See pp. 565-74). Likewise, separation from the Lutheran church entailed loss of "Swedish citizenship" and other inconveniences which could have no meaning whatever unless recourse was had to the usual interpretation of the word "Swedish." (See pp. 554 ff.) Instances of this sort could be multiplied indefinitely. It is to be noted that the changes or revisions of this law, to which reference is made in the title of the work, were changes effected by means of legislation before the completion of this edition. The changes did not include such things as substituting the word "Finnish" for "Swedish", "Finland" for "Sweden" and the like but consisted of revisions of the body of the law itself.

It is also worth noting that the question of constitutionality had never been raised before 1883. While the point had been made from time to time that the Diet should participate in the language legislation, the administrative character of the language situation had never been denied. With regard to the contested point in the Code of 1734, this very section of the Code was used by the Language Committee, in 1862, appointed to prepare the ground for the introduction of Finnish into court procedure, in support of the contention that specific provision for the use of Finnish should be made. The Government proposal of 1882, previously mentioned, was duly considered by the Committee on Laws composed of competent legal talent. Only one reference was made in its deliberations to the oftmentioned provision of the Code of 1734. It was appealed to in support of the idea that this very provision rendered imperative the completion of the language reform. See *Handlingar tillkomna vid Landtdagen i Helsingfors åren 1877-1878*, Vol. V, No. 25, pp. 1-26; *ibid.*, 1882, documents included in Proposition No. 6; *Protokol af Ridderskapet och Adeln 1882*, I, 272-83; II, 867-72.

20. *S.A.*, 1883, No. 40, pp. 4-7.

21. *Ibid.*, 1877, No. 6, p. 1.

22. *Ibid.*, 1887, No. 6, pp. 1-3. (Dated Apr. 4, 1887.)

23. *Ibid.*, 1902, No. 18, pp. 1-3. (Dated June 19, 1902.)

24. The following sources are given without any pretence that they include more than a fraction of the pertinent literature of the period. A.A.B., "Suomen kielen entisestä ja nykyisestä valtiollisesta asemasta," *Valvoja*, Vol. III (1883), No. 22, pp. 606-10; Buch, M., *Finnland und seine Nationalitätenfrage*, especially pp. 46-71; Castrén, J., *Mikä on oikea ohjelma suomalaisuuden asiassa?; Uuden Suomettaren ja sen miesten 'puoluemoraali'*; Churberg, W., "Nykyisen aseman johdosta," *Keski-Suomi*, Aug. 25, 1883; Danielson, J. R., "Vastustajilleni oikeus-ja virkakieltä koskevassa riidassa," *Valvoja*, Vol. III (1883), No. 22, pp. 621-29; E.H., "Papisto ja Suomenkieli," *ibid.*, VIII (1888), 336-42; Forsström, F., *Våra domstolsspråk inför lag*; "Framsynt," *Hvilken kurs styra vi?*; Gebhard, H., "Kirje Helsingistä," *Valvoja*, XII (1892), 586-92; "Suomalainen puolue kansanvaltaisemmaksi," *ibid.*, XIII (1893), 480-87; Grotenfelt, K., "Viime valtiopäiväin työstä," *ibid.*, XIV (1894), 279-85; F. H. (Felix Heikel), *Centralt eller moderat?*: Hallström, E., "Kansanihailu," *Valvoja*, XVI (1896), 288-93; Heikel, I. A., *Kieli-puolueet ja Työväenkysymys*; Lagus, F. H. B., *Muistelmia ja kuvauksia kielitaistelun ajoilta*; En Fennoman (Agaton Meurman), *Hwad är en Fennoman?; Kuinka Suomenkieli pääsi viralliseksi*; "Suomi virallisena kielenä," *Kirjallinen Kuukauslehti*, 1880, Nos. 8-9, pp. 171-81; E. N. (ervander), *Fädrens röst*; Neuter (A. W. Ervasti), *Om rätta förhållandet af svenskans och finskans likställighet*; Palmén, E. G., "Kieliky-

symyksen nykyinen asema," *Valvoja*, XVII (1897), 152-64; "Kirjeitä valtiopäiviltä," *ibid.*, XI (1891), 124-28, 309-14; "Käänne Suomen puolueoloissa," *ibid.*, VII (1887), 415-27; "Mietteitä vuoden vaiheilla," *ibid.*, XII (1892), 1-9; "Mitä sopii odottaa 1885 vuoden valtiopäiviltä?" *ibid.*, V (1885), 1-18; "Puolueitten nykyinen asema Suomessa," *ibid.*, IV (1884), 23-34, 117-41; "Valtiollisista lentokirjoistamme," *ibid.*, VII (1887), 97-112, 159-71; Parmanen, W, (?), *Uppfatta att du är Finlands medborgare*; Rein, Th., "Käskykirje virkakuntien kielestä," *Valvoja*, VI (1886), 198-203; "Mietteitä äsken päättyneiden valtiopäiväin johdosta," *ibid.*, V (1885), 277-84, 372-81, 421-33, and cf. 116-26; "Uudenvuoden mietteitä 1890," *ibid.*, X (1890), 28-43; "Valtiopäivät tulossa," *ibid.*, IV (1884), 612-23; 1-r-1 (W. Renvall), *Uppsatser i Språk — och Nationalitetsfrågan*; Vasenius, V., "Käsitteiden selvitykseksi kieliasiassa," *Valvoja*, XVII (1897), 216-23; *Suomenmielisyys ja vapaamielisyys*; X (A. Edelheim), *I brytningstid*; von Born, V. M., *Det svenska partiet*; Nemo (pseud.), *Partierna vid 1885-års landtdag I, II; Tankar i politiska frågor*; Estlander, C. G., "Min ställning i språkfragan," *Finsk Tidskrift*, XII (1887); Lille, A., *op. cit.*, Chaps. X-XVI; *Päivälehti*, Nov. 16, 1889, Jan. 3, 1890; *Nuori Suomi*, 1891-1892.

25. *Utdrag ur Publique Handlingar, Placater, Förordningar, Resolutioner Ock Publicationer*, I (1742), 529-34. This interesting ordinance stated in part: "Parents and guardians must see to it that their children learn to read their principles of Christianity. If the parents are not able to discharge their duty, they must employ a school master . . . ; nobody will be excused from this obligation unless he be in extreme poverty. Should anyone . . . fail to observe this ordinance, he shall pay, after having been twice warned, a fine of two marks in silver to be used in the instruction of the poor children of the parish, but this does not free him from his duty. . . . If there are parents too destitute to care for their children in this matter, His Royal Majesty assumes that the parish will appropriate the means required for this useful undertaking. . . ."

26. *Ibid.*, VII, 5296-97.

27. Vikman, K. O., *Suomen kansan lukutaidon synty ja kehitys Ruotsin vallan aikana*; Raitio, K., "Varhaisempi Kansanopetus," in Tarjanne, A. J., Ahtiala, K., *et al.*, (Ed.) *Suomen Kansakoulu 1866-1916*, pp. 11-30.

28. *Ibid.*, pp. 30-38.

29. *Litteraturbladet*, 1847, No. 11, p. 326; *ibid.*, 1847, No. 1, pp. 11-14; S-n, "Skolorne," *Helsingfors Tidningar*, 1841, Nos. 29, 30, 90; "Litteratur," *ibid.*, June 27, 1846, No. 49; "Om sockenskolor," *Morgonbladet*, 1846, Nos. 16-20.

30. E. [Nervander], *Fädrens röst,* p. 52.

31. *Ibid.,* p. 60.

32. A.M., "Uutena vuonna," *Kirjallinen Kuukauslehti,* 1875, No. 1, p. 2.

33. Tarjanne, A. J. *et al.* (Ed.), *op. cit.,* pp. 41-48.

34. *Ibid.,* pp. 49-67.

35. See Palmén, E. G., "Kansakoulumme aamusarastuksen ajoilta," in Tarjanne, A. J. *et al.* (Ed.), *op. cit.,* pp. 97-132.

36. *S.A.,* 1866, No. 12, pp. 1-88; Tarjanne, A. J., *op. cit.,* pp. 83-96.

37. Tables in *Oma Maa,* III, 459, 460. A good contemporary discussion of the school situation in 1886 is given in Schauman, A., *Nu och Förr,* pp. 139-56.

38. Compulsory school attendance was realized, despite the efforts of its friends, only after the attainment of independence, in 1921.

39. That is, in the Finnish-language schools. The act of 1866 provided equally for the two language groups. In the Swedish-language primary schools, no instruction was required in Finnish, nor is it required at present.

40. Mäkinen, K. K., "Kansakoulun opetustoiminnan kehitystä," Tarjanne, A. J. *et al.* (Ed.), *op. cit.,* pp. 111-28.

41. See *S.A.,* 1866, No. 12, pp. 11, 60, 61, 69-70, 76-80. The general results of the educational advance are suggested by the rapid growth in the number of schools and by the increase in attendance already noted. In 1880, the total number of lower schools was about 1550; by 1900 it had grown to roughly 3,500. The total attendance grew from 28,700 in 1880 to 111,800 in 1900. *Suomen Tilastollinen Vuosikirja,* Vol. XVIII (1920), Table 170, pp. 202-3.

42. Finland's population, education and related statistics usually divide the people into Finnish-speaking and Swedish-sepaking inhabitants. This is a misleading classification because it is in fact based upon the so-called "home language" or "mother tongue" of the individual citizen. Thus a Swede-Finn will be listed as Swedish-speaking, although he may, and frequently does, master Finnish equally well. This classification has been used here because it indicates, however roughly, the gains made by the Finnish movement in the field of education. On the Jyväskylä and Hämeenlinna institutions see Jalkanen, K. J., *Jyväskylän Lyseo 1858-1908,* and *Hämeenlinnan Normaalilyseo 1873-1887 ja Lyseo 1887-1923.*

43. *Suomen Tilastollinen Vuosikirja,* Vol. I (1903), Tables 178, 179, pp. 292-95; Vol. XXVI (1928), Table 183, pp. 200-1.

44. *Ibid.,* Vol. XVIII (1920), Table 183, pp. 210-211; Vol. III (1905),

Table 179, p. 287; Vol. XXVI (1928), Table 189, p. 205. But see statement concerning classification according to language, in note 42.

45. Setälä, E. N., *The Language Fight in Finland*, pp. 15-16; *S.A.*, 1894, No. 3, p. 9.

46. The Home Language Society's work assumed greater importance in the course of the nineties, especially after 1897 when it began to publish the *Virittäjä*, a journal devoted to the bringing forth and development of Finnish scientific terms.

47. Since 1884, it has published the *Duodecim*, a journal devoted to the interests of the medical profession, and in 1888 began the publication of the *Journal of Hygiene* which has done pioneer work among the people of Finland in promoting scientific and progressive advance in public health.

48. Several other organizations also participated in the task of providing the necessary tools for Finnish scholarship in all fields. The Finnish Literature Society continued the publication of works of every description. The Finnish Historical Society which had its inception in 1864 as one of the sections of the Finnish Literature Society, began its existence as an independent body in 1875. The *Historical Archives*, its most conspicuous publication, comprises over thirty substantial tomes. (See Suomen Historiallinen Seura, *Juhlajulkaisu 1875-1925*, Helsinki, 1925.) Finland's Antiquities Society, founded in 1870, became the main seat of the great variety of subjects dealing with Finnish and with north European antiquities. Its *Journal* began to appear in 1874, and in 1894 it began the publication of *Finland's Museum*. Both serve as repositories of scholarly production. The field of ecclesiastical history and studies became the domain of the Finnish Church History Society, founded in 1899. It has brought forth a considerable amount of source publications in its *Acts* and *Protocolls*. The Fenno-Ugric Society, founded in 1881, became the sponsor of philological and other studies dealing with the Fenno-Ugric language group. *Journal de la Société Finno-Ugrienne* and the *Memoires de la Société Finno-Urgienne*, published since 1886, have appeared mostly in French or in German and make no attempt to appeal to the layman. See Aspelin-Haapkylä, E., "Suomalaisen Tiedeakatemian edellytykset," *Suomalainen Tiedeakatemia. Esitelmät ja Pöytäkirjat*, I (1909), 50-64.

49. Setälä, E. N., *op. cit.*, p. 16.

50. This general objective was variously stated long before the act of 1866 was passed, and was frequently stressed after that date. See "Nationalitetens och Nationalandans historiska betydelse," *Helsingfors Tid-*

ningar, Jan. 3, 1846; "Folkskolan," *ibid.*, Apr. 20, 1850; "Privatgymnasium i Helsingfors," *ibid.*, Oct. 7, 1804; "Ännu ett ord om Finlands Folkskolor," *ibid.*, Sept. 2, 1857; "Ett besök i Finlands folkskollärareseminarium," *ibid.*, June 14, 1864; A.M. "Uutena Vuonna," *Kirjallinen Kuukauslehti*, 1875, No. 1, p. 2; *Valvoja*, 1885, V, 12, 122; 1890, X, 159-67; Lönnbeck, G. F., *Folkskoleidens utveckling i Finland från nittonde århundradets början till 1866*, pp. 87-89, 106 ff.

51. *Penni-Kirjasto Suomen Kansalle*, 1867-1880; *Pennibiblioteket*, 1866-1880. Another series of the latter, consisting of six essays, was published 1890-1900. The literature consisted for the most part of 15-25 page pamphlets. The writer has been unable to ascertain the circulation of this literature but it appears to have been considerable. Salovaara, H. A., "Varsinaissuomalaisen osakunnan kansanvalistuskomitean toiminnasta," *Lännetär. Uusi Jakso*, II, 175-80; "Kotimaista kirjallisuutta," *Kirjallinen Kuukauslehti*, 1867, No. 5, pp. 137-39; Meinander, V. B., "Nyländska afdelningens folkbildningsarbete," *Album Utgifvet af Nylänningar*, XI, 189-232, and cf. VII, xi; X, 302-03, 295-96; XI, 276, 297, 162-65.

Similar literature had been published earlier in large quantities, although under other auspices. Thus *Readings for the People*, consisting of no less than 183 titles, was published between 1852 and 1865, and a smaller series of 141 items in 1851-1855. In these series as well as in the later publications already mentioned, a great variety of subjects were treated. Among those in the first *Readings* was a life of Benjamin Franklin and a history of the American Revolutionary War. *Readings for Children* in fifteen parts was published in 1860-1862 Several less pretentious collections, likewise designed to provide instructive reading matter for the masses, were issued during these years.

52. B. F. G[odenhjelm], "Kansanvalistus-Seurasta," *Kirjallinen Kuukauslehti*, 1873, No. 2, p. 25.

53. A good treatment of the Adult Education Society and several similar organizations is found in Tolvanen, O., "Kansanvalistusjärjestöt," *Oma Maa*, III, 776-92; "Kuukauskirje," *Kirjallinen Kuukauslehti*, 1874, No. 12, pp. 314-16. A Swedish-language society, which proceeded to work on much the same lines as the Adult Education Society, was founded in 1881.

54. *Suomen Nuorisoseuraliikkeen 25-vuotisjuhla ja Suomen Nuorison Liiton Yleinen Kokous 1906*, pp. 11-12; Liakka, N., "Suomen nuorisoseuraliike," *Oma Maa*, II, 419-30. Statistical information on the associations is given in Alkio, S. (Ed.), *Suomen Nuorison Liiton Vuosikirja*, Vol. I, Tables 1-12; II, 51; III, 64; VI, 24, 31, 35; VII, 23, 25, 33; IX, 17, 19,

23; X, 16, 22; *Kansannuorison Sivistystarve ja Nuorisoseuraliike*, pp. 34-41. In 1925, the number of local Young Peoples Associations exceeded 1,300, and their membership approximated 65,000. *Finland, the Country, Its People and Institutions*, p. 447. For the nationalist complexion of these organizations, see Seppälä, J., (Ed.), *Suomen Ensimäinen Yleinen Nuorisoseurain Kokous Jyväskylässä 1895*, pp. 4-5, 13-22, 43-83, 89-103, 119-23; Rikala, K., *Pöytäkirja Tampereella 1897 pidetystä Toisesta Yleisestä Nuorisoseurain Kokouksesta*, pp. 10, 14, 77, 38, 44, 87, 91-96; *Pöytäkirja Viipurissa 1899 pidetystä Kolmannesta yleisestä Nuorison Liiton Kokouksesta*, pp. 5, 8-12, 47, 68-69; *Suomen Nuorison Liiton Kokous Mikkelissä 1901. Pöytäkirja*, pp. 7, 8, 32, 38, 99-103; *Suomen Nuorisoseuraliikkeen 25-vuotisjuhla ja Suomen Nuorison Liiton Yleinen Kokous*, 1906, pp. 11-12, 26-27; and the second work by Alkio mentioned above, pp. 9-33, 42-52.

55. Kojonen, R., "Kansanopisto," *Oma Maa*, IV, 460-76; Engelberg, R., "Työväenopistot ja muut vapaat opistot," *ibid.*, VI, 187-212, and bibliography on pp. 212-13.

56. *Suometar*, Apr. 1, 1859; "Maiden ja Merien takaa," *Helsingfors Tidningar*, Jan. 28, 1865; Gebhard, H., "Suomenkieliset aikakauskir-jamme," *Valvoja*, 1889, IX, 495-96; *Kirjallinen Kuukauslehti*, 1871, No. 12, p. 307; Vasenius, V., "Sanomalehdistön suhde yleisöön," *Valvoja*, 1894, XIV, 359-78; Palmén, E. G., "Puolen vuosisadan sanomalehtitilas-toa," *ibid.*, 1897, XVII, 46-51; *Suomen Tilastollinen Vuosikirja*, Vol. IV (1906), Table 265, pp. 440-41. It is interesting to note that as late as the early eighties, the Fennoman group still included a sufficiently large number of Swedish-speaking enthusiasts for the cause to necessitate the publication of a Swedish-language newspaper to serve them. Twenty years later, however, the Finnization of the supporters of the Fennomen had proceeded to a point where such a sheet was unnecessary. See Hytönen, V., *Suomalaista sivistystaistelua 1858-1908*, pp. 8 ff.

57. Kovero, M., *Suomen vientiteollisuus*, pp. 61-94; Ramsay, H., *Suomen teollisuuden kehityksen pääpiirteet*, pp. 28-33. Schauman, A., *op. cit.*, II, 119-24; "Suomen voikaupasta," *Suometar*, June 20, 21, 29, 1865; "Vår ekonomiska utveckling," *Helsingfors Tidningar*, Nov. 12, 1866; "Handel och Sjöfart," *ibid.*, Sept. 23, 1854; Johnsson, Y., *Tut-kimuksia Suomen teollisuus työväen suojeluslainsäädännön Kehityksestä 1860-luvulta alkaen*, Chaps. I, III; Voionmaa, V., *Sosialismin vuosisata*, II, 510, 518-19; von Schoultz, J., *Bidrag till belysande af Finlands social-demokratiska partis historia*, I, 11-19.

58. Renström, K., *Tampereen Työväenyhdistyksen vuosikertomus*

vuodelta 1888, p. 3, and cf. pp. 13, 16-17; A.W., "Lyhyt silmäys työväen elämään entisinä aikoina erittäinkin Tampereella," *Työväen Kalenteri*, II (1894), 58-64; *ibid.*, 24-27; Turtonen, J., (Ed.) *Tampereen Työväenyhdistyksen vuosikertomus vuodelta 1895*, pp. 3-4; A.R., "Wilhelm Hackman," *ibid.*, IV, (1896), 1-9; Vintiö [V. Virta], "Hiukan työväenasiasta," *ibid.*, V (1897), 76-81; von Schoultz, J., *op. cit.*, pp. 31-34, 50-54.

59. Vaara, L., (Ed.), *Porin Työväenyhdistys 25-vuotias*, pp. 8-10; Voionmaa, V., *op. cit.*, II, 526-31; Renström, K. (Ed.), *Tampereen Työväenyhdistyksen vuosikertomus vuodelta 1890*, p. 23.

60. Vaara, L. (Ed.), *op. cit.*, pp. 28-31; Renström, K. (Ed.), *Tampereen Työväenyhdistyksen vuosikertomus vuodelta 1887*, p. 19; "Ohjelmamme," *Länsisuomen Työmies*, Dec. 19, 1898; *Arbetets Vänner i Helsingfors*, Jan. 1891-Mar. 1894, pp. 3, 31; *ibid.*, Mar. 1900-Mar. 1901, p. 8; *Arbetets Vänner i Helsingfors. De första tio åren af föreningens lif*, pp. 4-5.

61. *S.A.*, 1889, No. 18, pp. 1-8.

62. *Ibid.*, 1895, No. 44, pp. 1-11; 1897, No. 15, pp. 2-8. The law went into effect Jan. 1, 1898.

63. *Ibid.*, 1897, No. 15, pp. 2-8; No. 27, pp. 1-12; No. 36, pp. 7-18; No. 35, pp. 1-6; No. 40, pp. 3-14; No. 47, pp. 1-35; No. 45, pp. 4-7.

64. Voionmaa, V., *op. cit.*, II, 515-16, 525-26.

65. *Ibid.*, II, 532-40; cf. "Onko meidän työväenliikkeemme suomalaisella pohjalla?," *Uusimaa*, 1899, No. 134.

66. Mechelin, Leo, "Kansalaisitsehallinto," *Työväen kalenteri*, I (1893), 9-10.

67. Cf. *ibid.*, p. 39.

68. Brander, K. A., "Katsaus ensimmäisen työväenyhdistysten edustajain kokoukseen Helsingissä," *ibid.*, II (1894), 12-16.

69. *Ibid.*, pp. 11-12,

70. Hultin, T., "Työväen toivomukset 1894 v. valtiopäivillä," *ibid.*, III (1895), 76-87.

71. Von Wright, V., "Työväenpyrinnöt Suomessa v. 1892," *ibid.*, I, 39. An excellent description of the suffrage problem before the franchise reform of 1905 is given in Tuominen, O., "Äänioikeustaistelut Suomessa 1880-luvulla," *Historiallinen Aikakauskirja*, 1931, No. 1, pp. 1-33.

72. Turtonen, J. (Ed.), *op. cit.*, pp. 4-15; Aronen, H., "Piirteitä työväenliikkeemme murrosajalta 1890-luvulla," *Kymmenen vuotta Suomen Työväenpuolueen muistoja ja ennätyksiä 1899-1909*, pp. 54-60; J.A.L., "Suomen työväenyhdistysten edustajain toinen yleinen kokous Tamperella,

1896," *Työväen kalenteri*, IV (1896), 51-81; VI (1898), Introduction; VII (1901), 19.

73. Printed in *Kymmenen vuotta Suomen työväenpuolueen muistoja ja ennätyksiä 1899-1909*, p. 26.

74. *Finland, the Country, Its People and Institutions*, p. 152.

75. Petäjäniemi, K. W. (Ed.), *Tampereen Työväenyhdistyksen Vuosikertomus Vuodelta 1898*, p. 7.

76. *Työväen kalenteri*, VII (1901), 24, and cf. V (1897), 38-50.

77. M.H-g, "Minkälainen kanta Työmieslehdellä tulisi olla?," *Työmies*, Aug. 24, 1900.

78. *Työväen kalenteri*, VII (1901), 30.

79. Paasivuori, M., "Irti Porvareista," *Kymmenen vuotta Suomen Työväenpuolueen muistoja ja ennätyksiä 1899-1909*, pp. 62-65, and cf. *ibid.*, pp. 66-69; *Työväen kalenteri*, V (1897), 17-20, 94-98.

80. *Ibid.*, V (1897), 93-97.

81. *Ibid.*, VII (1901), 37, and cf. *ibid.*, VI (1898), 73-79, 58-68; *Työmies*, Aug. 24, 1900. It is worth noting that the Swede-Finn nationalist movement was sharply condemned because, according to the labor view, it represented undisguised and selfish class interests. Cf. *Työväen kalenteri*, V (1897), 74.

82. *Arbetets Vänner i Helsingfors*, Feb. 26, 1893-Mar. 11, 1894, pp. 28-29.

83. *Ibid.*, Mar. 1898-Apr. 1899, pp. 38-39.

84. *Ibid.*, Feb. 24, 1895-Mar. 15, 1896, pp. 55, 61.

85. *Arbetets Vänner i Helsingfors. De första tio åren af föreningens lif*, p. 5 and cf. *Kertomus Vaasan Työväenyhdistyksen toimista vuonna 1890*, pp. 3-8, and *ibid.*, 1891-1892, pp. 40-41.

86. *Arbetets Vänner i Helsingfors*, Mar. 1900-Mar. 1901, pp. 10-11; Mar. 1901-Mar. 1902, p. 12; Mar. 1902-Mar. 1903, p. 17.

87. *Ibid.*, Mar. 11, 1894-Feb. 24, 1895, p. 10.

88. *Ibid.*, Feb. 24, 1895-Mar. 15, 1896, pp. 36-38, 43, 44-45; Mar. 1900-Mar. 1901, p. 11.

89. An illustration of the surrender of the Friends of Labor to the Swecoman group was the decision, in 1901, concerning the establishment of a newspaper for the organizations. It was decided that the *Hufvudstadsbladet* should be considered the organ of those associations that desired to use a newspaper as their forum. The *Hufvudstadsbladet* was at the time one of the main Swecoman sheets, *ibid.*, Mar. 1901-Mar. 1902, pp. 6, 12, 36-37.

90. *Ibid.*, Mar. 1901-Mar. 1902, pp. 32, 33, 34, 35.

91. "Modersmålet," *Arbetaren*, Sept. 23, 1905.

92. H. H., "Några synpunkter," *ibid.*, Oct. 28, 1905. Cf. Axelsson, E., "Några ord för vår svenska tidningspress att beakta," *ibid.*, Aug. 12, 1905 and *Svenska folkpartiet, vad det vill*, p. 12.

93. J. V. H[ellberg], *Tampereen Työväenyhdistyksen Vuosikertomus vuodelta 1899*, p. 4; von Schoultz, J., *op. cit.*, pp. 248-49, 246-47.

94. It has been estimated that more than one-fourth of the organized workers in the country were included in the membership of the so-called "revolutionary workers' groups" which actively coöperated with the radical anti-Russian opposition. Reuter, J. N., *"Kagalen," ett bidrag till Finland's historia 1899-1905*, pp. 75-78; von Schoultz, J., *op. cit.*, pp. 280-81; Estlander, B., *op. cit.*, III, 44, 167-172, 237, 245-46, 264, 265, 283, 291-94, 306, 323-33, 351; Ignatius, H., Theslöf, G., *et al.* (Ed.), *Suomen vapaussota vuonna 1918*, I, 70, 87; Estlander, E., "Det passiva motståndet," *Med lagen och svärdet*, p. 16: cf. A. K[omonen], *Vaasan Työväenyhdistyksen 25-vuotis historiikki*, pp. 49-53.

95. Fisher, J. R., *op. cit.*, Chaps. XIII-XIV contain a good discussion of the military question in the Finnish-Russian controversy.

96. Wrede, R. A., *Grunddragen af Finlands rätts- och samhällsordning*, I, 113-19.

97. Bergh, E., *Finland under det första årtiondet af Alexander III:s regering*, pp. 114-16.

98. Danielson, J. R., *Finland's Union with the Russian Empire* (1891), pp. 1-16; Estlander, B., *op. cit.*, pp. 272-82; Fisher, J. R., *op. cit.*, Chap. IX. On the Slavophile movement in Russia, see Masaryk, T. G., *The Spirit of Russia*, Vol. I, Chap. IX and Vol. II, Chap. XVI.

99. *S.A.*, 1890, No. 16, pp. 1-2; 1891, No. 13, pp. 1-2; Bergh, E., *op. cit.*, pp. 353-58. The manifesto of Feb. 28, 1891, issued for the purpose of quieting the fears which the postal decree of the preceding year had aroused, appears to have indicated the general objectives of the Russification policy which was being contemplated. It stated that no disregard of Finland's laws was intended and continued in part as follows: "However, the absence of complete correspondence between some of Finland's laws and those of the Empire, as well as the absence of sufficient clarity in the laws concerning the relations between the Grand Duchy and the Empire, give rise to regrettable misunderstandings as regards the real meaning of the measures which are taken in order that objectives common to all parts of the Russian Empire may be realized. It is My hope that the wisdom of the Finnish people will eliminate this misunderstanding, and that a true perception of their own advantages will enable them

to strive for the strengthening of the bonds that unite Finland with Russia. . . ." Nothing came of the attempt to amalgamate the Finnish customs service with the Russian, and the Finnish monetary system was likewise not wiped out.

100. *S.A.*, 1891 No. 19, p. 1.

101. *Ibid.*, 1891, No. 27, pp. 2-3; No. 39, pp. 1-2.

102. *Ibid.*, 1891, No. 26, pp. 1-17, and cf. *ibid.*, 1894, No. 18, pp. 2-3.

103. *Ibid.*, 1900, No. 20, pp. 2-4.

104. *Ibid.*, 1891, No. 24, pp. 1-2; No. 39, pp. 1-2; 1894, No. 41, pp. 4-5; 1890, No. 21, p. 4; No. 28, pp. 1-2; 1893, No. 10, pp. 1-2; No. 29, pp. 4-5; 1895, No. 31, pp. 3-4; and cf. 1891, No. 3, p. 17; 1898, No. 39, pp. 1-2.

105. *Ibid.*, 1899, No. 3, pp. 1-2.

106. *Ibid.*, 1899, No. 3, pp. 3-4.

107. Fisher, J. R., *op. cit.*, p. 169 and cf. pp. 147-77.

108. Nylander, J. W., *Den Stora Deputationen*; Estlander, B., *op. cit.*, III, 34-47; *Ur Finlands Nyaste Historia*, Vol. I, Chaps. IV-V. Governor-General Bobrikoff was appointed to his post on Aug. 31, 1898. The policy which he tried to carry out in Finland included among other things a complete amalgamation of the Finnish military forces with the armies of Russia; the discontinuation of the Finnish State Secretariat in St. Petersburg; the introduction of Russian into the Finnish Senate and the administrative offices; the appointment of Russians to the Finnish civil service; and the elimination of the customs boundary and the national currency of Finland. It appears that this general program was presented by Bobrikoff and approved by the Tsar at the audience at which Bobrikoff's appointment was made. Estlander, B., *op. cit.*, III, 3.

109. The idea of an international address in favor of Finland appears to have originated with an Englishwoman, Mrs. Gertrud Coupland, although several Finns, among them W. Söderhjelm, Y. Hirn, J. Reuter, A. Edelfelt, H. Pipping, E. Westermarck, and K. Zilliacus, were largely responsible for its success. The address consisted of eleven separate addresses, signed by representatives from the following countries: England, France, Germany, Norway, Sweden, Denmark, Holland, Belgium, Italy, Austria and Hungary. The eleven copies were inscribed upon parchment and bound in Stockholm. The original bound copy now reposes in the State Archives in Helsinki. A facsimile edition, *Pro Finlandia* was published a few years later. Zilliacus, K., *Sortovuosilta*, pp. 1-33; Westermarck, Edw., "In Memoriam." *Murrosajoilta*, II, 433-39; Estlander, B., *op. cit.*, III, 47-57; *Ur Finlands Nyaste Historia*, Vol. II, Chap. IX. After it became obvious that the international deputation would

not be received by Nicholas II, but before it had left the Russian capital, Trarieux, Brusa, van der Vlught and other members of the delegation agreed to further effort on behalf of Finland. An international jury composed of competent jurists and experts in constitutional questions was to be called together to study the facts in the conflict between Finland and Russia and render a verdict. President McKinley of the United States was to be approached with the request that the verdict of the contemplated jury be presented to the Tsar by the ambassador of the United States at St. Petersburg. McKinley, it was maintained by one of the sponsors of this idea, "could hardly refuse to grant this request, for in that case the papers and the speakers of the opposing Democratic party would attack him. They would utilize to the utmost [in the campaign of 1900?] his unwillingness to lend a helping hand to a small nation that has turned to him in its hour of need." The Finnish emissary who came to the United States to present the request to McKinley found upon his arrival that the President was at Lake Champlain, and before McKinley returned to Washington the whole scheme was abandoned at the suggestion of several influential Finns who feared that it might lead to still greater difficulties rather than an abandonment of the anti-Finnish Russian policy. See Zilliacus, K., *op. cit.*, pp. 34-41.

That the attention of the outside world began to be fixed upon the unequal constitutional struggle in Finland, was in no small measure due to the international deputation and the manner of its reception in Russia. However, even before its failure gave added publicity to the enterprise, the situation in Finland had become the subject of considerable comment in the press of the major European countries. On the whole, the European press was favorably disposed toward Finland, and the sympathetic publicity which many of the papers gave to the Finnish cause, was of no small importance in strengthening the opposition of the Finns. See Söderhjelm, W., "Ulkomaat ja me," *ibid.*, II, 523-39 and *Ur Finlands Nyaste Historia*, II, 27-66.

110. *Ibid.*, II, 1-26; Estlander, B., *op. cit.*, III, 107-14; *S.A.*, 1900, No. 3, pp. 1-2.

111. That Bobrikoff aimed at nothing less than a complete eradication of Finland's autonomy and the reduction of the Grand Duchy to the position of a Russian frontier province, in which the Russian language would be supreme, is clearly indicated in his lengthy report (dated Oct. 15, 1902) to the Tsar. I have used the Swedish translation *Generalguvernör Bobrikoffs Berättelse öfver Finlands Förvaltning från sept. 1898 till sept. 1902* (1905).

112. *S.A.*, 1901, No. 26, pp. 1-73; and cf. No. 2, p. 1, No. 7, pp. 2-3.

113. Reuter, J. N., *op. cit.*, Vol. I; Estlander, B., *op. cit.*, III, 167-73. Bobrikoff states in his report (p. 176) that the number of absentees was 51.1 per cent. No fully reliable statistics on the success of the levy exist (*Finland, the Country, its People and Institutions*, p. 187) but it appears that at least 13,000 absented themselves.

114. *S.A.*, 1900, No. 22, pp. 1-3; 1901, No. 30, pp. 2-3; 1905, No. 18, pp. 4-5; 1903, No. 43, pp. 4-5; No. 47, pp. 2-6. The general situation in the country is suggested by the following words in an imperial decree issued on Apr. 9, 1903. "Concerned about a closer political union of our realm," it stated, "we have prescribed measures for uniting . . . Finland to the original part of the Empire, but the realization of these measures has been prevented by the open opposition among a part of the population in Finland. Persons of ill-will have, in their attempts to lead the people to oppose the government, committed acts which threaten peace and tranquility. . . . Under ordinary circumstances order . . . could have been maintained by means provided by existing laws. However, these means are ineffective at present because certain government officials and civil employees, and particularly the law courts, not only refuse to co-operate in the maintenance of order but often serve as deplorable illustrations of resistance to law." To remedy the situation, the Tsar granted extraordinary powers to the Governor General, for a period of three years. In general, the Governor General was empowered to close book stores, hotels and industrial or commercial establishments; to prohibit all private and public meetings; to dissolve all private associations and clubs; to deport without trial all suspicious persons; to confirm the choice of members of town and village governing bodies; and to prevent all measures by local officials which, in the opinion of the Governor General, did not correspond to the demands of general imperial policy. These prerogatives invested the Governor General with dictatorial powers and constituted a complete negation of government by law. See *ibid.*, 1903, No. 35, pp. 1-44, and No. 57A, pp. 2-6.

115. Danielson, J. R., *Mihin suuntaan?*; Tenax (pseud.) *Taipuako vai tehdä vastarintaa?*; Toivo (Ignatius), *Oikea Tie*; Gripenberg, L., *Ur mina levnadsminnen*, pp. 56-95; Reuter, J. N., *op. cit.*, Vol. II; Estlander, E., "Det passiva motståndet," *Med lagen och svärdet*, pp. 1-31; Vapaussodan Historian Komitea, *Suomen vapaussota vuonna 1918*, I 52-74; Estlander, B., *op. cit.*, III, 26, 44-45 69-70, 74-75; *Murrosajoilta*, pp. 79-80, 397-98.

116. The organization program and methods of the Activist Party are

described in A. Söderhjelm's "Det aktiva motståndspartiet," *Med lagen och svärdet*, pp. 32-85; K. Zilliacus tells his story in *Sortovuosilta*, especially chaps. III-X. See also *Lennart Hohenthals Memoarer*; Estlander, B., *Eugen Schauman*; Hjelt, E., *Från händelserika år*, I, 160-74; Gripenberg, L., "Muutamia muistelmia vuodelta 1903," *Murrosajoilta*, I, 55-80.

117. Roos, S., *Nationalstrejken i Finland*, 2 vols.

CHAPTER VII

1. *S.A.*, 1906, No. 26, pp. 1-49; 1907, No. 1, pp. 1-44. The new Parliament Bill contained only one reference to the language question. Par. 50 stated: "At the sessions of the Diet, Finnish or Swedish shall be used."

2. *Suomen Tilastollinen Vuosikirja*, Vol. XXVI (1928), Table 18, p. 43.

3. The program is printed in Lille, A., *op. cit.*, pp. 889-92; cf. "Det svenska partimöte," *Nya Pressen*, May 20, 1906, and Reuter, O. M., *I dagens frågor*.

4. *Suomen Maalaisväeston Liiton ohjelma* (1906), p. 7. In 1908, the Agrarians added to these demands another to the effect that the "rights" of the two languages, and their use, etc., be fixed by means of a constitutional provision. See *ibid.*, (1908), pp. 4-5.

5. I have used the German version of the program issued by the Finnish Party, *Die Finnische Partei in Finnland, ihr jetziges Programm nebst einigen einleitenden Worten* (1907). It contains a good 32-page survey of the objectives of the party before 1906; cf. Danielson-Kalmari, J. R., *Ratkaisun edellä*.

6. *Nuorisuomalaisen eli perustuslaillisen suomenmielisen puolueen ohjelma*, pp. 2-3, 15-19; Castrén, Z., *Kielikysymys* (1906) pp. 10-12. Ingman, S., *Puolueiden suhteet toisiinsa*, p. 15, cf. Anon., *Nuorsuomalaisten kannasta suomalaisuuden asiassa; Nuorsuomalaisen puolueen ohjelmasta*, p. 2; *Vaalitaisteluohjeita*, II, 72-74; Ignatius, K. E. F., *Mietteitä muutamista päivän kysymyksistä*.

7. E. A.-io, "Kielikiihkon palvelukseenko?" *Sosialistinen aikakauslehti*, Vol. I (June, 1906), No. 11-12, pp. 283, and cf. *ibid.* (Nov. 1906) No. 19, pp. 434-435.

8. Wuolijoki, S., "Torpparit ja sosialistit," *ibid.* (Feb. 1907), No. 26, pp. 41-49; "Köyhälistöpuolueen vaaliohjelma ja herraspuolueitten hätälu-

paukset," *ibid.*, pp. 49-63; cf. "Iltakatsaus," *Työmies*, Jan. 2, 1905, and *Sosialistinen aikakauslehti*, Vol. II (March 1907), No. 27, pp. 85-87.

9. Program printed in *ibid.*, Vol. I (Sept. 1906), Nos. 15-16, p. 382; cf. O. W. K., "Porvarillinen puolue muodostus maassamme," *ibid.*, II (1907), 76-82.

10. *Suomen Tilastollinen Vuosikirja*, Vol. XXI (1923), Table 233, pp. 262-63. Swede-Finn Socialists contributed 10,000 votes to the Social-Democrats. It is interesting to note that the Socialists obtained 33 per cent of the urban vote, and 37 per cent of the non-urban vote. *Murros-ajoilta*, II, 326.

11. Ignatius, H., Theslöf, G., *et al.* (Ed.), *op. cit.*, Vol. I, Part 1, Chap. VII, Part. 2, Chaps II-III; Langhoff, A., *Seitsemän vuotta Suomen edustajana valtaistuimen edessä. Muistoja ja muistiinpanoja vuosilta 1906-1913*; Blomqvist, K., "The Second Period of Oppression," *Finland, the Country, Its People and Institutions*, pp. 189-99. The Russian side of the case was presented especially during the Duma debates in the spring of 1908. I have used a verbatim translation of the debates, which appeared in Helsinki under the title *Den finska frågan i tredje ryska riksduman* (1908). The following controversial pamphlets may probably be considered fair statements of the Russian interpretation of Finland's position in the empire during the controversial years 1899-1910. Borodkin, M. M., *Finland, Its Place in the Russian State*; it contains an appendix giving the so-called "Equality Law" of June 30, 1910; Feodoroff, E., *The Finnish Revolution in Preparation 1889-1905*. Transl. by G. Dobson; Korewo, N. N., *The Finnish Question*; Soovoroff, P., *The Finnish Question*; Valiszevsky, K., *The Finnish Question — The Ostrich and the Sparrow*. Trans. by G. Dobson; Berendts, E. N., *The Rights of Finland according to European Scholars: A Rejoinder*. The "Rejoinder" by Berendts was a refutation of the conclusions concerning Finland's rights in the controversy with Russia, formulated by a conference of scholars convened in London February 26-March 1, 1910. The conference found for Finland and issued a report signed by Professor G. Anschutz of the University of Berlin, Professor L. von Bar of the University of Göttingen, Professor A. de Lapradelle of the University of Paris, Professor Leon Michoud of the University of Grenoble, Ernest Nys, Councillor of the Brussels Court of Appeal, W. van der Vlugt, Professor at the University of Leyden, and two eminent English jurists, Sir Frederick Pollock and J. Westlake. Their conclusions are found in Jean-Jacques Caspar's *Finlande et Russie*, pp. 50-54. Chaps. III-V of this work contain an account of the Russification policy down to 1910.

12. Ruuth, O. Y., *Självständighetspolitiken och jägarrörelsens uppkomst*, pp. 35-57, contain an excellent summary of the trends of public opinion during the war. It goes without saying that the press was unable to give expression to preferences of this kind.

13. Gummerus, H., *Jääkärit ja aktivistit*, Chaps. I-XIII; Ruuth, O. Y., *op. cit.*, pp. 61-152; Söderhjelm, A., "Det aktiva motståndspartiet," *ibid.*, pp. 86-114; Zilliacus, W., "Jägarrörelsens financiering," *ibid.*, pp. 139-43; and cf. Numelin, R., "Politisk verksamhet i Sverige 1914-18," *ibid.*, pp. 115-38; Hultin, T., *Taistelun mies*, pp. 148-56.

14. Sources cited in the preceding note.

15. *S.A.*, 1917, No. 20, pp. 1-3.

16. *Ibid.*, 1917, No. 27, pp. 1-4.

17. *Ibid.*, 1917, No. 50, pp. 1-2.

18. *Ibid.*, 1917, No. 69, pp. 1-2; No. 82, p. 1. Curiously enough, nothing was said about foreign relations. However, it was provided' that in case the Governor General considered it necessary, matters should be submitted to the "supreme Executive Power."

19. See table on p. 213.

20. Source cited in note 2, p. 266.

21. *S.A.*, 1917, No. 92, p. 1; No. 96, pp. 1-10; No. 102, pp. 1-2. It is interesting to note that the first legislative result of the coup d'état was the passage of a law establishing an eight hour day for all workers. *Ibid.*, 1917, No. 103, pp. 1-6.

22. Ignatius, H., Theslöf, G., *et al.* (Ed.), *op. cit.*, Vol. II.

23. *S.A.*, 1919, No. 94, pp. 1-26. The constitution was dated July 17, 1919. Rosenqvist, G. G., *Vår kungafråga år 1918; I Regeringsformsfrågan; I dagens frågor. Besinning och tolerans*; von Wendt, E., *Ett politiskt aktstycke av september 1918*; Hjelt, E., *Finsk-svensk och finsk-tysk politik under krigsåren.*

24. Many of the Swede-Finn newspapers have been trying for years to spread the use of the word "Finlander," but its use is not general, nor is by any means consistently used even by the papers that take care not to use the word "Finn" when speaking of the citizens of the country.

25. Lille, A., *op. cit.*, pp. 899-974.

26. *Ibid.*, pp. 975-80.

27. *Ibid.*, p. 998.

28. *Ibid.*, pp. 999-1023. Passing mention should be made in this connection of the separatist movement among the Swedish-speaking inhabitants on the Åland Islands. They made an attempt in 1919 to obtain annexation of the islands by Sweden. The result was a dispute between

Sweden and Finland which was submitted to the League of Nations. The solution of the problem was in favor of Finland, and provision was later made for extensive local self-government for the Islanders. J. S. Bassett's *The League of Nations,* Chap. III contains a summary of the controversy.

The effort of the Ålanders to break loose from Finland was in no way connected with the aspirations of the majority of the Swede-Finns. The former specifically repudiated coöperation with the Swedish-language group in the matter of securing constitutional guarantees of the kind desired by the Swede-Finns on the mainland. Also, the latter opposed the efforts of the Islanders because they constituted some 25,000 out of the total of approximately 350,000 Swede-Finns. Their union with Sweden would have seriously depleted the number of Swedish-speaking inhabitants in the country. See Lille, A., *op. cit.*, pp. 973, 988 ff., 1003.

29. See first source cited in note 23, pars. 14 and 50.

30. *Ibid.*, 1921, No. 118, pp. 385-88; 1922, No. 148, pp. 591-96; No. 149, pp. 596-97, and cf. Nos. 311-12, pp. 1221-28. See also Lille, A., *Språkstriden i Finland; The New Language Law passed by the Riksdag of Finland;* von Wendt, G., *Några utvecklinslinjer och framtidsmål;* Rosenqvist, G. G., *Den nutida svenskhetsrörelsen i Finland. Mål och medel.*

In pursuance of the Language Law of June 1, 1922, which became effective on Jan. 1, 1923, the country was divided on Dec. 30, 1922 into language districts. The communes were listed either as bilingual or unilingual, and the classification arrived at was to hold until 1932. The results may be briefly stated as follows. Out of a total of 554 communes (exclusive of the Åland Islands whose population is almost solidly Swedish-speaking) 454 were listed as unilingual Finnish localities and 64 as bilingual. While there were Finnish-speaking people living in all communes, including Åland, there were 109 communes with no Swede-Finn population, and 165 additional communes in which the number of Swede-Finns was ten or less. *S.A.*, 1922, No. 337, pp. 1277-87. On the basis of the situation disclosed by this survey, the larger administrative regions — headed by provincial governors — were divided into three bilingual, and four Finnish districts, while one was to be considered bilingual with respect to one commune. As regards the judicial divisions, all the superior court districts were classified as bilingual. Exclusive of Åland, no lower court districts became unilingual Swedish-language districts. *Ibid.*, pp. 1269-76.

31. Dahlström, H., "Kielisuhteet Suomessa," *Oma Maa,* V, 471-81;

Suomen Tilastollinen Vuosikirja, 1928, Tables XVII-XIX, pp. 42-45. The percentage of other language groups varied from 0.3 to 0.5 per cent. Of this group, approximately 1,600 were Laplanders. At the time of writing, statistics for 1930 had not yet been published.

32. *Hufvudstadsbladet*, Feb. 19, 1931.

33. Dahlström, H., *loc. cit.* While no complete statistics have been collected on bilingualism throughout the country, it is probably true that fully fifty per cent of the Swede-Finns speak Finnish.

34. *Suomalainen Virallinen Lehti*, May 12, 1906. The *Official News* published an extra issue of 51 pages of four columns each in order to make room for all the names changed. Its issues throughout May contain hundreds of names that did not get into the famous No. 109. A Swede-Finn writer estimates that at the time some 100,000 Finnizations of surnames took place. Estlander, B., *op. cit.*, III, 387.

35. *Suomen Tilastollinen Vuosikirja*, 1928, Table 236, pp. 226-27; 1930, Table 240, pp. 278-79; *Helsingin Sanomat*, Jan. 24, 1931. The table does not include certain unimportant minor parties, such as the Christian Workers Party which obtained two seats in 1919, and the Small Farmers' Party that captured one seat in 1930. The Communists were outlawed in 1919. In the elections of 1922, 1924 and 1927, they masqueraded under three different party names, and were completely excluded from the election of 1930.

36. Wuorinen, John H., *The Prohibition Experiment in Finland,* especially Chaps. II, IV, IX, and pp. 199-211, 224-32.

37. *Svenska Pressen*, Sept. 25, 26, 29; Oct. 13; Dec. 8, 12, 16, 18, 23, 27, 1930; Jan. 10, 13, 23; Feb. 16; Mar. 2, 1931; *Hufvudstadsbladet*, Oct. 1, 13; Dec. 2, 13, 1930; Jan. 24, 27, 1931; *Helsingin Sanomat*, Oct. 21, 1930. I have summarized some of the main aspects of the Lapua movement in *Current History*, June, pp. 585-86, Aug., pp. 1012-13, Sept., p. 1225, Oct., pp. 146-47, Nov., pp. 305-6, Dec., 463-65, 1930; and Jan., pp. 623-24, Feb., 782, Mar., p. 950, Apr., pp. 147-48, 1931.

38. Cf. *Suomen Tilastollinen Vuosikirja*, 1923, Table 50, p. 70; Tudeer, A. E., "The Population of Finland," *Bank of Finland Mon. Bull.*, Oct. 1922, pp. 18-22; *Finsk Tidskrift*, 1917, LXXXII, 409-10.

39. The impression that the Swede-Finns represent an upper class element which has been contending for generations against the growing pretentions of Finnish-speaking lower classes, appears to be fairly general outside of Finland. For example, Eugene Van Cleef remarks, in his *Finland — The Republic Farthest North*, that during the Swedish period, the Swede-Finns were "politically dominant in Finland" and "had no

difficulty in maintaining their political position" down to the early part of the nineteenth century (p. 18). It must be obvious, in the light of the survey presented in Chap. I, that this statement is absurd. Likewise, we have seen that in composition the Swede-Finns do not represent a single social, economic or political class any more than does the Finnish-speaking part of the population.

40. W.A.L., "Kielikysymyksen nykyinen vaihe," *Helsingin Sanomat,* Aug. 31, 1927, and cf. Laurila, K. S., *Kielikysymyksestämme vieläkin hiukkasen.*

BIBLIOGRAPHY

1. UNPUBLISHED SOURCES

ACADEMICA ÅBO. INKOMNA HANDLINGAR. Skrifvelser från prokanslärn m. fl. 1725-1787. State Archives, Stockholm, Sweden.

ALCENIUS MANUSCRIPTS. 12 vols. Manuscript Collection, University of Helsinki, Helsinki, Finland.

ALLMOGENS BESVÄR. Finland 1; Egentliga Finland 1; Österbotten, Nos. 1, 2, 3; Österbotten 2; Södra Österbotten — 1731. State Archives, Stockholm, Sweden.

ARWIDSSON, A. J., Min Lefnads-Händelser. Royal Library, Stockholm, Sweden.

BREV TILL JOH. VILH. SNELLMAN II. Manuscript Collection, University of Helsinki, Helsinki, Finland.

GOTTLUND, C. A., BREFSAMLING, I. Manuscript Collection, University of Helsinki, Helsinki, Finland.

PALMÉN, J. PH., Allmän Inledning till Historiens Studium öfverhufvud; Föreläsningar, Vol. IV. Manuscript Collection, University of Helsinki, Helsinki, Finland.

2. PUBLIC RECORDS

ALLMÄNNA KUNGÖRELSER, 1804-1807. Turku, 1807.

HANDLINGAR TILLKOMNA VID LANDTDAGEN I HELSINGFORS, 1863-1894. 34 vols. Helsinki, 1863-1894.

KONGL. STADGAR, FÖRORDNINGAR, BREF OCH RESOLUTIONER, IFRÅN ÅHR 1528 IN TILL 1701. Angående Justitiae och Executions-Ährenden. Stockholm, 1706.

PROTOKOLLER FÖRDA I DET UTSKOTT AF FINLANDS FYRA STÅND, som till följd af Hans Kejserliga Majestets Nådiga Manifest af den 29 Mars (10 April) 1861 Sammanträdde i Helsingfors, den 20 Januari-6 Mars 1862. Helsinki, 1862.

PROTOKOLL FÖRDT HOS FINLANDS RIDDERSKAP OCH ADEL, 1863-1894. 27 vols. Helsinki, 1863-1894.

SAMLING AF DE TILL EFTERLEFNAD GÄLLANDE BREF, FÖRKLARINGAR OCH FÖRESKRIFTER, hvilka af Hans Kejserliga Majestät, äfvensom ifrån Expeditionerne i Dess Senat för Stor-Furstendömet Finland blifvit utfärdade uti Justitiae-, Economiae- och Polititiae-ärender, 1809-1859. By several editors. 6 vols. Helsinki, 1821-1862.

SUOMEN ASETUSKOKOELMA, 1861-1928. 67 vols. Helsinki, 1861-1928.

SUOMEN TILASTOLLINEN VUOSIKIRJA — ANNUAIRE STATISTIQUE DE FINLANDE, 1905-1930. Helsinki, 1906-1931.

SVERIGES RIKES LAG GILLAD OCH ANTAGEN PA RIKSDAGEN ÅHR 1734. Jemte Bihang, innehållande i sammandrag, under lagtexten, de intill år 1855 utkomne, i Storfurstendömet Finland gällande Stadgar och författningar som ändra eller förklara lagen eller närmare bestämma föreskrifterne i de ämnen densamma omfattar. Helsinki, 1856.

UTDRAG UTUR PUBLIQUE HANDLINGAR, PLACATER, FÖRORDNINGAR, RESOLUTIONER OCK PUBLICATIONER, 1718-1894. By several editors. 16 vols. Stockholm, 1730-129.

3. NEWSPAPERS AND PERIODICALS

AIKA. Helsinki, 1910.

AKTIVISTI. Kokkola, 1930.

ARBETAREN. Helsinki, 1904-1905.

AURA. Turku, 1817-1818.

BAROMETERN. Helsinki, 1861.

BORGÅ TIDNING. Porvoo, 1838-1845.

DAGENS NYHETER. Helsinki, 1877-1878.

FINLAND. Helsinki, 1885-1890.

FINSK TIDSKRIFT. Helsinki, 1880-1917.

FRISINNAD UNGDOM. Gothenburg, 1921.

HELSINGFORS DAGBLAD. Helsinki, 1862-1889.

HELSINGFORS MORGONBLAD. Helsinki, 1832-1844.

HELSINGFORS TIDNINGAR. Helsinki, 1829-1866.

HELSINGIN SANOMAT. Helsinki, 1927-1930.

HELSINGIN UUTISET. Helsinki, 1863.

HUFVUDSTADSBLADET. Helsinki, 1864-1890, 1919-1930.

ILMARINEN. Vaasa, 1848-1852.

KANAVA. Viipuri, 1845-1847.

KANSAN LEHTI. Helsinki, 1905.

KIRJALLINEN KUUKAUSLEHTI. Helsinki, 1866-1881.

LITTERATURBLAD FÖR ALLMÄN MEDBORGERLIG BILDNING. Kuopio, 1847-1849.
LÄNNETAR. Pori, 1863.
LÄNSISUOMEN TYÖMIES. Pori, 1899-1901.
LYCEUM. Stockholm, 1800.
MAAMIEHEN YSTÄVÄ. Kuopio, 1844-1845.
MEHILÄNEN. Oulu, Helsinki, 1836-1840, 1862.
MNEMOSYNE. Turku, 1819-1823.
MORGONBLADET. Helsinki, 1845-1855.
NYA PRESSEN. Helsinki, 1883-1900.
OULUN VIIKKO-SANOMIA. Oulu, 1829-1834, 1836-1837, 1840-1841.
PÄIVÄLEHTI. Helsinki, 1890-1900.
SAIMA. Kuopio, 1844-1846.
SANAN-SAATTAJA VIIPURISTA. Viipuri, 1833-1836, 1840-1841.
SOSIALISTINEN AIKAKAUSKIRJA. Helsinki, 1906-1907.
SUOMALAINEN VIRALLINEN LEHTI. Helsinki, 1906.
SUOMALAISET TIETOSANOMAT. Turku, 1775.
SUOMETAR. Helsinki, 1847-1866.
SVENSKA PRESSEN. Helsinki, 1927-1930.
SVENSKA TIDNINGEN. Stockholm, 1858.
TIDNINGAR IFRÅN HELSINGFORS. Helsinki, 1829-1831.
TIDNINGAR UTGIFNA AF ETT SÄLLSKAP I ÅBO. Turku, 1771-1778, 1782-1785.
TURUN VIIKKOSANOMAT. Turku, 1820-1827, 1829-1831.
TYÖMIES. Helsinki, 1900-1906.
TÄHTI. Turku, 1863-1867.
UUSIMAA. Porvoo, 1899.
UUSI PÄIVÄ. Helsinki, 1917-1918.
UUSI SUOMETAR. Helsinki, 1869-1900.
VALVOJA. Helsinki, 1881-1905.
VIKINGEN. Helsinki, 1870-1874.
WIBORGS TIDNING. Viipuri, 1854-1855, 1864.
ÅBO MORGONBLAD. Turku, 1821.
ÅBO TIDNINGAR. Turku, 1820-1844.

4. PAMPHLETS

ALKIO, S., Talonpoika ja Suomen vapaus. Vaasa, 1922.
——— Maalaisliitto, Vaasa, 1916.
ANDERSON, A., Den svenska folkstammens ställning i Finland. Helsinki, 1924.

CASTRÉN, J., Mikä on oikea ohjelma suomalaisuuden asiassa? Jyväskylä, 1887.

—— Uuden Suomettaren ja sen miesten "puoluemoraali." Helsinki, 1894.

CASTRÉN, Z., Kielikysymys. Helsinki, 1906.

CHURBERG, W., Nykyisen aseman johdosta. Helsinki, 1913.

DANIELSON, J. R., Mihin suuntaan? Porvoo, 1901.

DANIELSON-KALMARI, J. R., Ratkaisun edellä. Helsinki, 1906.

DIE DIREKTION DES LANDBUNDES, Das Program des Landbundes. Vaasa, 1921.

EDISTYSPUOLUE, Valtiollinen ohjelma. Helsinki, 1918.

EN FENNOMAN (AGATON MEURMAN), Hwad är en Fennoman? Helsinki, 1896.

ERKKO, E., Muistelmia Päivälehden perustamisesta. Helsinki, 1929.

DIE FINNISCHE PARTEI IN FINNLAND, ihr jetziges Program nebst einigen einleitenden Worten. Helsinki, 1907.

FORSSTRÖM, F., Meitteitä lainkäyntikielistämme. 1896.

—— Våra domstolsspråk inför lag. Helsinki, 1898.

FRAMSYNT-KAUKOSILMÄ, Hvilken kurs styra vi? Helsinki, 1895.

FREUDENTHAL, A. O., Om Ålands ortnamn. Helsinki, 1867.

GODENHJELM, B. F., Mikä on suomalainen sivistys? Helsinki, 1906.

GROTENFELT, K., Nuorsuomalaisen puolueen Ohjelmasta. Viipuri, 1908.

HANEMANN, M., I svenskhetsfrågan. Helsinki, 1924.

—— M H-nn (Max Hanemann), Svenska Folkpartiets vänster och höger. Helsinki, 1907.

HASTIG, J. Vår nationella framtidslösen. Vaasa, 1924.

HEIKEL, F., Centralt eller Moderat? Helsinki, 1886.

HEIKEL, I. A., Kielipuolueet ja Työväenkysymys. Helsinki, 1898.

HELSINGIN YLIOPISTON YLIOPPILASKUNNAN HALLITUKSEN ULKOASIAIN-VALIOKUNTA, Länsipohjan kysymys. Porvoo, 1929.

HERMANSON, R., 1917 års landtdag. Helsinki, 1917.

HJELT, E., Finsk-Svensk och finsk-tysk politik under krigsåren. Helsinki, 1920.

HULTIN, T., Perustuslaillinen hallitus ja suomettarelainen hallitus. Hämeenlinna, 1907.

—— Vielä kerran suomettarelainen hallitus. Helsinki, 1907.

HÄSTESKO, F. A., Kalevalan kuvakielestä. Supplement. Pori, 1909.

IGNATIUS, K. E. F., Mietteitä muutamista päivän kysymyksiastä. Helsinki, 1905.

INGMAN, S., Puoleiden suhteet toisiinsa. Helsinki, 1906.

ITSENÄISEN SUOMEN ALKUTAIPALEELTA. Kansallisen Edistyspuolueen viisivuotisen toiminnan selostusta. Helsinki, 1923.

JORMA (pseud.), Suomettarelaisen politiikan Jäniksenpolku. Viipuri, 1907.

JUHLAPUHEEN ELI ESITELMÄN SUUNNITELMA TOUKOK. 12 P. 1906 PIDETTÄVÄÄ SNELLMANIN JUHLAA VARTEN. (Nuorisuomalaisten Julkaisuja). Helsinki, 1906.

KOSKENHOWI, P. A., Kansallisuus- ja Kielikysymyksestämme. Turku, 1907.

LAURILA, K. S., Kielikysymyksestämme vieläkin hiukkasen. Helsinki, 1927.

L-R-L (WOLMAR RENVALL), Fyra Polemiska uppsatser. Turku, 1897.

―――― Uppsatser i Språk- och Nationalitetsfrågan. II. Turku, 1898.

LIKGILTIGT HVEM (A. MEURMAN), För det svenska partiet att beakta. Helsinki, 1896.

LILLE, A., Språkstriden i Finland. Helsinki, 1920.

―――― The New Language Law. Helsinki, 1921.

LINDSTRÖM, G., Miten ruotsinkieli tuli valtakieleksi Suomenmaassa? Helsinki, 1906.

MÄKINEN, K. K., Alustavia piirteitä koulualalla tehtäviin uudistuksiin. Helsinki, 1906.

M H-NN. See under Hanemann, M.

MÖRNE, A., Förfinskningen af vår svenska landsbygd och folk-bildningsarbetet därstädes. Helsinki, 1900.

NEMO (PSEUD.), Partierna vid 1885 års landtdag I, II. Helsinki, 1885.

NEUTER (A. A. ERVASTI), Om rätta förståndet af svenskans och finskans likställighet. Helsinki, 1894.

NUORSUOMALAINEN PUOLUE, Nuorsuomalaisen eli perustuslaillis- suomenmielisen puolueen ohjelma. Turku, 1906.

―――― Nuorsuomalaisen Puolueen Ohjelma. Turku, 1906.

―――― Nuorsuomalaisten kannasta suomalaisuuden asiassa. Hämeenlinna, 1908.

―――― Vaalitaisteluohjeita II. Helsinki, 1908.

PALME, S. Ställningar och förhållanden i Finland. Stockholm, 1891.

PARMANEN, W., Uppfatta att du är Finlands medborgare. Kristinestad, 1897.

RENVALL, H., Finlands självständighet. Helsinki, 1917.

REUTER, O. M., I dagens fråger. Turku, 1906.

ROSENQVIST, G. G., Besinning och tolerans. Helsinki, 1918.

―――― Den nutida svenskhetsrörelsen i Finland. Helsinki, 1920.

―――― I Regeringsfrågan. Helsinki, 1918.

—— Vår kungafråga år 1918. Helsinki, 1919.

SCHAUMAN, G., Det Svenska Problemet i Finland. Helsinki, 1921.

SETÄLÄ, E. N., Elias Lönnrot ja suomenmielisyys. Helsinki, 1898.

—— Nuorsuomalaisen puolueen tehtävästä. Helsinki, 1906.

—— The Language Fight in Finland. Helsinki, 1919.

SNELLMAN, J. V., Dagbladspartiets program. Helsinki, 1880.

SOHLMAN, A., Det unga Finland. Helsinki, 1880.

SPJUT, E., Svenskhetstanken. Vaasa, 1921.

STÅHLBERG, K. J., Valtiollisen aseman johdosta. Viipuri, 1908.

SUOMALAISEN NUIJAN NIMENSUOMALAISTUTTAMISKOMITEA, Kokoelma Suomalaisia nimiä. Helsinki, 1906.

SUOMEN MAALAISVÄESTON LIITTO, Suomen Maalaisväeston Liiton Ohjelma, 1907, 1908. Oulu, 1907, Kuopio, 1908.

SVENSKA FOLKPARTIET, VAD DET ÄR OCH VAD DET VILL. Helsinki, 1908.

TENAX (PSEUD.), Taipuako vai tehdä vastarintaa? Berlin (?), 1902.

TOIVO (PSEUD.), Oikea Tie. Stockholm, 1902.

TORCKELL, O., Vår svenska stam och vårt modersmål. Helsinki, 1909.

TULENHENHEIMO, A., Kielilainsäädäntömme. Helsinki, 1926.

VASENIUS, V., Suomenmielisyys ja vapaamielisyys. Helsinki, 1890.

WENDT, E. VON, Ett politiskt aktstycke av september 1918. Helsinki, 1923.

—— Svenskt och finskt i Finland. Helsinki, 1925.

WENDT, G. VON, Några utvecklingslinjer och framtidsmål. Helsinki, 1919.

WREDE, R. A., Själfständighetsfrågan och Finlands landtdag. Helsinki, 1917.

X (A. EDELHEIM), I Brytningstid. Helsinki, 1897.

5. GENERAL WORKS

AHLMAN, E. (EDITOR), Vanha ja uusi Turku. Porvoo, 1929.

AHO, JUHANI, Helsinkiin. Porvoo, 1889.

—— Kevät ja Takatalvi. 4th ed. Porvoo, 1920.

ALBUM UTGIFVET AF NYLÄNNINGAR. 11 vols. Helsinki, 1860-1903.

ALKIO, S., Kansannuorison Sivistystarve ja Nuorisoseuraliike. Porvoo, 1897.

ARBETETS VÄNNER I HELSINGFORS. 9 vols. Helsinki, 1894-1903.

ARBETETS VÄNNER I HELSINGFORS. De första tio åren i föreningens lif. Helsinki, 1901.

ARPPE, A. (EDITOR), Finska Vetenskaps-Societeten 1838-1888. Helsinki, 1888.

ARWIDSSON, A. I., Ingenii romantici, aevo medio orti, expositio historica. Turku, 1817.

——— Svenska Fornsånger. Stockholm, 1837. Vol. I.

BASSETT, JOHN SPENCER, The League of Nations. New York, 1928.

BERENDTS, N. N., The Rights of Finland according to European Scholars: A Rejoinder. St. Petersburg, 1910.

BERGH, E., Finland under det första årtiondet af Alexander III:s regering. Helsinki, 1893.

BOETHIUS, S. J. (EDITOR), Statsrådet John Albert Ehrenströms efterlemnade Historiska Anteckningar. 2 vols. Upsala, 1882.

BONSDORFF, CARL VON, Opinioner och stämningar i Finland 1808-1814. Helsinki, 1918.

BONSDORFF, L. G. VON, Den Ryska pacificeringen i Finland 1808-09. Helsinki, 1929.

BORODKIN, M. M., Finland, Its Place in the Russian State. St. Petersburg, 1911.

BUCH, M., Finnland und seine Nationalitätenfrage. Stuttgart, 1883.

CASPAR, JEAN-JACQUES, Finlande et Russie. Paris, 1911.

CASTRÉN, G., Josef Julius Wecksell. Samlade Dikter. 5th ed. Vol. I. Helsinki, 1919.

CHARPENTIER, A. (EDITOR), Till hundraårsminnet af Johan Philip Palmén 1811-1911. Skrifter. Helsinki, 1911.

CLAUSEN, J., Skandinavismen. Copenhagen, 1900.

CYGNAEUS, F., Drag ur våra kulturförhållanden och tänkesätt nuförtiden. Helsinki, 1874.

DANIELSON, J. R., Finland's Union with the Russian Empire. Porvoo, 1891.

DANIELSON-KALMARI, J. R., Aleksanteri I:n aika. 3 vols. Porvoo, 1923.

——— Kustavilainen aika. 2 vols. Porvoo, 1921.

——— Tien varrelta kansalliseen ja valtiolliseen itsenäisyyteen. 3 vols. Porvoo, 1928.

DEN FINSKA FRÅGAN I TREDJE RYSKA RIKSDUMAN. Helsinki, 1908.

DONNER, A. ET AL., (EDITOR), Finland, the Country, Its People and Institutions. Helsinki, 1926.

ERWAST, K., Hämeenlinnan Normalilyceumi. 2 vols. Hämeenlinna, 1876-1877.

ESTLANDER, B., Elva årtionden ur Finlands historia. 4 vols. Helsinki, 1919-1930.

ESTLANDER, C. G., Arwidsson som vitter författare. Helsinki, 1882.

——— Ungdomsminnen. Helsinki, 1918.

EUREN, G. E., Förhandlingar vid Första Allmänna Skolläraremöte i Finland. Hämeenlinna, 1864.

FAVÉN, A. E., Hämeenlinnan Vanhemmista Kouluista. Hämeenlinna, 1879.

FEODOROFF, E., The Finnish Revolution in Preparation 1889-1905. Trans. by G. Dobson. St. Petersburg, 1911.

FINLANDS MINNESVÄRDE MÄN. 2 vols. Helsinki, 1853-1857.

FISHER, J. R., Finland and the Tsars. London, 1899.

FORSMAN, J., Mistä syystä sosialismi levisi Suomen maalaisväestön keskuuteen? Helsinki, 1912.

FORSSTRÖM, O. A., Suomen historian oppikirja kansakouluja varten. Porvoo, 1893.

FRENCKELLIN LUKEMISIA. Turku, 1856.

FRIMAN, TH. (EDITOR), Lukemisia Suomen Rahwalle. Viipuri, 1849.

FURUHJELM, E., Ur Finlands kulturhistoria. Vol. I. Helsinki, 1902.

FÖRHANDLINGAR OCH UPPSATSER, Helsinki, 1904.

GEITLIN, J. G., Hämeenlinnan Normalilyceumi. 4 vols. Hämeenlinna, 1875-1880.

GENERALGUVENÖR BOBRIKOFFS BERÄTTELSE ÖFVER FINLANDS FÖRVALTNING FRÅN SEPT. 1898 TILL SEPT. 1902. Stockholm, 1905.

GRIPENBERG, L., Ur mina lefnadsminnen. Helsinki, 1922.

GROTENFELT, K., GUMMERUS, J. ET AL. (EDITOR), Juhlajulkaisu E. G. Palménnin 70-vuotis päiväksi. Porvoo, 1919.

GRÖNBLAD, E., Handlingar rörande Klubbekriget. Helsinki, 1843.

GUMMERUS, H., Jääkärit ja aktivistit. Porvoo, 1928.

GYLDÉN, N. A., Till åhörande af det offentliga föredrag, hvarmed Professoren i Finska Språket D:r Elias Lönnrot kommer att tillträda sitt ämbete. Helsinki, 1854.

HALLENDORFF, C., AND SCHUCK, A., History of Sweden. Stockholm, 1929.

HANDLINGAR RÖRANDE FINSKA AFDELNINGEN VID NORMALSKOLAN I HELSINGFORS. Helsinki, 1869.

HAYES, CARLTON J. H., Essays on Nationalism. New York, 1926.

—— Historical Evolution of Modern Nationalism. New York, 1931.

HELSINGIN TYÖVÄENYHDISTYS (EDITOR), Työväen Kalenteri I. Helsinki, 1893.

HISTORIALLINEN AIKAKAUSKIRJA, 1929-1931. Helsinki, 1929.

HISTORIALLINEN ARKISTO. 28 vols. Helsinki, 1866-1926.

HJELT, E., Finsk-svensk och finsk-tysk politik under krigsåren. Helsinki, 1920.

—— Från händelserika år. 2 vols. Helsinki, 1920.

HULTIN, A., Det Ekonomiska Tidevarvet i Finlands Litteraturhistoria. Helsinki, 1910.

—— Finlands Litteratur under Frihetstiden. Vol. I. Helsinki, 1906.
HULTIN, T., Taistelun mies. Helsinki, 1927.
—— Suomalaisuuden Herätys. Helsinki, 1892.
HYTÖNEN, V., Suomalaista sivistystaistelua 1858-1908. Helsinki, 1908.
IGNATIUS, H., THESLÖF, G., ET AL., (EDITOR), Suomen Vapaussota vuonna 1918. Vol. I. Helsinki, 1922.
IGNATIUS, K. H. I., (EDITOR), Lukemisia Suomen Kansalle. Helsinki, 1845.
INKILÄ, A. Suomen Nuorisoseuraliikkeen 25-vuotisjuhla ja Suomen Nuorison Liiton Yleinen Kokous Kauhawalla 1906. Jyväskylä, 1906.
JAHNSSON, Y., Tutkimuksia Suomen teollisuustyöväen suojeluslainsäädännön kehityksestä 1860-luvulta alkaen. Helsinki, 1910.
JALKANEN, K. J., Jyväskylän Lyseo 1858-1908. Jyväskylä, 1908.
JOHAN VILHELM SNELLMANS SAMLADE ARBETEN. Vol. II. Helsinki, 1910.
JOUKAHAINEN. Utgifven af Österbottningar (Since 1873, Pohjalais-Osakunnan Toimittama). 12 vols. Helsinki, 1843-1904.
JURIDISKA FÖRENINGENS I FINLAND TIDSKRIFT. Vol. II. Helsinki, 1866.
J. V. H. [ELLBERG], Tampereen Työväenyhdistyksen Vuosikertomus vuodelta 1899. Tampere, 1900.
JÄRNEFELT, A., Isänmaa. Helsinki, 1913.
KAJAANI, J. F., Suomen Historia, koetteeksi kerrottu lyhykäisessä järjestyksessä. Helsinki, 1839-1840.
KALLIO, O. A., Viipurin Läänin järjestämisestä muun Suomen yhteyteen. Helsinki, 1901.
KANSALAISEN OPINTOKIRJA. I. Helsinki, 1909.
KAPTEN PUFF (N. H. PINELLO), Små Berättelser och Tidsbilder. 4 vols. Turku, 1866-1875.
KEKÄLÄINEN, O. (A. I. ARWIDSSON), Finlands Nuvarande Stats-Författning. Stockholm, 1840.
KELLGREN, K., TENGSTRÖM, R., TIGERSTEDT, K., Fosterländskt Album. 2 vols. Helsinki, 1845.
KERTOMUS WAASAN TYÖVÄENYHDISTYKSEN TOIMISTA VUONNA 1890. Vaasa, 1891.
KERTOMUS WAASAN TYÖVÄENYHDISTYKSEN VAIKUTUKSESTA, VUOSINA 1891-1892. Vaasa, 1893.
KIRBY, W. F. (TRANS. AND EDITOR), Kalevala. Everyman's Library. 2 vols. London, 1907.
KOMONEN, A., Vaasan Työväenyhdistyksen 25-vuotis Historiikki vuosilta 1883-1908. Vaasa, 1908.

KOSKINEN, Y., Finnische Geschichte von den frühesten Zeiten bis auf die Gegenwart. Leipzig, 1874.
—— Kansallisia ja yhteiskunnallisia kirjoituksia. 2 vols. Helsinki, 1904-1906.
—— Klubbekriget. Trans. by E. O. Edlund. Helsinki, 1864. See also Yrjö-Koskinen, Y. S.

KOTKAN TYÖVÄENYHDISTYS (EDITOR), Työväen Kalenteri V. Kotka, 1897.

KOVERO, M., Suomen Vientiteollisuus. Helsinki, 1926.

KROHN, H. (EDITOR), Julius Krohn. Nuoren Ylioppilaan Kirjeitä 1850-luvulta. Helsinki, 1918.

KROOK, A., Finnish Songs. Helsinki, 1904.

LAGUS, F. H. B., Muistelmia ja kuvauksia kielitaistelun ajoilta. Porvoo, 1924.

LAGUS, W., Från Pojkåren och Gymnasiet. Helsinki, 1904.
—— Strödda Blad. Helsinki, 1878.

LANGHOFF, A., Seitsemän vuotta Suomen edustajana valtaistuimen edessä. Muistoja ja muistiinpanoja vuosilta 1906-1913. Porvoo, 1922.

LAURELL, A. A., Afhandlingar i Uppfostringsläran. 2 vols. Helsinki, 1831-1833.

LAUREN, L. L., Minnen från Skolan och Universitetet. Stockholm, 1877. Wasa Trivialskola 1684-1884. Nykarleby, 1884.

LEHOKAS, V. [?] (EDITOR), Kymmenen vuotta Suomen työväenpuolueen muistoja ja ennätyksia 1899-1909. Helsinki, 1909.

LEINBERG, K. G., Handlingar Rörande Finska Skolväsendets Historia. 4 vols. Jyväskylä and Helsinki, 1884-1901.

LENNART HOHENTHALS MEMOARER. Stockholm, 1908.

LILLE, A., Svenska nationalitetens i Finland Samlingsrörelse. Helsinki, 1921.

LILLJA, J. W. (EDITOR), Lukemisia Kansalle. 7 vols. Turku, 1852-1865.

LINDEQUIST, C. J. (EDITOR), Förhandlingar vid Andra allmänna Skolläraremötet i Finland. Helsinki, 1867.

LUKEMISIA. 3 vols. Turku, 1851-1855.

LUKEMISIA LAPSILLE. Kuopio, 1860-1862.

LÄNNETÄR. Album, utgifvet af vestfinnar. 7 vols. Helsinki, 1860-1882.

LÖNNBECK, A., Studier i Finska Vitterheten efter 1830. Helsinki, 1883.

LÖNNBECK, G. F., Folkskoleidéns utveckling i Finland från nittonde århundradets början till 1866. Helsinki, 1887.

MALMGREN, A. J. (EDITOR), Handlingar rörande skolfrågan i Finland. Helsinki, 1882.

MASARYK, T. G., The Spirit of Russia. Trans. by Eden and Cedar Paul. 2 vols. London, 1919.

MED LAGEN OCH SVÄRDET. Helsinki, 1919.

MELA, E., Suomen Nuorison Liiton seitsemäs yl. Kokous. Pori, 1907.

MEURMAN, A., Kuinka Suomenkieli pääsi viralliseksi. Helsinki, 1893.

MICKWITZ, A., De Finska Deputationerna till Riksdagen 1742-43 och Finska Ekonomikommissionen. Helsinki, 1912.

MODEE, K. G., Utdrag Utur Publique Handlingar, 1730-1739. Vol. III. Stockholm, 1746.

MURROSAJOILTA. MUISTOJA JA KOKEMUKSIA. 2 vols. Porvoo, 1913.

MÖRNE, A., Axel Olof Freudenthal och den finlandssvenska nationalitetstanken. Helsinki, 1927.

―――― Från "Saima" till "Vikingen." Porvoo, 1916.

NERVANDER, E., Fädrens röst. Helsinki, 1891.

―――― Isien ääni. Helsinki, 1891.

NESTOR (PSEUD.), Finska Förhållanden. Andra serien. Stockholm, 1892.

NIEMI, A. R., Kalevalan Kokoonpano. Helsinki, 1898.

NORDMAN, P. (EDITOR), Lilla Folkhögskolebiblioteket. 1-6. Helsinki, 1891-93.

―――― Suomen historian oppikirja kansakouluja varten. Porvoo, 1893.

NORDSTRÖM, J. J., Bidrag till den Svenska Samhällsförfattningens Historia. Vol. I. Helsinki, 1839.

NYBLOM, C. R., Johan Ludvig Runebergs Samlade Skrifter. 2 vols. Stockholm, 1903.

NYLANDER, J. W., Den Stora Deputationen. Helsinki, 1899.

OULUN TYÖVÄENYHDISTYS (EDITOR), Työväen Kalenteri VI. Oulu, 1899.

PALANDER, G., see Suolahti, G.

PALMÉN, E. G. (EDITOR), Oma Maa. 6 vols. Porvoo, 1920-1925.

―――― Suomen Valtiopäiväin Historia. Porvoo, 1910.

―――― Till hundraårsminnet af Johan Philip Palmén 1811-1911. 3 vols. Helsinki, 1917.

PEDER SÄRKILAX (E. VON QVANTEN), Fennomani och Scandinavism. Stockholm, 1855.

PENNIBIBLIOTHEK FÖR SWENSKA ALLMOGEN I FINLAND UTGIFWET AF NYLÄNDNINGAR. 43 items. Helsinki, 1866-1900.

PENNI-KIRJASTO SUOMEN KANSALLE. Helsinki, 1867-1880.

PETÄJÄNIEMI, K. W., Tampereen Työväenyhdistyksen Vuosikertomus. 2 vols. Tampere, 1898-1899.

PIETILÄ, A. J., Daniel Juslenius. Hänen Elämänsä ja Vaikutuksensa. 2 vols. Tampere, Porvoo, 1907-1910.

PORIN TYÖVÄENYHDISTYKSEN TOIMIKUNTA (EDITOR), Porin Työväenyhdistyksen toiminta. I. Pori, 1889.

PÖYTÄKIRJA VIIPURISSA 1899 PIDETYSTÄ KOLMANNESTA YLEISESTÄ
NUORISON LIITON KOKOUKSESTA. Helsinki, 1901.

PROGRAMMER UTGIFNA VID UNIVERSITETET I HELSINGFORS, 1853-1859, VI.
No date.

PÄRSSINEN, J., Kasvatusopilliset Virtaukset ja Koululaitoksen Kehitys
Suomessa vuosina 1801-1843. Helsinki, 1911.

QVANTEN, E. VON (EDITOR), Finska Förhållanden. Hft. 1-4. Stockholm,
1857-1861.

RAMSAY, H., Suomen teollisuuden kehityksen pääpiirteet. Trans. by
K. Metsävainio. Porvoo, 1919.

READE, A., Finland and the Finns. London, 1914.

REIN, TH., Johan Vilhelm Snellman. 2 vols. Helsinki, 1895-1899.

—— Muistelmia elämän varrelta. Helsinki, 1918.

RENSTRÖM, K., Tampereen Työväen-Yhdistyksen Vuosikertomus. 2 vols.
Tampere, 1888-1891.

RENWALL, G., Grammatiska Uppsatser. Turku, 1837.

REUTER, J. N., "Kagalen," ett bidrag till Finlands historia 1899-1905.
Vol. II. Helsinki, 1930.

RIKALA, K. Pöytäkirja Tampereella 1897 Pidetystä Toisesta Yleisestä
Nuorisoseurain Kokouksesta. Tampere, 1898.

ROOS, S. Nationalstrejken i Finland. 2 vols. Helsinki, 1906.

ROSENDAL, M., Suomen herännäisyyden historia XIX:lla vuosisadalla.
3 vols. Oulu, 1902-1913.

RUUTH, J. W., Åbo Stads Historia. Vol. III. Helsinki, 1916.

RUUTH, O. Y., Självständighetspolitiken och jägarrörelsens uppkomst.
Helsinki, 1919.

—— Uusi Suunta. Jyväskylä, 1920.

RÜHS, F., Finland och Dess Invånare. Trans. by A. I. Arwidsson. Stockholm, 1827.

SANTERI [INGMAN-IVALO], Hellaassa. Helsinki, 1890.

SAVO-KARJALAISET OPPIVAISET (EDITOR), Lukemisia Suomen Kansan
Hyödyksi. 2 vols. Helsinki, 1845-1847.

SCHAUMAN, A., Från Sex Årtionden i Finland. 2 vols. Helsinki, 1892-
1893.

—— Nu och Förr. Helsinki, 1886.

SCHOULTZ, J. VON, Bidrag till belysande av Finlands socialdemokratiska
partis historia. Vol. I. Helsinki, 1924.

SCHRÖTER, H. R., Finnische Runen. Upsala, 1819.

SCHYBERGSON, M. G., Bidrag till Finlands inre historia åren 1721-1731. Helsinki, 1875.

—— Finlands Historia. Vol. I. Helsinki, 1903.

—— Historiens Studium vid Åbo Universitet. Helsinki, 1891.

SEPPÄLÄ, J. (EDITOR), Suomen Ensimäinen Yleinen Nuorisoseurain Kokous Jyväskylässä 1895. Vaasa, 1895.

SKARSTEDT, S. (EDITOR), Sveriges Rikes Lag. Stockholm, 1926.

SNELLMAN, J. V., Dagbladspartiets program. Helsinki, 1880.

SOHLMAN, A., Det Unga Finland (2d ed.) Helsinki, 1880.

SOIKKELI, K., Suomen Sanomalehdistö vv. 1771-1900. Viipuri, 1910.

SOOVOROFF, P., The Finnish Question. St. Petersburg, 1910.

SUOLAHTI, G. (PALANDER, G.), Elämää Suomessa 1700-luvulla. Porvoo, 1909.

—— Henrik Gabriel Porthan. Helsinki, 1904.

—— Henrik Gabriel Porthan historianopettajana. Helsinki, 1901.

—— Henrik Gabriel Porthan Yliopiston Opettajana. Helsinki, 1903.

—— Suomen historia aikakausittain. Porvoo, 1906.

—— Suomen Papisto 1600- ja 1700-luvuilla. Porvoo, 1919.

—— Vuosisatain takaa. Porvoo, 1913.

SUOMALAINEN TIEDEAKATEMIA. ESITELMÄT JA PÖYTÄKIRJAT. Vol. I. Helsinki, 1909.

SUOMEN NUORISON LIITON KOKOUS MIKKELISSÄ 1901. PÖYTÄKIRJA. Hämeenlinna, 1902.

SUOMEN NUORISON LIITON VUOSIKIRJA. 12 vols. Oulu, Vaasa, Helsinki, 1908-1919.

SUOMEN NUORISON LIITON YLEINEN KOKOUS. Pori, 1909.

SUOMEN TYÖVÄEN PUOLUEHALLINTO (EDITOR), Työväen Kalenteri VII. Turku, 1901.

SÖDERHJELM, W., Åboromantiken och dess samband med utlädnska idéströmningar. Porvoo, 1915.

—— Johan Ludvig Runeberg. 2 vols. Helsinki, 1904-1906.

—— Johannes Linnankoski. Helsinki, 1918.

—— Kotimaisia Kulttuurikuvia. Trans. by H. Cannelin. Helsinki, 1920.

TAKALA, E. E. (EDITOR), Suomen Nuorison Liiton Kokous Paimiossa 1903. Laihia, 1903.

TAMPEREEN TYÖVÄENYHDISTYKSEN VUOSIKERTOMUS. 3 vols. Tampere, 1892-1897.

TAMPEREEN TYÖVÄENYHDISTYS (EDITOR), Työväen Kalenteri II. Tampere, 1894.

TARJANNE, A. J., AHTIALA, K. ET AL. (EDITOR), Suomen Kansakoulu 1866-1916. Porvoo, 1916.

TAVASTSTJERNA, K. A., Barndomsvänner, Porvoo, 1887.

TETTAU, W. J. A. VON, Ueber die epischen Dichtungen der Finnischen Völker, besonders die Kalevala. Reprint from Jahrbücher der Königlichen Akademie Gemeinnütziger Wissenschaften zu Erfurt, 1873. Neue Folge, 7 Heft, pp. 145-308.

TOIVONEN, E. J., Suomen Nuorison Liiton Yleinen Kokous. (Kymmenes Nuorisoseurakokous). No place or date of publication.

—— Suomen Nuorison Liiton Yleinen Kokous. (Yhdestoista Nuorisoseurakokous). Porvoo, 1911.

TOPELIUS, Z., Vincent Vågbrytaren. Porvoo, 1923.

TURTONEN, J., Tampereen Työväenyhdistyksen Vuosikertomus v. 1895. Tampere, 1896.

TURUN SUOMALAISEN YLIOPISTOSEURAN WUOSIKIRJA. 2 vols. Turku, 1920-1921.

TURUN TYÖVÄENYHDISTYS (EDITOR), Työväen Kalenteri III. Turku, 1895.

UR FINLANDS NYASTE HISTORIA. Stockholm, 1900.

VAARA, L. (EDITOR), Porin T. Y. 25-vuotias. 1912.

VALISZEVSKY, K., The Finnish Question — The Ostrich and the Sparrow. Trans. by G. Dobson. St. Petersburg, 1910.

VARSINAISSUOMALAINEN OSAKUNTA, Lännetär, Uusi jakso. 2 vols. Helsinki, 1908-1914.

VASENIUS, V., Zacharias Topelius. 6 vols. Helsinki, 1920-1930.

VESSBERG, G. V., Om Svenska Riksdagen, dess Sammansättning och Verksamhetsformer, 1772-1809. Stockholm, 1889.

VIIPURIN TYÖVÄENYHDISTYS (EDITOR), Työväen Kalenteri IV. Viipuri, 1896.

VIKMAN, K. O., Suomen kansan lukutaidon synty ja kehitys Ruotsin vallan aikana. Helsinki, 1910.

VOIONMAA, V., Sosialidemokratian vuosisata. Vol. II. Porvoo, 1909.

WESALA, K., Suomen historia. Kansakouluja varten. Porvoo, 1895.

WIDERHOLM, P. (EDITOR), Lukemisia Kansalle. Porvoo, 1885.

WREDE, R. A., Grunddragen af Finlands rätts- och samhällsordning. Helsinki, 1920.

WUORINEN, JOHN H., The Prohibition Experiment in Finland. New York, 1931.

YHTEINEN HISTORIA LYHYKÄISESTI SUOMEN KANSALLE. Kuopio, 1845.

YRJÖ-KOSKINEN, Y. K., Suomen historia. Porvoo, 1893.
   See also Koskinen, Y.

ZILLIACUS, K., Sortovuosilta. Porvoo, 1920.

INDEX

Aboa Vetus et Nova, 18

Academic Reading Club, 101

Act for the Organization of Elementary Schools, 1866, 158-59

Activist Opposition Party, and Russification, 199

Adult Education Society, 166-67

Agrarian Union, 205; language program of, 207-08; representation in Parliament, 1907-1916, 213; 1919-1930, 232

Alexander I, and annexation of Finland, 30, 33, 35, 36, 40; and Diet, 125

Alexander II, policies in Finland of, 104; and Diet, 126-27

Alkio, S., 167

Andrastea, 68

Annexation of Finland by Russia, 30-32; meaning of, 34-35

Anti-Communism, 233

Armfelt, G. M., and Russian annexation, 33-34, 37-38, 39

Arwidsson, Adolf Jwar, early nationalist, 47-54; importance of contribution, 54-55; 56, 57, 59, 70, 79, 83, 84, 88, 103

Association of Finnish Jurists, 164

Aurora Society, and patriotic studies, 24

Bell-Lancaster schools, 156-57

Bernadotte, heir apparent of Sweden, 39; views concerning Finland, 39-40

Bilingualism, since 1880, 228-31, 235

Björnstierne-Björnson, 194

Bobrikoff, N., Governor-General, 194, 196; assassinated, 200

Brahe, Pehr, 16

Brusa, E., 194-95

Carlsbad Decrees, 57

Castrén, M. A., contribution of, to nationalist cause, 98-99; meaning of contribution, 99-100; first professor in Finnish, 102; and independence aspirations, 111-12

Catholic Church, in Finland during Middle Ages, 6

Censorship, after 1809, 57-58, 94; act of 1850, 102, 103; Administration, 107; abolished, 218-19

Charles XII, 12, 18

Charles XIII and Russia's Annexation of Finland, 39

Cities, language groups in, 1900-1920, 230

Clergy, and Swedization before 1809, 45-46; Finnish-language requirements of, 102

Collection of Finland's Laws, 196

Committee of Five Hundred, 193-94

Constitution, and language legislation, 147-51; violated by Russia, 188-203, 214-15; language provisions in, 1919, 227

Constitutional Finnish Party, see Young Finnish Party

Constitutionalists and Russification, 199

Count de Broglie, 194

Crimean War, and Scandinavianism, 108-11, 113, 119

Customs Service in Finland, before 1809, 13

Cygnaeus, Fredrick, 95

Declaration of Independence, 1917, 150

Defense Guards, 221

Delbrück, Hans, 194

Diet, convened 1863, 125-27; and language question, 141, 142-44, 146-47, 148; and Russification, 192-93; reform of, 200, 204

"Discovery of the Swede-Finns," 115-19, 127

Dissertatio de Poesi Fennica, 23, 66

Duodecim Society, 163

Economic situation, in 1809, 29-30; after 1865, 169-70

Edda, Icelandic epic poem, 74

Education and Swedish language, before 1809, 42-47; and nationalist movement, 154-69

Educational work, before 1809, 155-56; trends in, after 1809, 156-63

Elgskyttarne (The Elk Hunters), 78, 79

English Liberalism in Finland, 123-24, 145

Erkko, E., and Constitutionalists, 198-99

Eucken, Rudolf, 194

Evolution of modern literary Finnish, 75-76, 80

February Manifesto, 1899, 190-92, 197, 201, 214

Fennomen, Young, 114, 127-36; and Liberal program, 145-46

Finland, as part of Swedish Kingdom, 3-9, 11-12; election of the King, in the Middle Ages, 7; as part of Russian Empire, 30-32

Finn and Swede-Finn, before 1809, 46-47

Finnische Runen, by Von Schröter, 70

Finnish language, social and economic advance before 1809, 42-47; use in religious services in Middle Ages, 46; in educational endeavor, after 1809, 62-66, 142-43; alleged relation to Turco-Tataric group and Ural-Altaic theory, 99-100; relationship to Hungarian, 100; requirements for public office, 102, 105-6, 128, 132-33, 142; use in public business, 104-5, 141-42; see also Language situation

Finnish Literature Society, 77-78, 79, 82, 98, 138, 170

Finnish particularism, during Swedish period, 9-18

Finnish representation in Riksdag, 11

Finnish State Secretariat, in St. Petersburg, 32

Finnization, of Swede-Finns, 230-31, 234-35

Finns, and governmental positions, in the Middle Ages, 8

Flora Day Celebration, 1848, 95-97

Folklore studies, before 1809, 23-25; after 1809, 66-76, 117

"Folkting of Swedish Finland," demands of, 226

Forsman, G., see Koskinen, Y.

France, Anatole, 194

Franchise Law, 1906, 204

Frederick of Hesse, 223

Freudenthal, A. O., Swede-Finn nationalist, 121-23, 236

Friends of Labor, Swede-Finn organization, 181-83

Fundamental Statutes, and Finland's constitution, 191-92

Fänrik Ståls Sägner (The Tales of Ensign Stål), 97, 98, 159

Germany, and Finnish independence, 217-18, 222, 223

Great Protest, against February Manifesto, 1899, 193-94, 201

Gripenberg, O. H., 156

Group for Coöperation with the Bourgeois Parties, 234

Grundtvig, N. F. S., 168

Gustavus Adolphus, 12, 224

Gustavus Vasa, 5, 6

Helsinki (Helsingfors), University of, Finnish studies at, 103 128, 142-43; language situation in, 129-30; and nationalist advance, 154-55, 161-63; linguistic groups in, 1920-1930, 229

Herder and nationalism in Finland, 23, 68, 69

Historical studies, after 1809, 59-62, 83

"History of the Fatherland," meaning of, after 1809, 61

Home Language Society, 163

Ibsen, Hendrick, 194

Imperial Senate of Finland, 31

Independence, schemes of, during Swedish period, 26, 27, 28; in forties, 111-12; during World War, 216-18, 219-20; established, 220-22

Institut de Droit International, 195

"Jaeger Movement," 217-18

Juslenius, Daniel, and Finnish patriotic studies, 18-20

Kagaali and Russification, 198, 199

Kalevala, the Finnish national epic 22, 67, 71; collected by Lönnrot, 72-74; how put together, 73-74; and critical scholarship, 74-75; and Finnish Literature Society, 77-78, 79, 82, 87, 98, 116, 159

Kalmar Union, 4, 5, 7

Kerensky, 220

King's Council, in Sweden, during the Middle Ages, 5

Koskinen, Y., Fennoman leader, 112; law suit, 130-32; nationalist ideas of, 133-35; and Swede-Finns, 137-38

Labor and nationalism, 169-87

Language and nationality, in Finland, 52-54

Language legislation, 102-06, 132, 141-42; constitutional aspects of, 147-51; in eighties, 151-52; 1902, 153; since 1918, 227-28

Language Ordinance of 1863, provisions of, 105-06; early application of, 130-33; Diet opinion concerning, 141; objects realized, 153-54

Language situation, during Swedish period, 42-47; after 1809, 41-42, 115-17, 128-33; 1880-1920, 229; at Helsinki University, 1920-1930, 229; bilingualism, 1900-1920, 230; in Parliament, 1919-1930, 232; see also Finnish language; Swedish language

Lapua anti-Communist movement, 233

Law of the Swedish Realm, 1734, 148-49

Lenin, N., 221

Liberals and language question, 123-25; program of, 144-46

Libraries, rural, 101

Lille, A., 206, 236

Liquor problem, 127

Literacy, before 1809, 155-56

Litteraturblad för Allmän Medborgerlig Bildning (The Literary News for the Citizens' Education), 94

Lutheran Church, 31-32; membership in since 1918, 235

Lyceum, founded 1831, 77

Lönnrot, Elias, and Finnish folklore studies, 71-76, 87; and evolution of modern literary Finnish, 75-76, 80

Maanmiehen Ystävä (The Farmer's Friend), 90

Magyars, alleged relation to Finns, 100

Manchester Liberalism and nationalist movement, 145

Manifesto of Feb. 15, 1899, 190-92, 197

Mehiläinen (The Bee), 80

Meurman, A., 158

Mill, John Stuart, and Finnish Liberals, 123-24

Mittag-Leffler, 194

Mommsen, Theodore, 194

Monetary reform, in sixties, 126, 170

Nansen, Frithiof, 194

National Coalition Party, 223; representation in Parliament, 1919-1930, 232

National Economic Society, 163

National Finnish Party, founding and program of, 208

National Progressive Party, 223; representation in Parliament, 1919-1930, 232

National Strike, 1905, 200, 201

Nationalist leaders, antecedents of, 87, 121, 133, 139

Nationality, theory of, Arwidsson's, 52-54; Snellman's, 91-93; Sohlman's interpretation, 119-20; Freudenthal's, 121-23; Koskinen's, 134-35

Nicholas I, 104; and Diet, 125

Nicholas II, 218

Nightingale, Florence, 194

Northern War, under Charles XII, 12, 45

Norway, compensation for Sweden's loss of Finland, 40

Nystad, peace of, 1721, 12, 45

O'Connel, Daniel, 82

Old Finns, and Russification, 198, 205

Ossian, Macpherson's, 23, 68

Oulun Viikkosanomia (*The Oulu Weekly News*), 80

"Our Country," Finland's national anthem, 95-97

Paris, Gaston, 194

Paris, Peace of, 1856, 112, 113

Parliament Bill, 1906, 204

Parliament, reform of, and nationalist movement, 174-75; in 1906, 200, 204; groups in, 1907-1916, 213; 1919-1930, 232

"Passive resistance," to Russification, 197-98

Patriotic studies during Swedish period, 18-26

People's High Schools, 168

Philology, Finnish, and nationalist movement, 98-100

Political independence, and nationalist aspirations, 2; in Finland, before 1850, 111-12; 1914-19, 17, 216-18

Popular education, and nationalist movements, 165-69; and Russification, 202-03

Population of Finland, in 1809, 29; in 1850, 116; in 1900, 205; 1880-1920, 229

Porthan, Henrik Gabriel, and Finnish studies before 1809, 22-26, 59, 66, 67, 69, 70

Porvoo (Borgå) Diet, 1809, 30, 48, 125

Post Office, Russification of, 189

Press, freedom of, after 1809, 57; instrument of nationalists, 1820-1840, 79-82, 83, 85-86, 101-02; Snellman's contribution to, 90-91; circulation of, 103; advance of, 169; and Russification, 195-96

Prohibition, as a dividing force, 223

Propaganda, and nationalist movements, 236-38

Public opinion, and Russia's annexation of Finland, 32-39

Rask, R. K., and Finnish folklore, 70

Readings for the Benefit of the People of Finland, 101

Red Guards, 221

Rein, Th., quoted, 65

"Retreaters" and Russification, 197-98, 205

Riksdag, Sweden's national parliament, 5, 7, 8, 10-11, 13

Romanticism, and Finnish nationalism, 67-70, 84

Royal Resolution of 1739, concerning appointments in Finland, 14, 17

Royalism, in Parliament of 1918, 223

Runeberg, Johan Ludvig, 76, 78, 86, 95, 97, 103

Russian language, introduction into Finland, 37, 196-97, 214-15

Russian Revolution, 1905, 200; effects on Finland, 200-01; 1917, 215-21

Russification, fear of, 1, 39, 41-42, 53, 55, 58, 69, 114, 121, 140, 185-86; appearance and objectives of, 187-203; and "passive resistance," 197-98; 1908-1917, 214-21

Russo-Japanese War, 1904, and Finnish Opposition, 199-200

Saima, 90, 93, 94, 95, 100, 101, 107

Sanansaattaja Viipurista (The Viipuri Messenger), 80

Saturday Club, 76-79, 87

Scandinavianism, aims of, 108-9; and Finnish nationalists, 109-11, 113, 119

School Resolution, 1760, 43

Schools, introduction of Russian language studies into, 37, 38-39; national system established, 158-59, 171; language instruction in, 230-31

Scientific societies, nationalist importance of, 163-64

Sjögren, A. J., 68

Smith, Adam, 125

Snellman, Johan Vilhelm, 76, 87-95; early program of, 89-90; theory of nationality of, 91-93; demands of, 92-94, 107; appointed professor, 103; on Swede-Finns' position, 116-17; on nation and language, 118; concerning education, 157-58

Social Democratic Party of Finland, 177-78, 205; language views

of, 210-11; independence, 218; representation in Parliament, 1907-1916, 213; 1919-1930, 232

Social legislation, 172-73

Society of Finnish Technologists, 163-64

Sohlman, A., and Swede-Finn nationalism, 119-20

Spanska Flugan (The Spanish Fly), 88

Spencer, Herbert, 194

Subject nationalities and nationalism, 1

Suometar, 103

Suomi, 78

Svinhufvud Senate, 222

Swecoman nationalists, Vikings, 114; representation in Burghers and Nobles, 147, 205

Swede-Finn nationalism, background and objectives, 115-23, 144

Swede-Finn particularism, since 1917, 225, 235

Swede-Finns, statistics concerning, 116; in schools, 161, 162; and Russification, 199; in 1900, 205; and independence, 218; 1880-1920, 229; representation in Parliament, 1907-1916, 213; 1919-1930, 232

Swedes and appointments in Finland, before 1809, 13, 18, 45

Swedish conquest of Finland, 4, 8-9

"Swedish Day," Swede-Finn national holiday, 224

Swedish Government, and Russia's Annexation of Finland, 39-40

Swedish language in Finland's

schools after 1809, 63-64; Sohlman's ideas of, 119-20; Liberals' views, 145; as official language, 148-49; *see also* Language situation

Swedish law, in Finland, 6, 148-49

Swedish People's Party, founding and program, 206-07; representation in Parliament, 1907-1916, 213; 1919-1930, 232, 233-34

Swedish traditions in Finland, 113; and Swecomen, 114, 119-23; and Liberals, 124; and Young Fennomen, 136-38

Swedization of the Finns, before 1809, 42-47, 63, 64 Arwidsson's notions concerning, 51-53; after 1809, 84-85, 87; Snellman's views, 92-94; change of surnames, 46

Tables, school attendance, 1874-1905, 159; political parties and Diet, 1907-1916, 213; strength of language groups, 1880-1920, 229; university attendance, 1920-1930, 229; bilingualism, 1900-1920, 230; parties in Parliament, 1919-1930, 232

Tales of Ensign Stål, 97, 98, 159

Tengström, Bishop, and advantages of Russian contacts, 38

Topelius, Z., and folklore studies, 71

Topelius, Zachris, 76; first professor in Finnish history, 102-3

Trarieux, L., 194

"Turanian," meaning of, 100

Turku fire, and collection of historical sources, 60-61

Turku (Åbo) University, and Finnish particularism before 1809, 16-17, 18, 20, 24; conditions at, after 1809, 56-57

Turun Viikkosanomia (*The Turku Weekly News*), 80, 81

Työmies (*The Worker*), 177-79

University students, nationalist efforts of, 100-1; and independence, 216-18

Uppsala University, 69

Vanamo Society, 163

Van der Vlugt, W., 194

Vikings, in Finland, 8; or Swecoman nationalists, 114

Vindiciae Fennorum, 19

Vipuset, 163

Von Becker, Reinhold, collector of folklore, 70-71

Von Heidenstam, Verner, 194

Von Qvanten, E., Finnish Scandinavian, 108-10, 112

Von Schröter, Hans Rudolf, and Finnish folklore, 70

Väinämöinen, 71

Wesltake, J., 194

World War, opinions in Finland concerning, 216-17

Women, laws concerning, 126-27; opponents of Russification, 199; political equality of, 204

Workers' Associations, 171-74

Workers' Institutes, 168-69

Young Fennomen, 114, 127-36; and Liberal program, 145-46

Young Finnish Party, language program of, 209

Young People's Associations, 167-68

Zilliacus, K., 199

Zola, Émile, 194

Åbo, Old and New, 19

Åbo Morgonblad (Åbo Morning News), 50, 56, 57, 58, 59, 79, 88

Åland Islanders and Finland's unity, 235

COLUMBIA UNIVERSITY PRESS
COLUMBIA UNIVERSITY
NEW YORK

———

FOREIGN AGENT
OXFORD UNIVERSITY PRESS
HUMPHREY MILFORD
AMEN HOUSE, LONDON, E. C.